With Vancouver in Inland
Washington Waters

Dick Blumenthal

for Noah, Joshua, and Jonah,
Enjoy these real-life accounts of
the discovery of Puget Sound.
— Capt. Steve Mayo

Also by Richard W. Blumenthal

The Early Exploration of Inland Washington Waters (McFarland, 2004)

With Vancouver in Inland Washington Waters

Journals of 12 Crewmen, April–June 1792

Richard W. Blumenthal

McFarland & Company, Inc., Publishers
Jefferson, North Carolina, and London

LIBRARY OF CONGRESS CATALOGUING-IN-PUBLICATION DATA

With Vancouver in inland Washington waters : journals of 12 crewmen, April–June 1792 / edited by Richard W. Blumenthal.
p. cm.
Includes bibliographical references and index.

ISBN-13: 978-0-7864-2669-0
ISBN-10: 0-7864-2669-1
(softcover : 50# alkaline paper) ♾

1. Washington (State)—Description and travel. 2. Washington (State)—Discovery and exploration. 3. Inland navigation—Washington (State)—History—18th century. 4. Washington (State)—History, Local. 5. Explorers—Washington (State)—Diaries. 6. Sailors—Washington (State)—Diaries. 7. Vancouver, George, 1757–1798—Friends and associates. 8. Vancouver, George, 1757–1798—Travel—Washington (State) 9. Seafaring life—Washington (State)—History—18th century. I. Blumenthal, Richard W., 1946–
F891.W84 2007
979.7'01–dc22 2006024662

British Library cataloguing data are available

On the cover: H.M.S. *Chatham* entering Cattle Pass, from an original watercolor by Steve Mayo (courtesy of Bob and Barbara Harnden)

Manufactured in the United States of America

McFarland & Company, Inc., Publishers
Box 611, Jefferson, North Carolina 28640
www.mcfarlandpub.com

To Connor and Tyler—
Neither can read yet
but I hope they'll also develop a love for our maritime
history and allow me to share this text with them soon

Contents

Preface

In my first book, *The Early Exploration of Inland Washington Waters: Journals and Logs from Six Expeditions, 1789–1792*, I examined the first six voyages into the inland waters of what is now Washington state. These included the explorations of John Meares, the early Spanish explorers and George Vancouver. This text presents the journals of Vancouver's men in 1792. Their journals provide additional detail of their exploration in inland areas not previously described. For example, they include Peter Puget's first-hand observations and exploration of Puget Sound as well as William Broughton's passage through the San Juan Islands. In addition, the journals go into more detail of the activities of the officers and enlisted men while onboard.

Some notes are appropriate. In almost cases, while underway, Vancouver's men used a six-column table format for their journals based upon an astronomical calendar which ran from noon of one day to noon on the following day. Entries on the upper half of the table occurred in the afternoon and evening of the day previous to that noted at the top of the table. The heading entries were as follows: H (hour), K (knots), F (fathoms), Courses (direction vessel is traveling), Winds (direction wind is coming from), and Remarks.

The "K" and "F" columns require some additional explanation. The explorers used a "ship's log" or "chip log" to determine speed. Early on, the log was just that, a piece of wood tied to a long line. During Vancouver's time, it evolved to the shape of a quarter circle, approximately twelve inches in diameter and weighted with lead on the arc portion. The shape acted as an efficient drogue. The line tied to the log was wound around a small drum with handles so that it would pay out with little friction. It was knotted at intervals. In Vancouver's case, I believe that the interval was seven fathoms. The log was lowered over the taffrail. After a sufficient amount of line was released so that the log cleared the ship's wake (perhaps ten fathoms), an "egg timer" was turned over. When the sand ran out, the line was stopped and the number of knots counted. In addition, the length from the final knot to the taffrail was also determined, as measured in fathoms. Thus, the "K" column reflected the physical number of knots passing over the rail. The "F" column reflected the length of the "partial knot," measured in fathoms. Broughton's first entry, 4K and 6F represent 204 feet of line (4 knots × 7 fathoms per knot × 6 feet per fathom + 6 fathoms × 6 feet per fathom). The egg timers were typically 28 or 30 seconds. It turns out that with the physical spacing, the count of the number of knots relates closely to the actual speed (for whatever reason, some men identified speed in miles per hour while others used nautical miles per hour—"knots").

While at anchor, some of the men interspersed this six-column format with a simple narrative. Others used a three-column format with the following headings: Day, Wind, and Remarks (some included a fourth column for the month). The astronomical calendar generally was used for this three-column format as well.

For brevity, I ignored the columnar format and simply transcribed the Remarks, except for one example aboard each ship to provide a sense of how the journals actually appeared. The entries in the remaining columns were mostly identical among the journals as the men simply copied this information from the official ship's log rather than observing it directly for themselves. Because the astronomical calendar is confusing, care must be used to determine the date to which the explorer referenced. In almost all cases, initial remarks are really the PM for the previous day to that noted. Where it is shown, AM remarks refer to the day that noted.

Readability and legibility of the journals varied greatly. In some, handwriting, spelling and sentence structure were generally good. That was not the case in others where writing habits such as, capitalization of nouns (common in that day), use of dashes instead of periods to end sentences, incomplete sentences, excessive use of commas instead of periods, or lack of marks at all to end a sentence introduced difficulties for reading. In order to make the text more clear, I took the liberty of adding commas as appropriate as well as periods to the end of sentences and capitalizing the first letter of the following sentence (in most cases). In many cases I could not read one or more various words. Where this occurred, I inserted brackets [ ]. When I was able to guess, I inserted words within the bracket. As a final note, I defaulted to the popular convention of reflecting the names of ships and Latin names in italics although they obviously did not appear that way in the handwritten journals. Where the source was previously typed and edited, I ignored other italics inserted by the editor.

In addition to those reflected here, I also found journals for Volant Ballard, John Stewart, Edward Roberts, James Scott, John Sherriff, Henry Humphries and John Sykes. These were virtually identical to those of their compatriots as in most cases, they simply copied from each other. Since, they contained nothing new, they are not included in this text.

As was the case in the first book, I added explanatory notes to assist in the understanding. Unlike Vancouver's journal, his men frequently used a nautical vernacular which is no longer in use. I apologize for the prolific number of these footnotes, but I hope the reader will find them of assistance.

I would appreciate receiving comments, criticisms, corrections, etc. and may be reached in care of the publisher.

Richard W. Blumenthal
Bellevue, Washington
Fall 2006

Charts

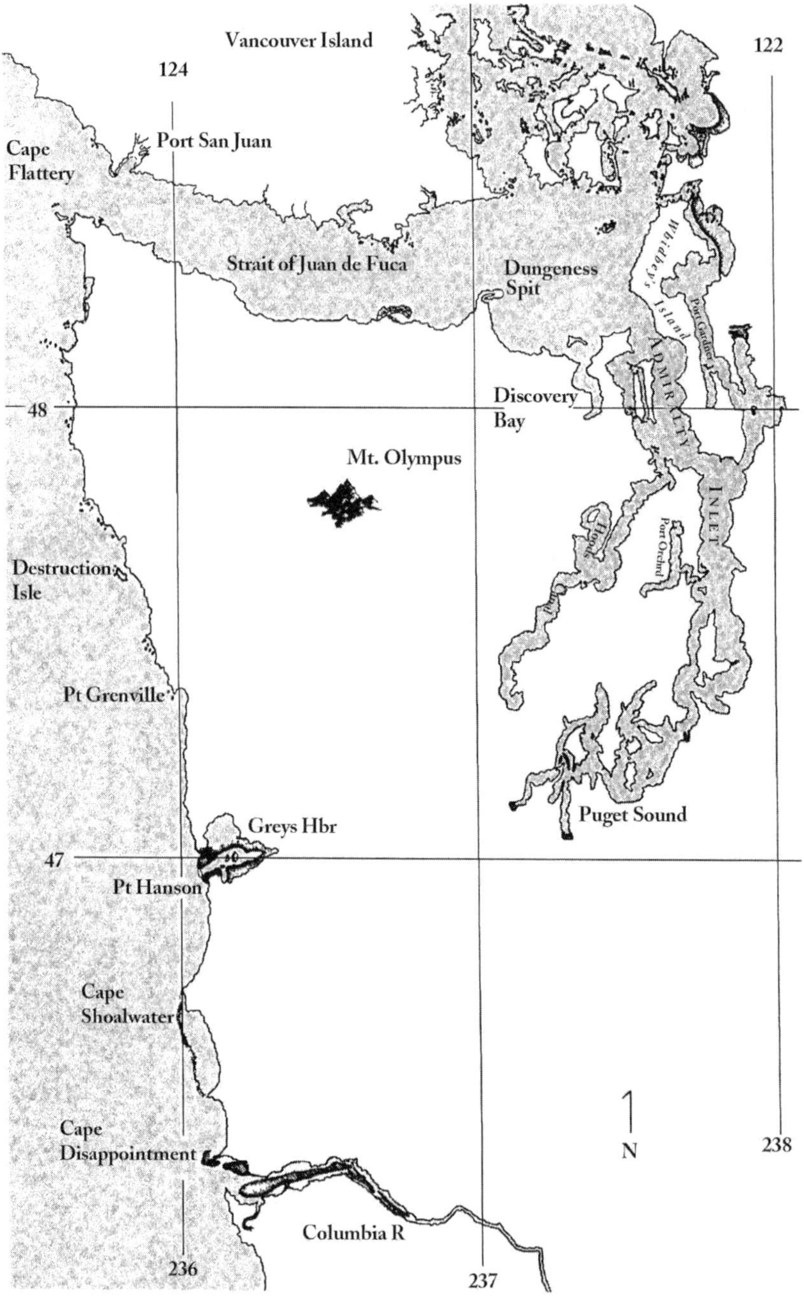

Vancouver, 1792, Washington coast and inland waters

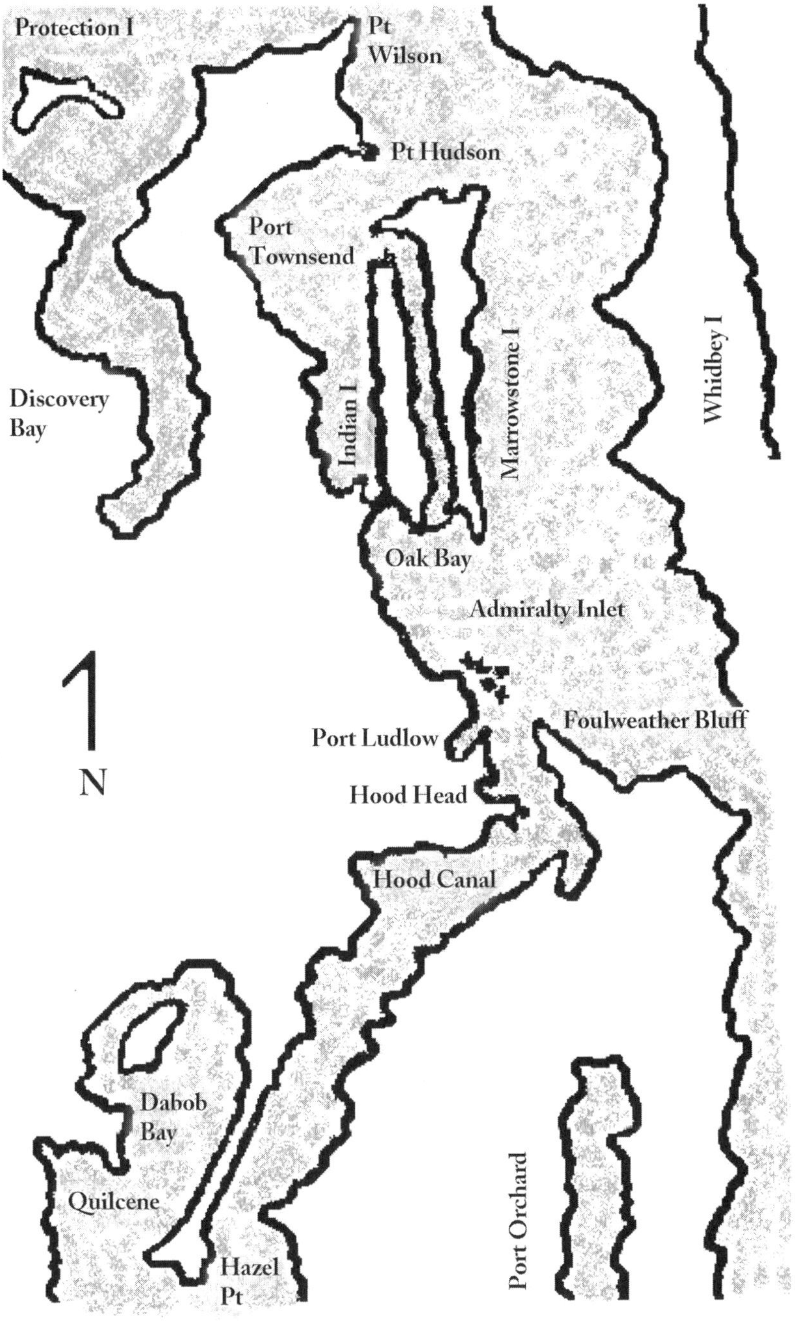

Vancouver, 1792, the northern portion of Admiralty Inlet

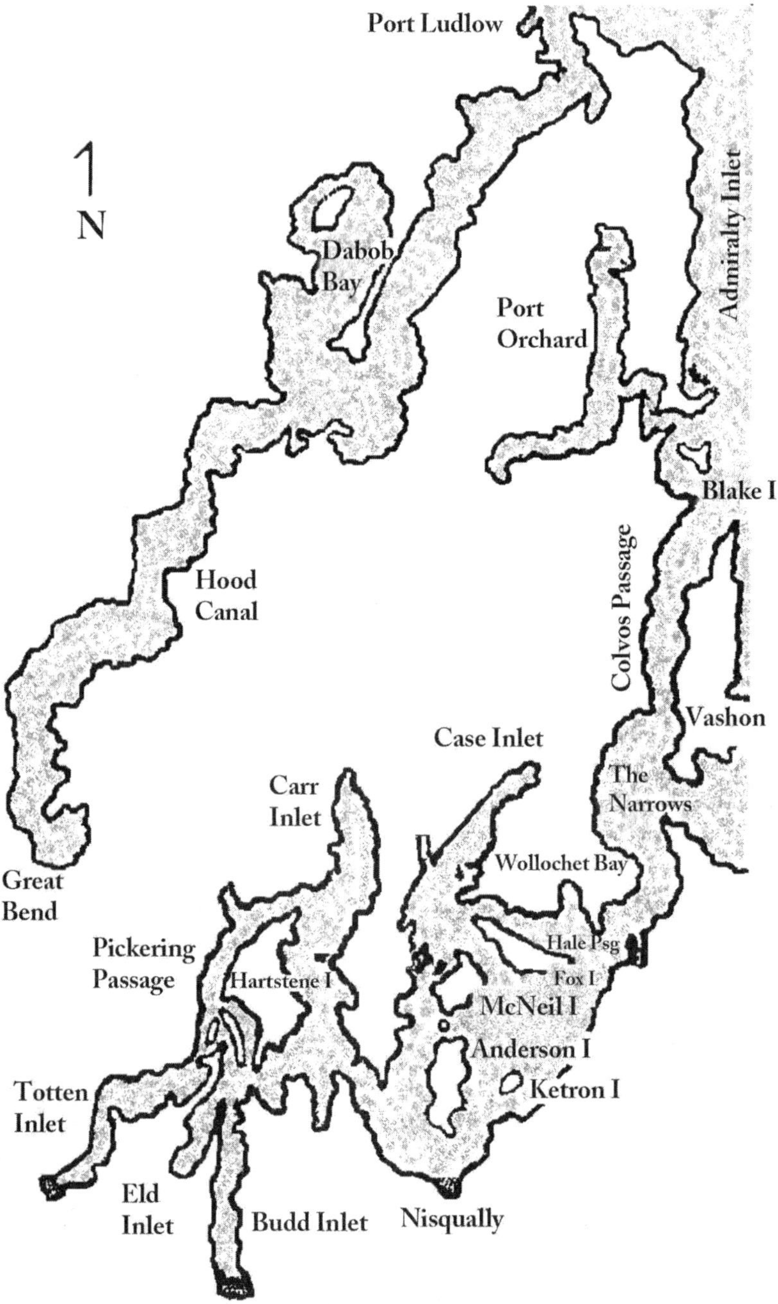

Vancouver, 1792, Hood Canal and Puget Sound

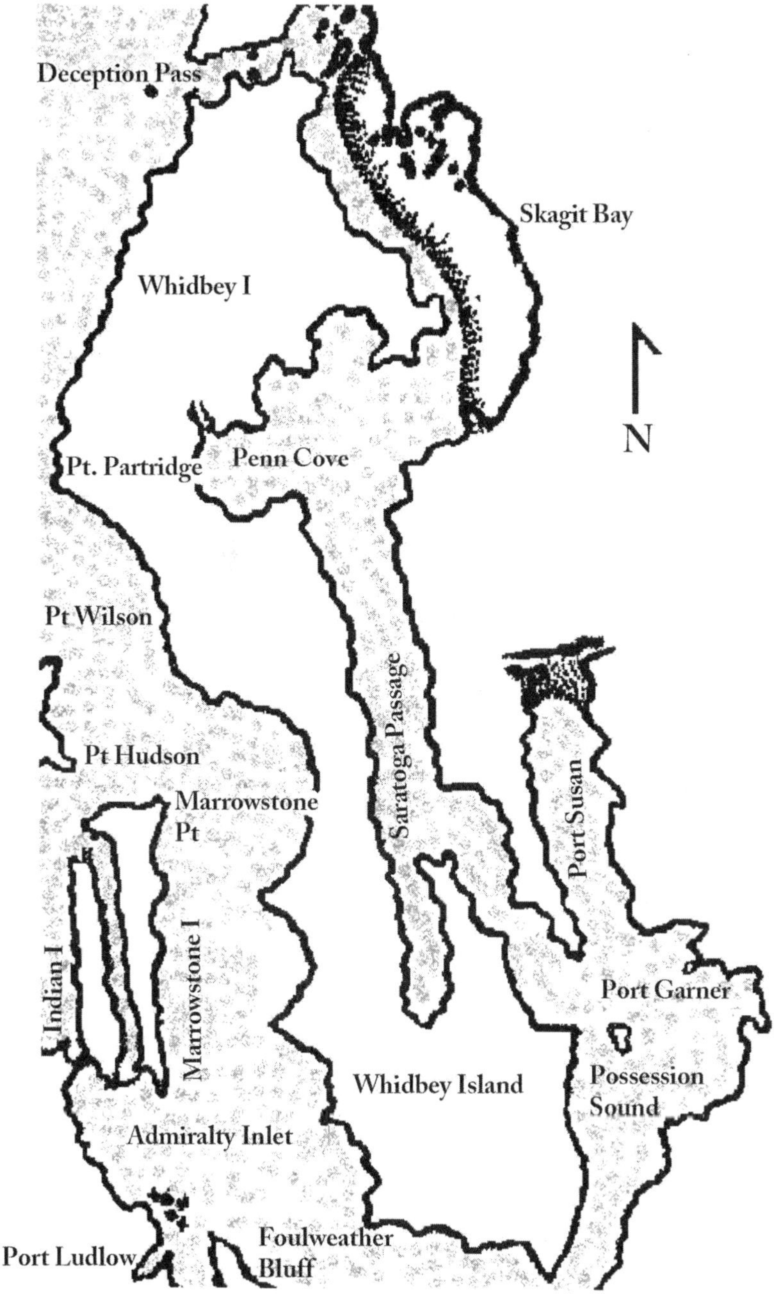

Vancouver, 1792, Whidbey Island

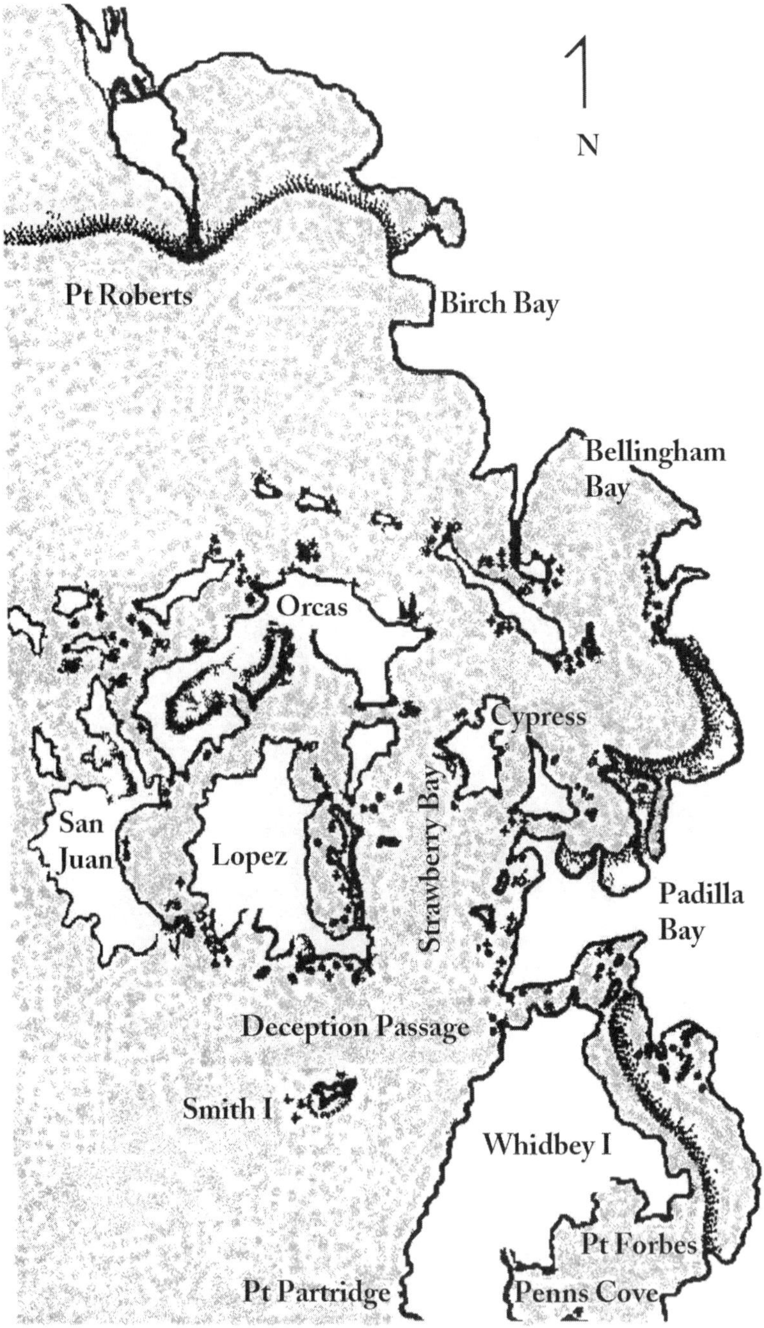

Vancouver, 1792, San Juan Islands

1

Peter Puget

Peter Puget was born on Winchester Street, London, in late October or early November 1765. His father, John, died in 1767. Puget entered the navy on August 1, 1778, at the age of twelve, aboard the *Dunkirk* commanded by John Milligan. He transferred to the *Syren* under Captain Edmund Dodd in December 1780 and battled the North Sea winter weather as well as the French. When Dodd was transferred to the *Lowestoft*, Puget joined him. In the Caribbean, the squadron commanded by Sir Samuel Hood was responsible for protecting English interests from the French. For the next two years, Puget fought admirably. In November 1782, he was transferred to *Thetis* under Captain John Blankett en route to the Mediterranean. In early 1783, he joined the *Europa* commanded by Captain Vashon, in Jamaica for a four-year tour. Also aboard *Europa* were First Lieutenant George Vancouver, midshipman Joseph Baker and Joseph Whidbey. Upon returning to England in 1787, Puget was paid off and furloughed. He resigned with Captain Dodd aboard *Lowestoff* for a couple months, but his naval career was on hold until he was assigned to the *Discovery* as master's mate.

Puget received his commission as Lieutenant on June 11, 1790, and remained aboard *Discovery* which served as a receiving ship during armament against Spain as a result of the Nootka problems. In October 1790, after signing of the Nootka Convention, Vancouver was promoted to Commander of the *Discovery* which departed England April 1, 1791. Throughout the expedition, Vancouver used Puget extensively in the long boats for surveying purposes. In January 1793, Lieutenant Broughton was dispatched to England for additional instructions relating to the Nootka issue. Puget was promoted to command of *Chatham* and continued in that capacity to the end of the voyage when he reached Portsmouth on October 16, 1795.

In February 1796, Puget accepted command of the transport *Adelphi*. The following year, on February 6, 1797, he married Hannah Elrington, the daughter of Army Captain William Elrington. During the next twenty-three years, they had seven boys and four girls. Puget commanded several other ships in the following years and was promoted to Captain. In late 1798, at the death of Vancouver, he assisted Vancouver's brother John with the completion of the final volume of the journal of the *Discovery*. In March of 1799, Puget received orders to join Admiral Whitshed's flagship *Temeraire* as flag captain, a prestigious appointment for a junior captain. This lasted a year, after which he was placed on inactive duty.

In February 1804, Puget took command of the *Foudroyant* as Flag Captain to Rear Admiral Sir Thomas Graves. For the next year and a half, he saw blockade duty in the English Channel against Napoleon and the French until he was seriously injured aboard. He recovered slowly over the following year, then faced disappointing inactivity until appointed to his final command aboard *Goliath* in early 1807. That summer, he had an active role with military activity against the Danes at Copenhagen.

In May 1810, he received orders to assume the duties of Commissioner of the Navy at Madras, India. For the next seven years, he threw himself into the work there, the responsibilities of which included contracting for supplies, construction materials and labor as well as the construction of an entirely new naval base at Trincomalee in Ceylon. He returned to England due to ill health in August 1816, arriving in Portsmouth early in 1818.

In 1821, at the age of fifty-six, Puget reached the top of the list of Post Captains and was commissioned Rear Admiral of the Blue. His health continued to fail. He died in Bath on October 31, 1822. His wife died on September 14, 1849.

Around 1960, H.W. McCurdy, the noted Seattle maritime historian, traveled to London to locate Puget's grave. He had little success until, at the suggestion of an English friend, he put an inquiry in the *London Times*. Three days later, a Mrs. Kitty Champion of Whoolley responded that Rear Admiral Puget was interred in the All Saints Churchyard in Bath. McCurdy verified the gravesite and arranged for a bronze plaque to be installed, donated by the Seattle Historical Society.

The following is an excerpt of the complete Puget journal consisting of two manuscript volumes and 315 pages. It was edited by Bern Anderson and printed in the *Pacific Northwest Quarterly*, V. 30, 1939, p. 177. The journal was handwritten in ink and probably based upon notes. The actual manuscript apparently is located at the Public Record Office in London, but Anderson used a microfilm copy at the University of Washington, which I was unable to locate. I did not use Anderson's footnotes as I believe some to be incorrect. Thus, the footnotes are mine.

For whatever reason, the text was not in chronological order. It began with the small boat trip from Discovery Bay to Port Townsend and Hood Canal. Puget's descriptions then reverted to entering the Strait of Juan de Fuca. For readability purposes, I rearranged the text in chronological sequence.

A LOG OF THE PROCEEDINGS OF HIS MAJESTY'S SLOOP *DISCOVERY*,
GEORGE VANCOUVER ESQ^{RE}, COMMANDER,
KEPT BY LIEUTENANT PETER PUGET
FROM THE 4TH DAY OF JANUARY 1791,
TO THE 14TH DAY OF JANUARY 1793
[p. 187] Streights of De Fuca 1792—

I am indebted to Mr Dalrymple in his Book "A Plan for promoting the Fur Trade"—for the only account I could procure of the Discoverer of these Streights in which he says "It is alledged that the Spaniards [p. 188] have recently found an Entrance in the Latitude of 47° .45' N^{o}. which in Twenty Seven Days Course brought them to the Vicinity of Hudsons Bay (a Note A.) (My Friend the Right Honble Charles Grenville, communicated to me this Intelligence, which Sir John McPherson got at the Cape of Good Hope from the Spaniards)—This Latitude exactly corresponds to the Ancient Relation of John De Fuca, the Greek Pilot, in 1592, who sailed into a Broad Inlet between 47° and 48° which led him into a far Broader Sea, wherein he sailed about 20 Days, there being at the Entrance, on the NW Coast, a great Head Land or Island with an Exceeding high Pinnacle or Spired Rock like a Pillar thereupon We have no other than verbal Information of De Fuca's Discovery, he communicated the Intelligence to a Mr Lock at Venice & offered to perform the Voyage on Condition of having Repayment of the Great Losses he had sustained to the Value of 60,000 Ducats, when captured by Sir Thomas Cavendish in the South Seas—The Amount of this Sum would have been an Obstacle to the Enterprize, however well convinced they may have been of the Reality of his Discoveries (a Note B) But De Fuca's Information only proves an Inland Sea & does not imply he sailed beyond America, Although he himself placed that Inference"—

By which we find by the best Accounts M^{r}. Dalrymple could obtain, that De Fuca was absolutely on this Coast between the Latitudes of 47° and 48° N^{o}. & this being Two Hundred Years ago it may be supposed the Latitude not very Accurate. Cape Flattery which forms the Entrance on the South Side of the Streights lies in the Latitude 48°.23' N°. Longitude 235°.38' East of Greenwich (as settled from the Observatory in Port Discovery).[1]

A Low Flat Green Island[2] laying off the Pitch of the Cape prevented our Rounding so close as we would wish, it lays in a [left blank] Direction from Cape Flattery & is about [left blank] in circumference. We passed pretty near the Island leaving a Bed of Rocks under Water on the Larboard[3] Hand, which bore from the Island [left blank] . Distance [left blank]—But no distinguishable Spiral Rock or Pillar made its appearance, to my knowledge, however Mr. Baker & Menzies say, that after rounding [p. 189] Green Island, a Rock of that Description came in Sight for a Minute or two—the Coast to the Southward of Cape Flattery is quite lined with them.——From this Cape we kept to the Eastward working up along the South Shore, & During the Afternoon were visited by some Indians from Classet,[4] a Village situated close to Cape Flattery, they came alongside without any Ceremonial Introduction; on their Parts or particular Invitation from us & appeared perfectly well acquainted with our Manners and Customs—One Man whom was supposed to be a Chief from his Dress, consisting of a Great Coat decorated with an Immense Quantity of Buttons sewed in the Seams Back or wherever they could be most conspicuous, was invited on board & presented with some Articles as a testimony of Friendship—In the Interim his Companions in the Canoes were not idle alongside, A traffic was commenced for what few Articles they had to dispose of & the Spirit of Commerce was carried on to such Lengths that a few Minutes stript both Men and Canoes of all

---

[1]For a thorough explanation of longitude references used aboard *Discovery*, as well as comparisons to modern charts for accuracy, refer to Blumenthal ... *Six Expeditions*. To avoid redundancy, it is briefly restated here. As was common in that day, British explorers used a 360° reference eastward from Greenwich, England when sailing around the Cape of Good Hope, to identify longitude. If the ship sailed around Cape Horn, the reference was west of Greenwich. Today our current system describes the value as (up to) 180° east or west of the Greenwich prime meridian with the international dateline at 180°. Thus, Puget's reference of longitude 235°.38' represents 124°22' in today's terms (360° minus 235° 38').

[2]Tatoosh Island.

[3]Larboard was an older term for the port or left side of a ship when standing at the stern or back of the vessel, looking forward. A larboard or port tack is achieved when the wind blows from left to right when standing at the stern. The term port referred to the opening on the left side of the ship from which cargo was loaded. Early sailors began using the term as starboard and larboard sounded similar and could be confused. The U.S. Navy officially adopted port and starboard in 1846.

[4]Classet was Vancouver's name for Cape Flattery. The village was about halfway between Cape Flattery and Neah Bay.

their Fishing Gear skin Implements Garments &c & though it rained exceeding hard, the Indians did not at all appear to be incommoded by the Rain — Copper & Iron they held in high Estimation as also were Yellow Buttons, Other trinkets they would accept as Presents, but not in Exchange for a Single Article; Three or four Sea Otters were purchased but indifferent in their Quality, other Garments made of Raccoon & the Black bear were in plenty. These with Bows Arrows and Fish Hooks composed the whole of their Merchandize — We Anchored that Night under the South Shore in 23 fths About ½ a Mile from the Land with these bearings Entrance of the Streight S°. 88 W N°. D°.[5] N 68 W^{t}.[6] The Streights here [left blank] Miles Broad at the Entrance [left blank] Miles. — Next Morning May 1st the Weather had again resumed its former Serenity & by ½ p^{t} 6 we were enabled to weigh with a light Westerly Breeze, which as the Day advanced, it increased. At Noon the Latitude observed was 48° .18' N°. The Course was directed along the Starboard Shore as the Continent which trended up East & EbN° by Compass, it being Cap^{tn} Vancouvers Intention to either Stop at the first Opening or Harbour to refit. Towards Sun Set a Low Sandy Point, which from its Similarity to Dungeness obtained that Name made its Appearance behind which was a Lagoon [p. 190] or Harbour for that we kept, but hauling too close to the Point we suddenly Shoaled the Water to three fathoms At a little further Distance was 8 & 9 fths. At 8 we Anchored in 14 fths Soft Bottom with the following Bearings — Distant low Bluff N35W — Lowpoint Point N24W Apparent Harbour Bluff S50E^{t} Nearest Shore South three Miles — Early in the Morning a Boat was sent to examine the Lagoon or Harbour that we had seen running down, she returned about 8 with an unsuccessful Report of that & also of the Apparent Harbour which bore S50E^{t} — Capt Vancouver therefore determined as the Vessels stood in Need of Repair & a supply of Wood and Water, to set out immediately after Breakfast in quest of a Convenient Place to carry on our Operations——About 9 we left the Ships with two of the *Discoverys* Boats & one from the *Chatham* — & at the Back of apparent Island[7] which bore N87E^{t} about Eleven Miles from our Present Anchorage a most excellent [harbour?] was found — with Conveniences of all Kinds for the Tents & a fine Rivulet of fresh Water close to the Situation we had pitched on for them — It was not till Eleven at Night that we got on board; where we were informed that during our absence Some Canoes had been alongside and sold some Halibut, that the Indians conducted themselves with Honesty & appeared perfectly inoffensive. The

[5]As used in this and later journals, the term is an abbreviation for "ditto."

[6]Approximately five miles east of Baadah Point.

[7]Protection Island.

People however notwithstanding their present pacific Dispositions must be of the same Tribe that attacked Mr Mears Longboat under the Direction of M^{r}. Duffin; therefore to our Force alone their good Behaviour was attributed —[8]

The Land to the Southward of Cape Flattery is of a Moderate

---

[8]Puget no doubt had reviewed the actual events, as explained by Meares, which are worthy of reproduction. At anchor in Barclay Sound, the longboat was dispatched to explore the Strait of Juan de Fuca (Meares, 1, 280).

"We embraced the present favourable opportunity to dispatch the long boat, not only to explore the straits of de Fuca, but to procure, if possible, some knowledge of the people of Shoalwater-Bay. She was, therefore, properly equipped for the occasion, was manned with thirteen of our people, and furnished with provisions for a month. The command of her was given to Mr. Robert Duffin, our first officer, to whom written instructions were delivered.— On the 13th, [July 1788] the boat departed on its voyage of discovery.

"...On the evening of the 20th, we saw the sails of the long-boat in the offing; but the sudden impulse of our unreflecting joy on the occasion, was immediately checked by the apprehensions that naturally arose in our minds from her early return. The interval of her arrival at the ship was a period of vary painful suspense to every one on board: at length, to our inexpressible satisfaction, we observed, on her coming alongside, that not an individual was missing.— Our immediate attention, however, was called to the assistance of some wounded men, who had suffered severely in a very violent conflict the boat had sustained with the natives of the straits, and which was the cause of her sudden return.

"The whole attention of the ship was now transferred to our wounded people, but though several of them were much hurt, we were consoled with finding that no mortal injury had been received by any. The officer was wounded by a barbed arrow in the head, which would have killed him on the spot, if a thick hat had not deadened the force of the weapon. One of the seamen was pierced in the breast, and another in the calf of the leg, into which the arrow had entered so far as to render a very large incision absolutely necessary, in order to discharge it. A fourth received a wound very near the heart, but the weapon which gave it, very fortunately fell short of the vital parts. The rest of the people were bruised in a terrible manner by the stones and clubs of the enemy; even the boat itself was pierced in a thousand places by arrows, many of which remained in the awning that covered the back part of it; and which, by receiving the arrows, and breaking the fall of large stones thrown from slings, in a great measure saved our party from inevitable destruction.

"In this engagement the natives behaved with a spirit and resolution that resisted the usual terror of fire-arms among a savage people; for the contest was close, and for some time our men fought for their lives.— One of them had been singled out by an individual savage for his victim, and a fierce engagement took place between them.— The native was armed with a stone bludgeon, and the sailor with a cutlass. They both manifested, for some time, equal courage and dexterity; but if an intervening oar had not broke a blow, armed with all the force of his enemy, our brave countryman must have sunk beneath it. It however failed its object, and gave him an opportunity, by a severe stroke of the cutlass, to deprive the native of an arm, who, notwithstanding such a loss, and several other wounds, contrived to swim from the boat, indebted for his life to the noble mercy of his conqueror, who disdained to kill him in the water.

"The seaman who was wounded in the leg, continued, (*note continued on next page*)

Height & as far as the Eye could reach one continued Forest, Towards the Sea are a few Spots sufficiently clear for Cultivation which have a pleasing Effect contrasted with the Hills at their Back & the Lofty Chain of Snowy mountains far Inland. If the Soil was good, that Situation might with a little Assistance to the bountiful Hand of Nature be made truly beautiful — We had a very imperfect view of the Country in the Afternoon after passing Cape Flattery — the Land was much higher towards the Sea but equally covered with Wood.—

Next Morning May 2[d] we left our Anchorage early & with a Light Westerly Breeze made Sail for the Harbour we had found the preceding [p. 191] afternoon — The Island which lays off its entrance obtained the Name of Protection Island & the Harbour [left blank]

[p. 180] An Account of the Expedition in the Boats & Remarks on Port Discovery

On the 7th of May we left the Ship on a Surveying Expedition with three Boats, provided with a Weeks Provision and well armed, in which were Cap[t]. Vancouver M[r]. Johnstone, Menzies & myself. We proceeded along the Continental Shore in an ENE direction for the Distance of

---

8. (cont.) during the action, with the arrow in his flesh; and with out attempting to rid himself of the torturing weapon, became, by his courageous and active exertions, a very principal instrument in preserving the boat.

"Though we had never had any intercourse or communication with the inhabitants of the straits, we had indulged ourselves with the hope that our friendly conduct towards their neighbours, might, by some means, have reached the district of their habitation, and given them favourable impressions of us: but their conduct marked the most savage and blood hostility; and the fury of their onset compelled a similar spirit of resistance: but to do justice to the humanity of our people, — notwithstanding the actual sufferings of many of them, and the cruel fate which they well knew would have been the certain allotment of them all, had they lost the day, — they never failed, in recounting the circumstances of it, to express an unfeigned concern for the unhappy people who had so rashly courted their own destruction.

"The attack was begun by the savages, — who boarded the boat, with the design of taking her, in two canoes, containing between forty and fifty men, who were most probably some of their choicest warriors. Several other canoes also remained at a small distance, to assist in the attempt; and the shore was every where lined with people, who discharged at our vessel continual showers of stones and arrows. A chief in one of the canoes, who encouraged the advance of the others, was most fortunately shot in the head with a single ball, while in the very act of throwing a spear of a most enormous length at the cockswain. This circumstance caused the canoes to draw back, and deprived the natives who were already engaged, of that support which must have ensured them the victory.— Indeed, as it was, when we consider that the boat's company consisted only of thirteen men, who were attacked with the most courageous fury by superior numbers, and galled as these were, at the same moment, by the numerous weapons constantly discharged from the shore, their escape is to be numbered among those favourable events of life, which never fail to excite, in well ordered minds, a mingled sensation of gratitude and astonishment."

four Miles, here the Coast headed to the SE[9] forming an Excellent Harbour,[10] with Regular Soundings from Nine to Seventeen fathoms, the Land towards the Beach rather Low & beautifully covered with Verdure. It was not till the Evening that we Reached the Head of this Place, there we found a Run of Water,[11] which I should imagine not perpetual, but merely occasioned by the heavy Rains we experienced on Entering De Fuca's Streights From the Entrance to the termination of this Harbour is Six Miles, where it is closed by low land, over which we could see another Spacious Inlet trending to the SE.[12] We waited with some [p. 181] anxiety for the Arrival of M[r]. Johnstone in the *Chathams* Cutter[13] who had been Dispatched to examine the opposite Side or Northern Shore of this Harbour; but his not joining the Party by Eight at Night obliged us to remain, where we had reached at Sun Set. Early next morning the Report of a Swivel[14] relieved us from the Fears of a total Separation, which we answered by firing another, & shortly after had the Satisfaction to see, the Boat pulling towards us—M[r]. Johnstone reported, he had been led into a Narrow passage where he found Four & five fathoms Water, & the hopes of finding it communicate, from the Rapidity of the Tide, to some other extensive Sound, induced him to continue on in a SE Direction for the Distance of Six Miles, here it was closed by a Sand Bank & Passable to Boats only at half Tide; as he had been so much deceived in this Passage, we called it Johnstone's Decoy.[15] As it was necessary to replenish our water every Opportunity for that

---

[9]Toward Point Wilson.

[10]Port Townsend.

[11]According to Vancouver's journal, the boats set a rendezvous near Kala Point. They discovered the run of water, perhaps Chimacum Creek, the following morning (Blumenthal, 127, 128).

[12]Puget was looking into Oak Bay and Admiralty Inlet.

[13]A cutter, yawl and pinnace were similar in appearance with as many as ten oars, five to a side. Early on, they were distinctively different but all evolved by the late 1700s to look essentially the same. For example, an early cutter was likely a lapstrake design while a yawl was smooth planked. *Chatham's* cutter was twenty-two feet in length, *Discovery's* was eighteen feet with six oars and a single mast. The yawl was twenty-six foot three-masted vessel with eight oars. The journals of the other "Gentlemen" referred to the yawl as the Pinnace. Launch and longboat are used interchangeably in the journals. These were the workboats, and generally larger than the cutters or yawls. Technically, a longboat is the largest of the workboats. Because it had a full keel, it was more easily sailed than the launch. However, the launch was more easily beached. The main recognizable difference between the boats is in the stern. The stern of a yawl and cutter was wineglass in shape, the entire transom was out of the water. The transom of the longboat and launch was broad and flat, and extended into the water.

[14]Small boat cannon which swivels or rotates on a mount.

[15]Kilisut Harbor.

purpose we were left behind in the Launch to fill the Empty Casks and Kegs, whilst the Pinnace and Cutter proceeded on to the further Examination of the Continental Shore—. . Here we had the Misfortune to ground nor Could our utmost Endeavours get the Boat afloat before the flood came in though every article had been taken out of her—, Through which accident it was not till two that we joined the Party round the Point which forms the Opposite Point of the Harbour[16]—Not far from this Situation our Astonishment was much excited by a Sight so truly horrid, that it awakened all New Ideas, that naturally crowd in the Imagination; of the Savage Customs and Manners of the Indians who inhabit these extensive Countries—A Long Pole & two others of Smaller Size were put upright in the Ground each having a Human Scull on the Top, through which the Poles Penetrated.; these appeared to have been lately put there, as the Hair & Flesh Still adhered to the Bone, & Though I have heard & read of this mode of Punishment in England, for very Capital Offenses where it was necessary as an Example, by such an Ignominious Testimony of the Crime committed, that it should have the public Exposal to deter others from falling into the same Snare, but here ignorant of the Motives which had caused the present unhappy fate of these three persons, it was therefore attributed more to the Barbarity of the Manners and Customs of the Indians, than to any Merited [?] Punishment—though they might have been Enemies or might have forfeited their Lives to the particular Laws under which they were governed—But these Considerations were now totally out of the Question—the Effect was judged without a Knowledge of the Cause—[p. 182] On this Point we stopped to Dinner & a pleasant Situation it was, at the Back of the Beach which was low and Sandy, was some Quantity of low Land, well covered with verdure & on which were plenty of Gooseberry Bushes & wild Roses.—We had now an Extensive Inlet before us to the SE with an immense Rapid Tide, the Flood coming in from the Entrance.—About three we again set off. Mr Johnstone was dispatched in the *Chathams* Cutter to Sound the Opposite or NE Shore.[17] I was in the Launch to keep Mid Channel whilst Capt. Vancouver in the Pinnace pursued the Continent fixing the Rendezvous in case of Separation to a very Distant Bluff bearing about SbE.[18] In our Station we frequently Sounded with Eighty fathoms no Ground ... & though we had a Fresh Breeze from the NW yet the Rapidity of the Ebb was so great that we went up Stream by the Land; its Rate must have been nearly five knots. Though the day had continued exceeding fine yet towards the Eve-

[16]Near Walan Point on Indian Island.

[17]The western shore of Whidbey Island.

[18]Foulweather Bluff.

ning the Hills became covered with a thick Vapour, & by 7 in the Evening the Weather had undergone a total Change — a SE Breeze & heavy Rain precluded any possibility of our being able to reach the Rendezvous that Night & as a total Separation appeared to have taken Place, I continued pulling towards the Rendezvous Bluff firing Swivels frequently to form a junction which were as often answered by the *Chatham* Cutter. It was not till 9 that I met Mr Johnstone at which time, it blew Strong, was extremely dark with a perfect torrent of Rain, and an Ebb Tide to pull against, these Obstacles induced us to return to the Continental Shore for the remainder of the Night: The Pinnace was afterwards joined & we three all proceeded on this Plan but it was till 2 in the Morning on the 9th that a Place could be found, that would answer our purpose — At Day Light we looked round with Anxiety to ascertain what kind of a Situation we had fixt on, as on the preceding Evening the Fire Arms had got wet & even not yet put in Order that should this Station have been near a large Village we would have proved but a Weak force — But we appeared to have pitched in a very eligible Spot, it was a Snug cove which formed the termination to Johnstones Decoy — .[19] The Native Inhabitants by the Remains of Fire & Huts must have been lately here, we however saw none — During the whole of the 9th it Rained & blew hard which prevented our moving, we were therefore employed putting the Fire Arms in order — The Surrounding Country appears like a thick Forest of Pines it is low — & abounds near the Beaches with some very pleasant Spots — In this Cove were some Small Oak Trees, Maple, Pines of various Sorts, Gooseberry & Raspberry Bushes — Of Birds, there were [p. 183] the White Headed & Brown Eagle, Crows Ravens Curlews & some Oceanic Birds — At Low Water the Beaches afforded us an Excellent Supply of Clams but a Small Seine we had was unsuccessful —

We were detained by this tempestuous Weather till the 10th in the M^{rng} when we quitted our Quarters early & made but little progress against a very Strong Southerly Wind — A Cove with a Smoak at its head about two Leagues along the Continental Shore from our Sleeping Place, induced Capt. Vancouver /after sounding it out/ to Stop there to Breakfast[20]; Seventeen Indians who had previously watched our Motions, landed at a little distance from the Boats, leaving their Arms in the Canoes — They approached with all the Confidence imaginable & were well contented to take their Seats beyond a Line marked out to divide the two Parties, here they remained to gratify their Curiosity & at our

---

[19]Near Kinney Point on the south end of Marrowstone Island.

[20]It is difficult to place this location. It was somewhere along the western shore between Olele Point and Port Ludlow.

Departure Some Medals and other Trinkets were given them, with which they appeared highly Pleased — The People in their Persons were Low & Ill made with broad faces & Small Eyes— Their Foreheads appear to be Deformed or out of Shape comparatively Speaking with those of Europeans— The Head has something of a Conical Shape — They wear the Hair Long with Quantities of Red Ochre intermixed with whale Oil or some other Greasy Substance that has a Similar disagreeable Smell.— Only One Man had a thick Beard, the others, wore a Small Tuft of Hair on the Point of the Chin & on the Upper Lip like Mustachios & on other parts of the Body they suffered Nature to have its Course, which were as well supplied as in the Common Run of Men except the Breasts, which were all totally destitute of Hair.— Square pieces of ear Shells were hung to small perforations in their Ears with small Rolls of Copper — Necklaces of the same Materials as the Latter were used as also round the Ankles & wrists.— Their Garments consisted of the Skins of an Animal tied at the two Corners over one Shoulder the upper Edge coming under the Opposite Arm — by which both Hands were free — The Rest of the Body was perfectly naked.— They had no other Arms but Bows and Arrows pointed with barbed Flints & long Spears in their Canoes, These were of simple Workmanship as also were the Canoes— The last consisted only of a log hollowed out Sharp at both Ends & tolerably well constructed for paddling — The Paddles were Short and pointed at the Ends.— There was no diminution of the Wind when we set off it continued Southerly & we had likewise a Strong Tide of Ebb to encounter — After a fatiguing pull of four hours we were under the Necessity of Stopping as the Boats did not get the least past the Land. This was about four Miles from the Cove where we saw the Indians that we Stopped to take some Refreshment — From this Situation a Small Round Island bore SE[21] & to the [p. 184] SE of the Point where this Rendezvous of the Boats had been appointed was an Extensive Inlet trending to the SE[22] but as this was the Continental Shore it was necessary to round it out as beyond the Round Island it appeared to terminate, from thence we should come to the Rendezvous Point as the Continent in the Afternoon.— It will be unnecessary to mention the variety of Coves & a full description of the Shore as we passed it, the Chart more fully explain their Situation, We left this Place about 3 in the Afternoon & sent the Boats on towards the Island, whilst Capt. Vancouver & ourselves walked along the Beach but without meeting any occurrence worth mentioning — The Island was found to be connected to the Main by a low Spit of Land beyond which

[21]Hood Head.

[22]The continuation of Admiralty Inlet.

was another Extensive Inlet trending to the Southward, but from the Supposed round Island to the Opposite Shore was no more than ¾ of a Mile Wide. Thus were we deceived in the termination we had from our last Stoppage expected; Passing the Narrows the Continent took a more Southerly Direction & the Inlet[23] widened to three Miles and an Half— Mr Johnstone was dispatched to sound in Mid Channel & the Launch to the Opposite Shore. The Wind attracted by the Surrounding Hills blew likewise Strong down the Reach, however with the rapid Flood we made some Progress. It was not till 8 that we pitched the Tent on a Pleasant Spot on the Eastern Shore—Indeed every Place we passed in the Afternoon on that side of the Inlet was equally agreeable. The Country was greatly beautified by the advanced State of the Spring, every tree appeared in Blossom & these small projecting Points in particular were every where covered with a Sort of Pale Crimson Flower[24]—We had some Expectation of finding a Communication with the Grand SE Arm[25]; Here we remained till Friday morning the 11th of May when we crossed the Inlet[26] after Breakfast after Determining the non existence of any Eastern passage in this Branch to the one we had left off Yesterday Afternoon— The Weather had now regained its usual Serenity that we were enabled to make great Progress.—& After a hard Days pull we Stopped for our Nights Quarters about five Miles to the Southward of a Smoak from which we had no Visitors. In this Days Examination we had passed a Branch trending about SW from the Breakfast Place & another with an Apparent Island at its termination of a No. Direction[27]; the Inlet we were now in trended about SbE—After being greatly tormented by Musquito's and Flies &c[28] we left our Quarters early & continued the further investigation of this Branch: [p. 185] Seeing a Smoak on the Western Shore we pulled in & landed[29] at a Small Village where we found a few Indians under two or three Miserable Sheds, or huts preparing Clams and Fish for the Winter Season /as was supposed/—From them we bought a Small Quantity of each for which they took any Article we offered—The Stench of this Place was Intolerable, though close to a fine fresh Water Run, yet the Indolence of the Inhabitants appear so great; that the filth is left close to the Habitations, which if carried but a few yards would be swept away

[23]Hood Canal

[24]Perhaps the rhododendron.

[25]Puget evidently believed the eastern shore to be an island.

[26]To Hazel Point.

[27]Dabob Bay.

[28]Throughout Puget's and other journals, "&c" is used for "etc."

[29]Near the Great Bend.

into the Stream. The People are nearly the Same in Appearance as those seen in the Cove on Thursday Morning—They willingly disposed of the Bows and Arrows, some of which were barbed with Iron—This gave rise to various Conjectures, but it was generally supposed that either Europeans had before visited this Tribe or they must have some Mercantile Communication with those situated near the Sea—As we saw the termination of this Inlet from our present Situation, which lies in the Latitude 47°–20' N°. Longitude. [left blank] Capt. Vancouver determined to make the best of His Way for the Ships as the Provisions were nearly exhausted.—From this village we kept to the opposite Shore, to visit some more Indians collected on a Point[30] which forms part of the Banks & Entrance of a Fresh Water Run.[31]—There we found People of all ages & Descriptions to the Amount of Forty or Fifty, they beheld the approach of the Boats without the least Apprehension or evident Signs of Fear.—They immediately on our Request began a barter for Fish or whatever Articles we wished for in their Possession. The Conduct of these People impressed me with an high Idea of their Honesty, for whatever they had to barter, was suffered to be taken away, without an Exchange & it would be sometimes ten Minutes or a Quarter of an Hour before the person returned from the Boats the Things he intended to give. Yet this Delay did not cause any murmuring or Discontent on the Contrary they appeared perfectly well satisfied of our friendly Intentions.—Surely then, if these People behave with such Confidence to Strangers, may we not infer, that Innate Principles of Honesty actuated their Conduct on this Occasion? Some have attributed that Confidence to Fear of the largeness of the Party, that they were glad to receive whatever we offered in Exchange, as they expected, their Property to be wrested from their Possession.—however I am willing to allow them Credit for Appearances & say they differ in Character from the General Body of their Neighbors, who by Report of former Visitors [p. 186] [seem to be] most arrant Rogues—The Women are not distinguishable by any Effeminacy or Softness of Features, they are nearly in appearance similar to the Men, & those we noticed, were discovered by suckling some Children—They wear their Hair long which is Black & as filthy as the Men's but are more decently covered with Garments as no part of the Body is visible, but the Heads Hands & Feet; some were solicited to grant their favors but they refused I believe for want of more Secret Opportunity, nor did the Men appear at all jealous of the Liberties taken with their Women—Having now finished our Visit we began returning along the Opposite or Eastern

[30]Likely Ayres or Musqueti Point.

[31]Rendsland Creek.

Shore & about two Miles from these Friendly Indians we pitched our Tents for the Night.— nor did a Single Canoe attempt to follow us.[32] Early next morning Sunday 13th of May we set out again on our Return to the Ships & as we were now certain of the Continent as far as the Rendezvous Point, we only stopped for our Meals— The Pinnace having pulled ahead in the Evening, and night having set in made us apprehensive we had already missed her, we however continued on close in by the Shore & about Ten found them on a Narrow Spit of Low Land, from this Situation the Tide very near floated us out, but it was too late to recede as the Tents & things were already on Shore — The water came close up which we were glad to see was its height.— During the Night the Weather had undergone a total Change & in the Morning the Hills were covered with vapours.— We however set out early on Monday the 14th & by the Afternoon reached the Rendezvous Point, where the Rain & threatening exposures of the Evening induced us to bring too thus early to secure the Boats— The Night proved full as bad as we expected, blowing and Raining from the SE, — thus prevented our Moving as early as usual however finding a Continuance of the Gale after Noon & having a Strong Ebb Tide in our favor with little or no Provisions left, induced Capt Vancouver to run for Port Discovery, we therefore about 12 on the 15th of May left our Quarters & as the Wind was fair & still blew hard, our progress was considerable along the Land, which was mostly obscured by the Incessant Deluge of Rain that fell the whole time we were running for the Ships— which we reached about three.[33] From this Place Capt. Vancouver determined to move as [soon as?] possible & with the Vessels pursue the great SE Inlet we had left Monday in that Direction from Rendezvous Point — In the Last Excursion we found the Country Low & thick covered with wood, of the same Sorts as I have before noticed in the Early part of the Expedition on the Beaches we found Stones in which were sufficient Iron to attract the Magnet round but [p. 187] no other Appearance of Minerals. The Oaks were all to Small for ordinary Use ——

As we had by this Examination discovered the Termination of an

---

[32]Vancouver's journal indicated that some of the Indians followed along the beach but returned to their camp as night fell (Blumenthal 138).

[33]The distance from Foulweather Bluff to Port Discovery is twenty-four miles. Puget's departure and arrival times would yield an average speed of eight knots. Vancouver's Narrative indicated they departed at 10:00 and arrived at 4:00 for an average speed of four knots (Blumenthal 138). Menzies indicated they left "early" and arrived at 3:00. Vital statistics on the *Townshend*, a replica of Vancouver's yawl located at the Point Hudson Marina in Port Townsend indicate that it travels at four to six knots. With a four knot push from the current, not uncommon in Admiralty Inlet, and favorable winds, an average speed of eight knots is very possible.

Inlet into which the Flood amazingly strong, & the Ebb returned with still more Rapidity, from this Circumstance various were the Conjectures, of which the Principal appeared that the Streight of De Fuca was prove a long Sound branching off in various Directions—& that we should have to return again to Cape Flattery[34]: M^r. Mears in his Account of the probable Existence of a N W Passage, makes the Sloop *Washington* commanded by M^r. Grey in the year [left blank]Sail Round to the Latitude of [left blank] N° by an Inland Navigation—but having now luckily seen M^r. Grey he assured me, that when he Commanded the *Washington* he had been, in the Streights of De Fuca but had never proceeded more than fifteen or Sixteen Leagues in an Easterly Direction up them: So that M^r. Mears must have trusted to bad Information in that Respect—but certain it is, that whilst the Flood has its Source from the Entrance of De Fuca, no passage can Exist.—M^r. Grey likewise informed me that in the Latitude of 55°.30' N°. he lost an Officer and 2 or 3 Men who were barbarously murdered by the Natives, when in a Fishing Party in a Small Boat, but obscured from the Vessel, he could never learn what caused their Death.—The Bodies were Stabbed in several Places. Mr Grey had wintered at Clioquat an Harbour situated on the Outer Coast between the Entrance of De Fuca and Nootka, where he was attacked by the Natives whom he repulsed with some Loss——

[p. 191] That of——**Port Discovery**

It is necessary in going the Western passage into the Harbour to give the West Point a Good Birth as there is a Shoal[35] which extends in the Channel [left blank] to the Main or Deep Water & between it & the Shoal 35fths Water, The Passage free from Danger is one Mile & one half wide—When past the Island the Inlet or Harbour trends up in a SEly Direction for Seven Miles & one half to a Low Point on the SW Shore, beyond this the Vessels Anchored in 34 fths Water about a Cables Length[36] from the Point, where we moored a Cable each way[37] with the

---

[34]Tidal direction was continually noted by the men. They assumed, given no change in direction, that the inlets they explored were not connected to the Pacific except from the Strait of Juan de Fuca.

[35]Dallas Bank which extends north and west of Protection Island.

[36]Cables attached to the anchor were generally 120 fathoms (720 feet) in length, hence the term "cable length."

[37]"Mooring" is the act of setting out two anchors in opposite directions. Thus, with changing currents and winds, the ship always pulls on an individual anchor from the same direction. If a single anchor was used, it must "reset" itself with each current change as the ship shifts from one side to the other. The risk of the anchor breaking loose is much greater.

following Bearings East Entrance Point N48W^{t} Center of Protection Island N50W^{t} West Entrance Point N54W^{t} & Observatory Point[38] S80W.—Protection Island lies S73E true 72 Miles from Cape Flattery.—The Harbour runs up four Miles and an half beyond our Anchorage in a winding SE Direction—Immediately after our Arrival the Sails were unbent & Tents & Observatories erected under the Guard of a Party of Marines——& the other Operations of Wooding watering brewing Spruce Beer & drying the Powder were put in forwardness——

The Land about Port Discovery is in some Places low but at a Short Distance from the Beach it Rizes to Hills of a Moderate Height & is everywhere covered with large Pine Trees, who Dimensions would answer for Masts or Yards for any Frigate in the Service—As to its Productions either Vegetables or Animals may be comprized in a very few Words—Pines of various Sorts chiefly composed the Woods—some of them sufficiently large to mast the *Discovery* there were other Small Trees, but of what Sort I do not remember wild cellery & Sanephud [?] were found in some Small Quantities—Of Birds there were many the Brown and White Headed Eagle, Crows Ravens, Curlews, & many Oceanic Birds.——

[p. 192] The seine supplied us occasionally with Salmon Trout a sort of Flat Fish perfectly insipid but large; another Sort equally bad called Gulpin.

The Natives I have Reason to believe do not much frequent this Place but on the most Solemn Occasions, either the Burial of the Dead or Human Sacrifice.—Close to the Tents were the Remains of an immense large Fire & among the Embers were several Human Sculls & Bones the former in general fractured & all much burnt. Not far from this Situation was found a Canoe suspended to a Tree with a perfect Skeleton in the Inside & others in a forward State of Decay—There were likewise Square Boxes, Bows & Arrows Fishing Implements and a stick or two of Clams laid by them;—The Canoe was hung by Ropes to the Branches & in another Place we Discovered a Basket suspended in a Similar Manner, which contained the Remains of a young Child, that from the putrified State of the Flesh could not have been there above a Month or Six Weeks. From these Circumstances I should suppose that the bones which had partly been consumed by Fire were the Remains of People taken in War who had been sacrificed to the Skeletons suspended to the Tree, & who had fell in the Engagement: but these were merely conjectural Ideas, as we had not yet sufficient acquaintance with the Native Inhabitants to

[38]Carr or Contractors Point.

assume at any Knowledge of their Manners or Customs This certainly appears to me to be the only probable way of accounting for such a horrid Sight: though it was first supposed from the Scattered & mangled State of the Bones, that the Indians had devoured the Flesh. A Minutes Reflection soon corrected such an Idea for however Strong Appearances may be in favor of such a Supposition, yet with ocular Demonstration as the most uncontestable Proofs of the existence of such a Savage Custom, I cannot think any Person authorized to fix such an indelible Stain on the Character of any Tribe, & much more so on the Numerous inhabitants of NW America whose Manners Customs Religion Laws & Government we are yet perfect Strangers to—

The Bones round the Fire Place were left undisturbed but the Curiosity of some of our People had induced them to cut the Canoe and Basket down & instead of replacing them in their former Situation they were left on the Beach.—

During our absence in the Boats, the Vessels secured a Small supply of Venison & Fish from the Indians which were purchased for Copper & other Trinkets, not one however; were perceived to go near the Burial Place, or even to notice it.—They were likewise on Shore when the Tents were struck, of which they were Silent Spectators nor did they Shew the Least Curiosity in the Examination of them, or a Single Article belonging to us, except the Musquets with which they appeared [p. 193] highly delighted & to convince them of the destructive Power of that Weapon, a Ball was several times fired through a Mail; which they beheld with a Mixture of fear and Admiration—Most of these People were perfectly naked, not even a part was covered from the Wind, this was owing to the Heat, as they in general use a Garment which reaches from the Shoulders to the Knees.—"Buffon mentions that the People of the New World are distinguished by only having hair on the Head; from those of the Old, our present Visitors by no Means answered to that Assertion; for in that particular they resembled Europeans—except on the Breast which in every one I have seen, was there perfectly destitute. In their Persons these People were but slenderly made, their colour was of a light Brown, but so much obscured by Dirt, Oil or Paint, that it was almost impossible to distinguish it. Their Faces were broad & had the Appearance of being deformed from their Natural Shape; they wore Ornaments suspended to the Ears which were perforated in three or four Places, also Neck Ancles & Wrists—Their Colour appeared of a light Brown—Their Bows were rather Short & had a remarkable Curve, making, when unstrung, a half Circle, but in use they are bent the contrary way, & the part which is under is straightened [strengthened?] by the Skin of some Animal affixed to the Bow by a Cement, of which Turpentine appears to be the Chief Ingredient — The Arrows are from 3½ to three feet in length & principally pointed with Flint Barbed. For Fishing Lines they have an Excellent Substitute, in the long Sea Weed, which among these People are in general use. — The Canoe was large that brought this Party to the Vessels — she was about thirty five feet in length & proportionately broad. — The bottom was made out of a Single Tree on which other pieces were neatly fixed, sown together by Sea Weed or something of that description. — They were inoffensive in their Conduct & honest in their dealings with us——

Latitude Observation —— 48° ..2' ..30" N°.
Longitude Mean of Lunars Watches &c 237° ..22' E^t^.
Variation of the Compass 20° East^y^
High Water full and Change
Rise and Fall of the Tide

Further Examination of De Fuca's Streights 1792..
Saturday May 19th

As the Large Inlet which we had left in the Boats might terminate in the same Manner as the one we had already Explored & as a Separation [p. 194] of the Vessels would greatly facilitate the Investigation of the Streight, Capt Vancouver therefore determined to send the *Chatham* to explore two large Openings apparently trending to the NW.[39] — as they might find a Communication with the Inlet we were about to enter. For that Purpose she Parted company —— & we kept on for the SE Branch with a fine Moderate Breeze from the Westward & pleasant Weather — At 4 we tried for Soundings but could not reach Bottom with 100 fths of Line — & as the Ebb shortly after came down we hauled in on the NE Shore & at ½ pt 4 Came to with the Bower Anchor in 28 fths about ½ a Mile from the Shore[40] — The Seine was sent immediately to be hauled but the Tide prevented their being successful. Here we remained till ½ pt 8 Next Morning when we weighed with a light Westerly Breeze — In hoisting the Foretopsail the Yard was carried away in the Slings — which on Examination proved to have been rotten half way through. The Spare Yard was Immediately got up in its Room & all Sail made — The Course was directed according to the trending of the Inlet from SEbS to EbS with a Rapid Flood Tide we continued running without any Boat a head sounding or knowing what was before us, though we frequently Sounded but had no Bottom with 50 or 60 fths of Line. At Noon the Latitude Observed was 47° .59' with these Bearings South Extreme S°28Et Western

---

[39]I.e., the San Juan Islands.

[40]Near Bush Point on the western side of Whidbey Island.

Extreme on the Larboard Shore N59W[t] Western Extreme of the Starboard Shore in one with the Larboard Shore. Water alongside perfectly Salt. We had now made considerable Progress up the Inlet left to the NE of Rendezvous Point[41] & it was intended to continue up to [where?] we should find sufficient work for the Boats & a good Place for the Ship — Fine Pleasant Weather ——

Sunday, May 20th 1792

Our course in the Afternoon was directed SbE½E & having run on till the Inlet was considerably decreased in its Breadth we came too with the Bower in 35 fths at ½ p[t] 6 not far from an Indian Village[42] — here it branched off in two Different Directions trending to the Southward & SE — As two Boats appeared to be of sufficient force to prevent any accident or attack from the Natives, It was determined that I should early set out with the Launch accompanied by M[r] Whidbey[43] in the Cutter Who was sent to make a Survey of the Various Branches & explore the Starboard Inlet[44] that being the Continental Shore —— In the Evening [p. 195] we visited the Indian Village, the Inhabitants of which were busily employed in preparing Clams & Fish for the Winter — NB (the Amount of the People & Village I have by some Accident lost). — however to the best of my Recollection they did not differ from what I have already described — In the Morning I received the following Memorandum from Captain Vancouver

Mem°

Concerning a further Examination of the Inlet we are in Necessary and capable of being executed by the Boats You are at 4 oClock tomorrow Morning to proceed with the Launch accompanied by Mr Whidbey

---

[41]Foulweather Bluff.

[42]Near Restoration Point.

[43]Vancouver relied heavily on Joseph Whidbey's abilities for virtually all of the small boat excursions during the three years of exploration on the northwest coast. Following the return to England, Whidbey continued to serve in the British Navy retiring in May 1805. In 1806, Whidbey (along with others) issued a report on the feasibility and design of a breakwater in Plymouth. He returned to his position as Master Attendant of Woolwich dockyard and in 1811, was selected as the superintendent for construction of the long delayed breakwater. He held the position until his resignation for health reasons, in 1830. Actual construction began in 1812 and was completed in 1841 at a cost of £1.5 million. A colossal feat, the freestanding breakwater (it is not anchored to land at either end) stretched nearly a mile; it was 40 feet wide at the top and 200 feet at the base and contained some four million tons of rocks. In 1833, the 78 year old Whidbey died at Taunton, Somersetshire, and was buried there in the churchyard of the Parish Church of St. James.

[44]Colvos Passage.

in the Cutter, whose Directions You will follow in such points as appertain to the Surveying the Shore &c &c being provided with a Weeks Provisions you will proceed up the said Inlet Keeping the Starboard or Continental Shore on board & having proceeded three Days up the Inlet, should it then appear to you of that Extent that you cannot finally determine its limits, and return to the Ship by Thursday next, You are then to return on board, reporting to me an account of your Proceedings as also noticing the appearance of the Country, its Productions and Inhabitants, if varying from what we have already seen

To Lieutenant Peter Puget
of His Britannic Majesty's
Sloop *Discovery* (a Copy)

Given on board his Britannic
Majesty's Sloop the
6th of June 1792
Geo Vancouver

I have inserted this order out of its Place as Similar Directions were given verbally before it took Place——...

Early in the Morning we left the Ships with the two Boats well Armed, the Launch carried two Swivels beside Wall pieces Musquetoons & Musquetts & provided with a Weeks Provisions we began the Examination of the Inlet.[45] We found it trend nearly South for about 4 leagues & in that Distance preserving the Breadth of One Mile, we were there induced to stop to Breakfast in hopes of enticing two Indians, who had deserted their Canoe & fled to the Woods to come to us—she was hauled up close to the Trees & before we went away some Beads Medals & Trinkets were put among their other Articles in the Canoe as a Proof that our Intentions were friendly—At the Back of this Place is a Small Lagoon[46] & as the Tide was out the Water was perfectly fresh in it. The Entrance is sufficiently broad to admit the *Chatham*, to go in at high Water as the Tide had by the High Water Mark then fallen fourteen feet.—The Land here is in general Low & rizing gradually a little [p. 196] Distance from the Beach to Hills of a Moderate Height & is everywhere covered with wood consisting chiefly of tall Straight Pine Trees.—About Nine we left the Breakfast Place with a fine fair Wind & Tide & proceeded on a further Investigation of the Inlet which still continued its Breadth & Direction, Soundings were frequently tried for but no Bottom could be reached with 40 fths of line—About 4 Miles from the Breakfast Place the Eastern Shore

---

[45]Colvos Passage.

[46]Olalla Cove.

which had hitherto been compact branched off to the Eastward[47] & afforded us a view of an excessive high Snowy Mountain,[48] which though frequently seen before I have omitted noting it.—The Snow was yet, notwithstanding the Heat more than ⅔ down & its Summit perfectly white appeared to reach the Clouds.—From the Foot of the Mountain, we were of Opinion that the Inlet branched off to the North[d] or NW, in which Case, it may communicate with the SE Branch[49] that was seen from the Ship on our Departure, admitting that the Supposition we must now be in the Main Inlet an Island[50]—— Passing the Eastern Branch we continued our Progress along the Star[b] or Continental Shore, which still was in a Southerly Direction & of the same Breadth. A Most Rapid Tide from the Northward hurried us so fast past the Shore that we could scarce land—— In Mid Channel[51] we found 30 fths. water—soft Bottom—Two Canoes who had for some time been seen paddling in Shore, One with Four the other with two Indians in them, immediately on our hauling in with an Intention to land, struck off in the Stream & endeavouring to increase their Distance from us—Nor could all the Signs emblematical of Friendship, such as a white Handkerchief—a Green Bough & many other Methods induce them to venture near us, on the Contrary, it appeared to have another Effect, that of redoubling their Efforts in getting away—At the distance of about Six Leagues from the Breakfast Place the Continent took a Sudden turn to the Westward[52] & from this Direction the Flood came so Strong that all our Efforts could not make way against it, we therefore landed to dine on the Point.[53]—This we left about 3 in the Afternoon & proceeded along the Shore of this Western Branch. About a Mile from the Dinner Point we found a Small Cove[54] at the head of which were a Party of Seventeen or Eighteen Indians in temporary Habitations drying Clams Fish &c which they readily parted with [p. 197] for Buttons Trinkets &c they did not appear the least Alarmed at our Approach but immediately offered their Articles for Sale—In their Persons these People are slenderly made they wear their Hair long which is quite Black and exceeding Dirty—Both Nose & Ears are perforated, to the which were affixed Copper Ornaments & Beads, the whole Party was Naked—— The Land is here Flat for the Space of a Quarter of a Mile rising Gradually

[47]Dalco Passage.

[48]Mount Rainier.

[49]East Passage.

[50]Vashon Island.

[51]The Narrows.

[52]Hale Passage. The distance from Olalla is closer to eleven miles (or four leagues).

[53]Point Fosdick.

[54]Wollochet Bay.

to the Back Hills, which every where is thickly covered with large Pines, & difficult of being penetrated through; The Soil appeared good & produced a Quantity of Gooseberry Raspberry & Currant Bushes now highly in Blossom which intermixed with Roses, exhibited a Strange variegation of Flowers but by no Means unpleasant to the Eye — We left Indian Cove & proceeded along the Continental Shore which Still trended to the Westward & about three Leagues from the Dinner Point at 8 we brought too for the Night[55] where we found the Larboard or Southern Shore composed of Islands. — to this Situation two Canoes had been our Attendants from the last Cove & they now lay on their Paddles about One Hundred Yards from the Beach attentively viewing our operations. In the Boats were some fire Arms that in the Course of Day had been found defective & we now wished them to be discharged but the fear of alarming the Indians, prevented me at present doing it: finding however they still kept hovering about the Boats & being apprehensive they would be endeavouring to commit Depredations during the Night I then ordered a Musquett to be fired but so far was it from intimidating or alarming them, that they remained stationary, only exclaiming *Pop* at every Report in way of Derision — they however soon after left us, nor did they trouble us afterwards——

We quitted our Quarters early on Monday Morning May 21st though it Rained. We proceeded on to the further Examination of this Western Branch — which still held its former Direction. The Tide prevented our making any considerable Progress before Breakfast to which we Stopped on a Small Island[56] about 6 Miles from Last Nights sleeping Place — This Island was called after its only Inhabitants, an astonishing Quantity of Crows. Between it & the Main it was almost too Shoal for the Boats. From this Situation we could see the Termination of this Western Branch[57] & the Land compact on the opposite Shore, however after Breakfast more clearly to ascertain, what appeared almost a Certainty, we continued pulling up for its head till near Eleven, when the Beach was close to the Boats & in the SW Corner of the Cove was a Small Village among the Trees — beyond the termination the Country had the Appearance [p. 198] of a Level Forest, but close to the Water, it was covered with Small Green Bushes — We pulled in towards the Village but seeing a Canoe paddling from it towards us, induced us to lay on our Oars to wait their Approach, but neither Copper nor any Article in our Possession had

---

[55]Behind the small hook east of Green Point in Hale Passage, locally know as Shaw's Cove. Puget's distance of three leagues was also overstated. From Point Fosdick, (Dinner Point), Green Point is approximately four miles.

[56]Presumably Cutts Island.

[57]Henderson Bay, with Burley Lagoon beyond.

sufficient allurement to get them close to the Boats. They lay about Twenty Yards from us & kept continually pointing to the Eastward, expressive of a Wish that our Departure would be more agreeable than our Visit— Finding all our Solicitations could not bring on a Reciprocal Friendship & we were only loosing time I therefore left those Surly Gentlemen & kept along the Opposite or Southern Shore of this Western Branch, however I did not like to quit those Indians altogether without giving some evident Proof that our Intention was perfectly friendly & an Expedient was hit on that soon answered our Purpose. Some Copper Medals, Looking Glasses & other Articles were tied on a Piece of Wood & left floating on the Water, then pulling away to a Small Distance, the Indians immediately Picked them up, this was repeated two or three times & as often proved successfull, at length by Intreaties they ventured alongside the Boat but not with that Confidence I would have wished In their Persons they were apparently more Stout than any Indians we have hitherto seen on the Coast. Two of the three in the Canoe had lost the Right Eye & were much pitted with the Small Pox,[58] which Disorder in all probability is the Cause of that Defect— During this Effort to conciliate their Friendship, we kept paddling easily along the Southern Shore; that no time might be lost in the prosecution of the Service; The Indians finding we were increasing our Distance from the Village immediately quitted the Boats to return back though Not till they had received an additional Quantity of Presents & by the Subsequent Circumstances I am of Opinion that they had the Ingratitude to impute our Friendship to a fear of their Power, & the Temerity with which they conducted themselves afterwards had near proved fatal to themselves and Companions—During the Time the three Indians were alongside the Boats they appeared exceedingly shy & distrustful notwithstanding our Liberality towards them, Nor would they understand the Common Words we had learnt from other Natives. But in that Case our own bad pronunciation might have been the Cause—to all our Questions they only answered Poh Poh & pointing to Crow Island, alluding as we supposed to the Report of the Musquets at Breakfast—Though they wanted Copper from us they would not part with their Bows or Arrows in Exchange, which were very neat & well constructed & of which they had plenty—

About four Miles from the Village on the South Shore of this Western Branch is a Small Cove[59] into which we had pulled to dine, the

[58]The theory of Nathaniel Portlock, who served with Vancouver under Captain Cook, was that Spanish introduced the disease to the northern Indians in 1775. It quickly worked its way down the coast decimating native tribes along the way (Howay 371).

[59]Puget's geographical descriptions do not match well with modern charts. Thus, it is difficult to place this location. It is perhaps Von Geldern Cove.

Weather was here extremely sultry, the Thermometer was at 90°. At [p. 199] the head of the Cove were two Runs of fresh Water — We were about to try the Seine for Salmon when the Appearance of Six Canoes & other following Circumstances prevented me. These Canoes contained about Twenty Men all Armed among whom I perceived the three Men who had before been to us, they paddled close to the Boats & some immediately landed. On their Approach a Line was drawn to divide the two Parties, the Intent of which the Indians perfectly understood & I was glad to see we had no Difficulty to keep them in order —— It is necessary to mention our Situation with Respect to the Communication we had with the Boats. It had been an invariable Rule to always have three or four Musquets with their Appendages landed with us, & on this Occasion it luckily had not been forgot; as it would have appeared extremely unguarded to have procured our Arms from the Boats after the Arrival of this Party & it might have caused more harm, than their hostile Intentions for such they afterwards appeared to be —— near Six Yards from the Place where the Boats were laying the land rose almost perpendicular Sixteen Feet. On this Cliff we had proposed to Dine previous to the Arrival of the Natives who were by this time joined by Another Canoe increasing their Numbers to Twenty four, & though there was a peaceable Appearance in the Conduct, yet for our own Security we took every precaution to prevent a Surprize, which entirely originated from their own distrustfull Behaviour, they were divided some on the Beach & others in the Canoes but the Greater part were armed with Bows and Arrows. But as Good Order appeared to be pretty well established we went to Dinner ourselves on the Hill & the Boat Crews in their Respective Boats ready with their Fire Arms.—

Nearly after our sitting down the Indians quitted the Beach & repaired to their Canoes where an Apparent Consultation was held, about our Party as they frequently pointed to the Boats & us on the Hill; I now began to think they seriously meant to attack us during the Division of the Party, we however took no Notice of their Proceedings as I did not wish, they should even suppose we were making any preparation to oppose such Measures, as they might then have in Agitation, but on the Contrary impress them with an Idea we were always on our Guard During their Consultations, three Canoes were stealing towards the Boats but on perceiving they were discovered by us on the Hill, immediately retreated to their former Situation — Another Canoe had now nearly joined the Party and as she Approached, they suddenly jumped on the Beach stringing their Bows & apparently preparing for an Attack — This reduced me to a most awkward predicament, for unwilling to fire on these poor People, who might have been unacquainted with the advantage we had over them, & not wishing to run the Risk of having the People wounded by the first discharge of their Arrows I absolutely felt [p. 200] at a Loss how to Act, as it might be preparations to oppose the Landing of the last Canoe—, but this Conjecture was soon removed by perceiving a Young Man ascending the Hill about five Yards from us with his Bow and Arrow ready, however he was not suffered to proceed, & unwillingly joined his Companions on the Beach, as also the Indians who arrived in the Last Canoe. As I now no longer could doubt their hostile Intention we remained on the Hill ready to return their first Salute. In the Meantime the People were removing the things to the Boats to prepare for our Departure. During which time the whole Party remained in deep Consultation on the Beach sharpening their Arrows, & their Bows ready Strung for use—The only Circumstance to be dreaded was the Execution they would do in having the Advantage of the first Discharge however had their Temerity carried them to begin the Attack I am afraid it would have proved fatal to their whole Party & indeed they deserved it after our Liberality and Kindness to the three whom we had first seen, had a Single Arrow been discharged either at us or the Boats I certainly have had that Person Shot, let the Consequence be what it would; They by that time appeared irresolute how to act, I therefore thought it a good Opportunity to order a Swivel to be fired with Grape Shot, that they might see we had other Resources besides those in our Hands, but contrary to our Expectation they did not express any Astonishment or fear at the Report or the Effect of the Shot, By this time our Party were united & the Major part under Arms & I believe they then totally relinquished all Idea of an Attack for they now offered their Bows and Arrows for Sale Which had Shortly before been strung for the worst of Purposes & solicited our Friendship by the most abject Submission—I now felt Real Satisfaction in not having carried Matters to an Extremity, But I still am of Opinion, that the Desire with which we entreated the first Canoe off the Village to come alongside & the Presents made him, had impressed them with an Idea we were purchasing their Friendship out of fear of the Numbers; For when they first came into the Cove, we were particularly anxious to purchase their Bows &c, but which they would not part with on any Account, how extraordinary then, that they should so soon Alter their Opinion, but the Reason is obvious, they had on the Eve of our Departure seen their Error & were now glad to sell the Garments from their Backs—These People were rather more Stout than any of our former Visitors, & were nearly Similar in their Ornaments &c of what we had before seen——We did not perceive a Single Sea Otter Skin among the whole Party but Plenty [p. 201] of Bear Raccoon Rabbit and Deer

used as Garments— these they willingly parted with in exchange for our Articles. Some of them had thick Bushy Beards, others with a Tuft only on their Chins & upper Lips like Mustachios— They had likewise Hair in profusion on those Parts of the Body in Common with ourselves except the Breast, which was perfectly destitute.——We now had quitted the Cove & were pulling to the Eastward along the South Shore of the Western Arm, followed by the Canoes to dispose of what remaining Articles were in their Possession, but finding we were drawing fast from their Habitation, they began to leave us, that in half an hour; we were again left to ourselves; but we had the Satisfaction of having convinced them of our Friendship before their Departure — The Weather had by this time undergone a total Alteration, A SE Breeze had brought with it a perfect deluge of Rain —& the Approach of Night obliged us to seek Shelter on the West Point of a Narrow Passage[60] trending to the Southward & about five Miles from Dinner Cove which had from the Conduct of the Indians obtained the name of Alarm Cove — Here we remained unmolested by Indians till Tuesday Morning 22^{d} May when we early proceeded to the further Examination of this Inlet — We had in first entering the Western Branch seen a Continuation of the Southern Arm as far as the Eye could reach, & by meeting with such various sets of the Tide in the former, we concluded that the Intervening Land, between the Southern Arm & the Western Branch would prove a Cluster of Islands.[61]——We had to pull against a most Rapid Stream in this narrow South Channel, & with great Difficulty got through. From thence we kept along the South Side of an Island, which for Distinction was called Pidgeon Island.[62] At the East Point of this Island[63] we found ourselves in the Main Southern Branch again. From that Situation we pulled over on the Eastern Shore for a Long flat Island[64] to obtain a Latitude which showed — [left blank]
From last Nights Sleeping Place the Continent ran away SSW to this therefore we should be obliged to return, it therefore became necessary we should make some Dispatch in reaching that Situation as that Shore with the Opposite Land formed an Excellent Channel of a Mile wide which I intended to pursue — The Morning was fine but no Wind — The Land which formed the West Side of the Main Southern Arm opposite to Long Island, from its Situation will prove I believe an Island,[65] we

[60]On the sand spit in Pitt Passage to the SW of Pitt Island.

[61]Fox, McNeil and Anderson Islands.

[62]McNeil Island, They're traveling through Balch Passage.

[63]Near Hyde Point.

[64]Ketron Island.

[65]Anderson Island.

therefore intend keep to the Southward along the East Side & by rounding it, we should again fall in with the Continent in the SSW Channel — But immediately [p. 202] after Noon the Sky blackened to the SE & in a Quarter of an Hour every Place was perfectly over Cast. The Squall came on with Thunder Lightening and Rain & obliged us to bear away for a Cove on the East Side of Supposed Island,[66] We landed about three & intended after Dinner to have proceeded on, but the extreme badness of the Weather prevented our Stirring, we therefore pitched the Tents, resolved if possible to set out the Earlier in the Morning——In the Meantime the Cutter being dispatched for Water saw clearly in the SSW Channel we had left, which clearly proved the Land we were now on to be an Island. In the Evening three Canoes visited our Encampment from a Village to the Southward with some Vegetables like Cellery[67] (the Natural Production of the Country for Sale) these were immediately purchased together with Some Bear Skins——They paddled away quietly at Dark — & though Situated close to them, yet we met no Interruption during the Night — We were disappointed in our Expectations on Wednesday Morning May 23^{d} for though the Rain had ceased yet it was succeeded by so thick a Fog that the Boats were scarcely perceptable from the Tents that detained us to 8 in the Morning when we again set out & pulled for the Supposed termination of the Southern Arm[68] where from the Appearance of the Low Country we expected to find a River; In stretching over we were joined by some Canoes with various Articles for traffic such as Bows Arrows &c their behaviour was the Opposite to what we had experienced from the Indians in Alarm Cove, these came alongside the Boats with the greatest Confidence & behaved themselves with much propriety a Commerce was therefore established for their Different Articles which was carried on with the Strictest Honesty and Apparently to the Satisfaction of both Parties; The Water had Shoaled quite across to four and five feet that Stopped our further progress towards the Shore as it was falling Tide, & I was fearfull of causing more detention, which would have been the Case had we grounded — This however terminated the Main Southern Arm about Nineteen Miles from the Point of the West Branch & four Miles from Last Nights Quarters, where the Continent takes a Sudden turn to the Westward — These Friendly Indians followed the Boats a Considerable Distance up the West Arm which we were now pursuing[69]

---

[66]Oro Bay.

[67]According to the Menzies journal, these were young shoots of raspberries.

[68]Nisqually Flats.

[69]At this point, the boats reached Nisqually Flats, turned northwest and were in the passage between Anderson Island and the mainland.

though they had sold all their Articles— In their Persons Customs and Manners they appeared to be of the same Tribe with those in Alarm Cove the only Difference is a friendly Disposition — Their Canoes Weapons & Paddles are of the Same Construction ——They did not leave us to after we had passed the SSW Channel & still conducted themselves in the most inoffensive & peacable Manner — By Noon we had reached the Continental Shore that now trended about West & pursued it for Ten Miles to an Island,[70] [p. 203] where we were glad to stop and erect our Tents to avoid a threatening Squall from the SE. About two it came on with Thunder Lightening & a heavy Gust which continued without Intermission all the Afternoon. The Rain fell in perfect torrents; we therefore were obliged to remain in our Quarters Till Next Morning Thursday May 24th. We again set out Early & pursuing the Continent which now trended to the Northward of West. By 8 we had determined the termination of this Branch about 12 Miles from Wednesday Island, here we tried the Seine & caught only one Salmon trout. From this termination we entered another Branch[71] trending in a SW & Southerly & in various Directions but not more than ¼ or ½ a Mile Broad. We continued on till 6 in the Evening

---

[70]Herron Island in Case Inlet. Puget named this "Wednesday Island."

[71]Pickering Passage.

[72]The explorer's route and evening camp present a conundrum. The evidence and conflicting information are as follows: Menzies noted viewing "...the large opening we passed yesterday..." (Dana Passage). It is more likely this passage could be seen from the south end of Hartstene rather than Squaxin. However, it is obvious that Menzies wrote this journal much later than the events actually happened. For example, knowledge of the name of Port Quadra for Discovery Bay was not known until meeting with the Spaniards in mid–June. Thus, Menzies wrote from the perspective of "hindsight" and could not have been certain of the "opening we passed yesterday" until they actually confirmed it a few days later. Puget noted seeing "...a Channel to the SE by which we hoped to return into the Main Branch through an Opening in the Opposite Shore...." In reviewing modern charts, it appears he is viewing Squaxin Passage with Dana Passage in the background, thus implying they camped on Squaxin Island. Both Puget and Menzies are complete with respect to their excellent descriptions of the country. While traveling on the west side of Hartstene, neither mentioned Hammersley or Totten Inlets which took a west and south western direction respectively from the west side of Squaxin Island. This implied they journeyed through Peale Passage on the east side of Squaxin Island, and hence, did not see either inlet as they are not visible except from the west side of Squaxin. Further, Menzies noted "making the land on the left of us a large Island, on the south side of which we encampd for the night...." Based upon their relative size, it is more likely he applied this reference to Hartstene, and provides further argument that they passed through Peale Passage. However, this is entirely inconsistent with their general practice of maintaining the continental shore on their starboard hand. Menzies noted in his journal: "Next morning [May 25] we *again* [emphasis added] pursued the arm keeping the Starboard Shore on board..." implying that in fact they did journey on the west side of Squaxin. Menzies' journal entries continued with the exploration of an arm which, at noon, terminated in an extensive mud flat: "...we could not get with the Boats (*note continued on next page*)

when we brought too for the Night & Dinner,[72] from this Situation we could see a Channel to the SE by which we hoped to return into the Main Branch through an Opening in the Opposite Shore where the last Canoes had left us.—Early Next Morning Friday May 25th we had a Survey on the Provisions which we found would last till Wednesday next. I therefore thought it best to determine this alternate Navigation & save the trouble of a Second Expedition to this Extent. We had likewise been successfull in procuring a good Quantity of Clams which with Nettle tops Fat Hen & Gooseberry Tops greatly assisted the customary allowance of Provisions & Yesterday during a hard Shower of Rain we were particularly fortunate in that Respect —— for the Boats could have loaded with the former, & the People were not averse to eating Crows of which we could always procure plenty. Therefore as our continuance out could not be attended with any Inconvenience, but would be saving time, We pursued our Examination of the Southern narrow Inlet[73] the termination of which we sounded out by Noon—In this Branch were many beautiful Spots the Low Surrounding Country though thickly covered with Wood had a very pleasant Appearance, now in the height of Spring. We had already passed during this Expedition several Small deserted Villages which were supposed to be only the temporary Habitations of Fishermen, we took advantage of the Remaining part of the Tide to come down as far as possible & about five Miles from the termination stopped to Dine[74]—In the Evening we were fortunate in reaching the SE passage seen from last Nights Sleeping Place where we pitched our Tents in a very pleasant Situation[75]; Early next morning Saturday May 26th with a continuance of favorable Weather we pursued another Small Branch[76] that nearly ran parallel to the one we [p. 204] had determined yesterday.

---

within two Miles of it...." This is consistent with Oyster Bay in Totten Inlet, again implying the west side of Squaxin. If they had camped at Brisco Point, they would have backtracked to the entrance of Totten Inlet, which neither journal references. Finally, Menzies mentions "...passing on the other side [the left side] some Islands that were divided by two or three branches leading off to the Eastward...." The only other island in the area is Hope on the west side of Squaxin (Menzies reference to the plural islands makes no sense). With the above in mind, my guess is they camped on the west side of Squaxin, north of Hope Island, perhaps Potlatch Point. For whatever reason, they did not explore Hammersley Inlet, likely because it takes a sharp "dogleg" to the south at the entrance and the appearance from the water is nothing more than a small bay.

73Totten Inlet.

74Perhaps near Windy Point in Totten Inlet.

75According to Menzies' journal, they "...encamped on the point of another arm leading to the Southward." This would place them near Hunter Point at the southeast end of Squaxin Passage.

76Eld Inlet.

About an Hour after we had set out, An Indian Village made its Appearance from whence some Canoes came off perfectly unarmed.[77] He pointed that we were near the Termination of this Arm, which Intelligence we found true; In our Way down we landed for a Short time & were received by the Inhabitants with all the Friendship and Hospitality we could have expected—These people I should suppose were about Sixty in Number of all Ages and Descriptions they lived under a Kind of Shed open at the Front and Sides. The Women appeared employed in the Domestic Duties such as curing Clams & Fish, making Baskets, of various Colours & as neatly woven that they are perfectly watertight. The Occupations of the Men I believe consists chiefly in Fishing, constructing Canoes & performing all the Labourious Work of the Village; Though it was perfectly Curiosity which had induced us to land, yet that was the sooner satisfied, by the horrid Stench which came from all parts of these Habitations, with which they were highly delighted. The Natives had but Two Sea Otter Skins which were purchased & a variety of Marmot, Rabbit Raccoon Deer & Bear Skins were also procured. The Men had a War Garment on, it consisted of a very thick Hide supposed made from the Moose Deer, & well prepared——I have no doubt but it is a Sufficient Shield against Arrows, though not against Fire Arms. The Garment reaches from the Shoulders down to the Knees, this however was got in exchange for a Small piece of Copper, from which we may suppose that they were not of much Value, they likewise disposed of some well constructed Bows and Arrows, in Short it was only to ask, & have your Wish gratified, the only Difference, I perceived between our present Companions and former Visitors, were the Extravagance with Which their Faces were Ornamented. Streaks of Red Ochre and Black Glimmer, were on some, others entirely with the Former, & a few that gave the Preference to the Latter—every Person had a fashion of his own, & to us who were Strangers to Indians, this Sight conveyed a Stronger Force of the Savageness of the Native Inhabitants, than any other Circumstance we had hitherto met with; not but their Conduct, friendly & inoffensive, had already merited our warmest Approbation, but their Appearance was absolutely terrific. & it will frequently occur, that the Imagination receives a much greater Shock by such unusual Objects, than it would otherwise would, was that Object divested of its Exterior Ornaments or Dress, or the Sight was more familiarized to People in a State of Nature & Though we could not behold these Ornaments with the same satisfactory Eye as themselves, yet in receiving the looking Glasses, each appeared well Satisfied with his own Fashion, at least the Paint was not [p. 205] at all altered.—They

---

[77]Perhaps southwest of Flapjack Point, locally known as Young Cove.

likewise had the Hair covered with the Down of Birds; which certainly was a good substitute for Powder, & the Paint only differed in the Colours & not the Quantity used by our own Fair Country women—In these two Instances we meet with some Resemblance to our Customs & I believe the above mentioned Ornaments were of a Ceremonious Nature for our Reception at the Village——

From Friendly Inlet we pulled up another[78] in the same Direction & landed not far from its termination to Breakfast whither the Indians from the last Arm had followed us. Here they made Signs, that this Branch was the Same as their own, which after a Quarter of an hours Row we found to be the case—from this we pursued the Continental Shore[79] till One in the Afternoon, when [which?] soon carried us into the former Western Branch which we had examined on Wednesday morning——& as All the Shore of the Southern Inlet is compact on its East Side, we are certain of the Continent to the Branch we left on Sunday in that Direction, where we had a view of the high Snowy Mountain—I therefore determined to return immediately to the Ships that no time might be lost in the Examination of that Branch—In the Evening we reached the Southern Branch; from whence we saw a Fire on Long Island[80] where we had landed on Tuesday last, but supposing it to be Indians & having a fair Wind & Tide, we proceeded down towards the Ships, now carrying as much Breeze as the Sails could Bear. It was not till Two in the Morning that we got on board & were glad to find Captain Vancouver had gone to examine the other Branch,[81] this he completed the Day after our Arrival, & which branch brought him by the Foot of the high Snowy Mountain into our Southern Inlet. Therefore we have now determined the Continent to the Entrance of the Great SE Branch except an Opening on its NE Shore[82] [left blank] Distant from the Entrance Point as seen from Protection Island—Capt Vancouver had left Orders for the *Chatham*, who had arrived during our Absence to take the *Discovery's* Launch & sailed to this Opening & begin its Examination along its Starboard or Continental Shore. We were to follow immediately on the Return of our Boats. The *Chatham* in her last Investigation of the NW Arms trending from the Heights had been among a perfect Archipelago of Islands[83] & from their

[78]Budd Inlet.

[79]Through Dana Passage and back toward the Nisqually River.

[80]Puget was observing Vancouver's fire on Ketron Island.

[81]East Passage along the east side of Vashon Island.

[82]Possession Sound and the east side of Whidbey Island.

[83]The San Juan Islands.

Accounts it was probable we should find much Inland work in that Direction — they always observed the Flood coming from the Southward ——— [p. 206] The Boats likewise found a Small Inlet to the Westward of the Village which obtained the Name of Port Orchard and the Inlet we had examined During the last Expedition Pugets Sound. The Snowy Mountain was named Mount Baker[84] —— The Latitude of the Southernmost of the Branches was 47°-3' Longitude 237°-18' East of Greenwich ——

Port Orchard Latitude [left blank] Long.° [left blank]

Mount Baker 48°-39' N°. Longitude 238°-20' E^{t}.

Transactions on board during my Absence in the Boats[85]

Monday 21st. Light Breezes and Clear Employed occasionally. A.M. Sent the Carpenters on Shore to make two new topSail Yards. Employed brewing Fishing & Several Canoes alongside.

Tuesday 22^{d}. Light Breezes and Pleasant Weather. Employed as before. AM. Light Breezes with Rain. At 9 fair Weather. Loosed Sails to Dry. Employed Brewing Fishing & Carpenters as before. Sailmakers repairing the jib and Fore topMast Staysail —

Wednesday 23^{d}. The first Part light Breezes and Clear, furled Sails; Middle part fresh Breezes & Squally with heavy Rain Thunder and Lightning — Punished James Button & George Raybold the first with 36 and the other with 24 Lashes for Theft. AM. Light Breezes and Pleasant Weather. Loosed sails to Dry. Sent Empty Casks on Shore. Several Canoes alongside.

[p. 207] Thursday 24th. PM Squally with Rain, furled Sails— Lost two Puncheons which broke from the Raft Rope. AM. Light Breezes and Clear. People employed about the Rigging — Sailmakers repairing the Main top Gallant Sail & Stay Sails— Carpenters making a New Top Gallant Mast and Yard —

Friday 25th. Light Breezes and Clear Weather. Employed brewing Fishing &c. Unbent the Foretopsail & shifted the Yard with a New One. Bent the Sail again. Several Canoes alongside, Indians very Quiet & Honest —

Saturday 26th. Light Breezes and Clear W^{r}. Sent the Empty Casks on Shore. Anchored here the *Chatham*. AM. Captain Vancouver with one Boat from the *Discovery* & one from the *Chatham* set out on a Surveying Expedition. Employed Brewing Fishing &c, Carpenters about the Main top Gallant Mast and Yard — At 9 Weighed and Shifted our Berth further in Shore — Three Canoes alongside.

---

[84] Puget meant to reference Mt. Rainier.

[85] Puget used astronomical dates in this section which began at noon. Thus the first notes for each date really represented the afternoon and evening for the previous day.

Sunday 27th. Do.Wr. Employed occasionally. AM. At 1 the Launch and Cutter returned from the Southward. Mustered the Ships Company.

Monday 28th. Moderate Breezes and Cloudy Wr. Sailed the *Chatham* accompanied by our Launch with an Officer in her. Employed Fishing Brewing &c.

Tuesday 29th. Moderate and Cloudy with Rain at times. Employed occasionally brewing Spruce Beer, Fishing &c. AM. Washed the Lower Deck. Sailmakers employed repairing the Staysails—Fired 17 Guns it being the Anniversary of King Charles happy Restoration.

[p. 208] Wednesday 30th. Light Breezes and Cloudy Wr. At 9 Boats returned with Capt Vancouver. AM. ½ pt 8 Weighed & came to Sail under TopSails, Top Gallant Sails and Fore Sail. At 9 Set Steering Sails. At Noon returned by the SE Branch Village Point S3Et. Punished Willm Wooderson Seaman with 24 Lashes for Insolence.

Thursday 31st. Light Breezes and Cloudy. Employed working up an Inlet[86] trending to the Northward, having its Entrance from the NE Shore & the Great SE Branch—At 11 Anchored with the Small Bower in 32fths Water. In working up the Tide had such a hold of the Ship that though a Fresh Breeze, she came round against the Helm—here we found the *Chatham*, who had sent our Launch & one of her own Boats to survey the Present Inlet which from its Appearance promises to communicate with the One before Explored by Mr Broughton. AM. Light Airs. Employed about the Rigging, hauled the Seine with some Success—

Friday June 1st. Light Breezes inclinable to Calms. Employed occasionally. At 7 light Breezes. Weighed and came to Sail under whole Topsails Top Gallant and Fore Sail Standing to the Northward for the Rendezvous appointed for the Boats. At 11 Fired a Gun & made the Signal to Anchor, Came too with the Small Bower in 20 fths In a Narrow Branch. AM. ½ pt 6 Weighed and made Sail Standing up a Northern Arm. At Noon Calm. Western Shore from N22W to S20E. Eastern Shore from N17W to S69Et. An Island in the Entrance S31E to S41Et.[87] Nearest Eastern Shore NEbN 1 Mile. Nearest Western Shore SWbW ½ a Mile—Fine Pleasant Weather. No Soundings. No great Irregularity in the Tides especially the Stream which Set in various Directions. *Chatham* in Company.

[p. 209] Saturday 2nd. Light Breezes & Clear. Standing to the Northward. At ½ pt 2 Came too with the Bower Anchor in 20 fths The *Chatham* on Shore a little to the Northward of us,[88] Out Boats & sent

---

[86]Possession Sound.

[87]Gedney Island.

[88]*Chatham* was aground at the head of Port Susan.

them to her Assistance with an Officer. AM. Moderate and Cloudy with Rain. At 1 the *Chatham* got off without Damage. ½ p^{t} 10 Made the Signal and weighed working down the Arm. Punished Jos. Murgatroyd Seaman with 12 Lashes for disobedience of Orders. Fired a Gun as a Signal to the Boats. At Noon light Breezes & fair Weather. Standing to the Southward.

Sunday 3^{d}. Light Airs inclinable to Calm. At 2 Anchored with the Bower in 50 fths—about 3 Cables from the Shore.[89] ½ p^{t} 8 & Shortly after fired two Guns to denote our Situation to the Boats. At 9 M^{r}. Whidbey came on board having determined the Extent of this Branch during his Expedition. He saw a large Indian Village whose Inhabitants treated him with great Friendship & Hospitality—We had now to return out again into the Streights by the SE Branch & pursue the first NW Arm seen by the *Chatham* as its Starboard or NE Shore now proved to be the Continent. AM. Light Breezes. Mustered the Ships Company and read the Articles of War—hauled the Seine with Success.

Monday 4th. Light Breezes and Clear. Hauling the seine—Capt Vancouver postponed sailing this Day that the People might have tomorrow to celebrate His Majesty's Birth with double Allowance of Grog. AM. In the Forenoon the Captain attended by M^{r}. Broughton & other Officers took possession of the Country in His Majesty's Name & hoisted the British Flag, on which Occasion 21 Guns were fired—Some Canoes alongside from the Village that Mr Whidbey had met with—

Tuesday 5th. Light Breezes and Cloudy. AM. ½ pt 7 Weighed and came to Sail, under Top Sail, Fore Sail & Top Gallant Sails—Turning down the Arm. Several Canoes Alongside. At Noon Moderate and Cloudy. Entrance Point N44W & Opposite Bluff N47W. *Chatham* in Company Latitude 47°. .49' N^{o}.[90]

Wednesday 6th. Moderate Breezes and Cloudy W^{r}. Tacked occasionally working out of the Inlet. At 12 came too with the Best Bower in 22 fths. AM. At 7 Made the Signal and weighed Working out of the Inlet. Starboard Extreme West Larb^{d} D^{o}. N60W^{t} & At 11 we passed over a Bank with 20fths on it & a great Rippling without us. Punished John Thomas with 36 Lashes for Neglect of Duty. At Noon we again had got out into the Streights East Point of Port Discovery S3W East Point of Protection

---

[89]Tulalip Bay.

[90]This is confusing. The observed latitude would place *Discovery* off Edmonds. Vancouver noted the shoaling off Cultus Bay, obviously Edmonds is several miles further south. In addition, the directions to the entrance point and opposite bluff make little sense. It is possible that the opposite bluff lay at N 47 E. If so, the ships were still working out of Possession Sound with the entrance point as Possession Point and the opposite bluff Elliot Point. Subsequent journals carry this same error.

Island S15W Dungeness Point S54W Nearest Shore EbN Entrance for which we steer N6E^{t}. *Chatham* in Com^{y}.

Thursday 7th. Calm and Pleasant Weather. At 3 Came too with Bower in 20 fths Sand — Sandy Island[91] N34W Protection Island S24W. Nearest Shore N60E 2 Miles— AM. ½ p^{t} 7 Weighed & at 10 Anchored again in 37 fths to wait Tide. Employed occasionally. *Chatham* in Company —

Friday 8th. Light Airs and Pleasant Weather. ½ p^{t} 6 Weighed under Topsails, Top Gallant Sails & Foresail drifting up the Reach with the Tide to the N West.— To this Situation we had seen the Continent but it now appeared to be broken. At ½ p^{t} 8 We again Anchored in 37 fths with the Small Bower, (it being now Capt Vancouvers Intention to dispatch me & Mr Whidbey to examine the Continent, intending after that to carry the Ship to a Situation pitched on by M^{r}. Broughton called Strawberry Bay where we were again to join him, after having traced the Continent to the Latitude of that Place). Cutter & Launch left the Ship on a Surveying Expedition with an Officer in Each. AM. Moderate and Cloudy W^{r}. Employed making Nippers.[92] Carpenters Sawing Planks— Latitude Obs^{d}— 48° .29' N°.

[p. 211] Third Boat Expedition in Surveying De Fuca's Streights—

On the 8 of June we left the *Discovery* at an Anchor off Sandy Island with the Launch and Cutter, Mr Whidbey in the Latter, attended by our usual Party & proceeded immediately on a further Examination of three Branches of this Arm on the Eastern Shore — Captain Vancouver intending to move the Ships during our Absence fixed the Rendezvous at a Place where the *Chatham* anchored & which M^{r}. Broughton had named Strawberry Bay, it lay considerably to the NW of our present Situation — That Evening assisted by a Strong Flood Tide we Arrived off the first Opening[93] trending to the Eastward, but it was so narrow that we imagined it almost impossible it could communicate with any other Branch, a Short time however convinced us of our Error for the Tide of Ebb came down with such force that, its Rapidity checked our utmost Efforts to stem the Stream, & effectually stopped our Progress for the Night, We

---

[91]Smith Island.

[92]Rather than raising an anchor by wrapping the large and inflexible mooring line around the capstan, a long length of smaller line called a *voyal* or messenger was seized around the cable in several places by nippers and then led to the capstan. As each nipper approached the capstan, it was removed, taken forward and reattached to the *voyal* and line. The responsibility of binding the line and *voyal* was that of the "nipper-men" who were assisted by the boys of the ship.

[93]Deception Pass.

therefore brought up near the Entrance from whence we Saw the Vessels dropping up in the NW Reach with the Tide——The force of the Tide gave us some hopes of finding an Extensive Inland Navigation though from the Smallness of the Entrance, there was some probability of its only being a large Cove but independent of these Suppositions we have hitherto made it a Maxim to see the Termination of every Branch however small it might appear, there [fore?] exclusive of the Tide this place would not have passed unnoticed. In our Row to this Opening we found a long Oceanic Swell from the Westward, that caused some Break on the Shore—All the beautifull Views & Beaches we hade met in the N Branch, were now supplanted by others of a far different Aspect, the Land lost its fertile Appearance & in the Place of a fine Country nothing was to be seen but Rocks of a Moderate height, thinly covered with Trees & the Shores equally destitute of affording Shelter——

On Saturday 9th June we again proceeded to the Examination of this Branch through this Narrow Channel not exceeding Forty Yards in Breadth & having Twenty fathoms in Mid Channel [left blank] passing the entrance the Continent took a more Southerly Direction & widened considerably—By Nine Mr Whidbey was perfectly satisfied of its Communication with the Arm he Surveyed; when dispatched on that Service, previous to our Arrival at the Place, where Possession was taken of the Country & which I have before noticed, however to ascertain it with more Certainty we continued on till he was enabled to take up his Old Angles & from them pursue the Continent——In the Fore Noon we Saw a very fine Deer, but were not able to kill it, though repeatedly fired at—[p. 212] The Rocks likewise abound with Seals & a variety of Oceanic Birds——In Sounding across we found Shoal Water; insomuch so, that I was afraid the Boats would Ground, from this and other concurring Circumstances I was sufficiently convinced, that this Passage cannot be navigated with Safety by Vessels of our tonnage, it may afford great Convenience to others of a Smaller Burthen, should any settlement be formed to the Southward, where it may be necessary to have a Communication with the Natives in the Northern Inlet. The Shoal Water lays on the Larboard Shore going in but on its Opposite, there are regular & good Soundings.—The chief objection are the Narrows—therefore we have now Determined the Intervening Land between the North Branch in the SE Arm on the NE Shore & the Narrows to be a large Island, which Captn Vancouver named after Mr Whidbey———

We now kept the Opposite Shore on board pursuing the Continent from Mr Whidbeys Old Angles & by the Afternoon had compleated rounded it out to the Narrows, but here we were again impeded by the Flood, its Rapidity was so great that we lost ground in the Stream, this detained us till the Evening—The Natives had attended to our Motions from the Morning & behaved in a most friendly Manner, their Numbers were not great, yet they approached us without any visible Fear or diffidence In which Sentiment I endeavoured to encourage them by Presents or whatever appeared. We passed their Village without landing, which seemed not a little to astonish the whole Party, especially after the Repeated Solicitations we had to visit their Habitations

In all these Excursions I should be happy to dedicate a few Minutes to satisfy the Curiosity of those Gentlemen who accompany us by landing at the different Villages we meet with—In this particular I should be equally happy to gratify my own Inclinations, which lead us to their Abodes, to obtain some knowledge of their Customs and Manners & by a proper Distribution of the Presents to more firmly cultivate their Friendship.—I have often found that by a Great Display of various Articles with which Government have so liberally supplied this Expedition that it frequently causes long Consultations among the Natives, who have come from their Habitations with fish, Refreshments & Curiosities to dispose of & for the which a certain proportion of Buttons Medals & other Trinkets have been given & though they Appeared perfectly satisfied with the exchange, yet their Eyes were continually fixed on what remained in the Boats. I do not mean to assert from this, that their Intentions were hostile, it might be Admiration or Curiosity and on the other Hand, we may equally suppose, their Consultations were not held [p. 213] for any good Purpose but merely to possess by Strategem or Force what they could not by Trade[94]——To carry such a Plan into execution I believe we have frequently been invited to their Villages, but as Prevention is at all times better than Punishment I have as often declined going——& however determined the Native Inhabitants may be to preserve strictly the Rules of Hospitality, still if these Temptations are thrown in his way the Resistless Desire of Gain entirely overbalance all natural benevolence and the Possession of what they have seen becomes their Chief Object. Therefore in frequently landing we might run some danger of being surprized, & the Knowledge we should obtain would be so superficial in so Short Visits, that Mr Whidbey agreed with me it was not worth the Risk——This however had not always prevented my stopping at their Habitations, where they have not been too Numerous & on these Occasions we have taken such Necessary precautions to guard against any Surprize, that the Indians must have perceived it & therefore were equally Cautions how they offended, But speaking in general Terms of their Conduct, we found

[94]The trinkets provided by the Admiralty were difficult to conceal in the boat. The Indians were perhaps curious and very envious of all this stuff.

them happy to supply our Wants in whatever their Village afforded & inoffensive in their Behaviour, & a Barter established carried on with the Strictest Honesty on both Sides—This however I greatly attributed to a proper treatment of these People on our parts, for we would never accept of any Article till the owner was satisfied with what was offered in Exchange —The Flood prevented us getting through the Narrows till the Evening & having rowed about four Miles NNE from the first Opening leaving two Islands[95] to the Westward of us; at the back of the second we brought up the Night on the Continental Shore on a narrow Spit of Low Sandy Soil on which was immense Quantities of Drift Wood this however is to be found on every Beach behind this Neck of Land is a Large Lagoon[96] with some Remnants of Huts where the Indians must have been very recently—Here we passed a most uncomfortable Night tormented by Musquito's & Sand Flies, which however was in some measure forgot in the morning by a large Supply of Strawberries and Wild Onions, which were found growing Spontaneously close to the Tents. The Country here is of a Moderate Height the Shores in general Rocky & the Appearance of the Land the direct Reverse of the Pleasant Prospects & delightfull Situation of the SE Arm, the Opposite Shore from the first Opening to our present Place seems broken as if forming a large Archipelago of Islands—The Continent abounds with the Remains of Indian Habitations but whether temporary or fixed we could not find out —The Productions of the Land are nearly Similar to [p. 214] what we have before observed, it abounds with Tall Streight Pines a few Maples & plants of Gooseberry Raspberry & Currant Bushes & is every where well supplied with Water. The Natives are likewise the same as our former Visitors in their Persons nor is there any visible Difference in their Manners Customs or Weapons.

Next Morning Sunday June 10th we left our Quarters early & proceeded along the Continental Shore till ½ pt 7 when the *Chatham* was seen at an Anchor near an Island[97] to the NW.—as she might have been ordered to wait there to furnish us with additional Instructions & a further Supply of Provisions I thought it best to pull over to her.—We Reached the *Chatham* at 8 & found her detained by the loss of an Anchor for which they were Sweeping—The Tide here ran three Knots & before we left the Vessel it increased to five. As Mr Broughton had no Orders for me; we again pursued our Examination of the Second Opening[98]

[95]Allan and Burrows Islands, they rowed through Burrows Bay.

[96]Flounder Bay.

[97]Cypress Island.

[98]Guemes Channel.

Through which we found the Tide so rapid, that the Boats could scarcely pull ahead — In the Afternoon we came into a large kind of Sound[99] which we might suppose would lead us into an Extensive Inland Navigation but its principal Direction being to the SE we were certain it could not possibly run far without coming into some of our Old Ground. — we landed on an Island[100] to take a more Distinct view of the Channel before us. About 3 Miles to the SE Low Sandy Spit were discovered extending from Shore to Shore about which were Several Natives busily employed in Canoes The Opposite or Eastern Land is Low — & to the Northward were some Islands. From this Island we kept to the SE along the SW Shore till the soundings decreased to two fathoms to only three feet. The Distant from the termination about a Mile and an half. — In this Depth to five feet to the Opposite Shore, — I have no Doubt but there is a Communication by Rivulets into the Place where Mr Whidbey took up his Old Angles as both Places have Similar Appearances in the low Swampy Country.[101] The Natives continued at the Work which was supposed fishing & never came near us — we could perceive a kind of Weir among the Shoals made of Small Sticks, probably for Salmon —— Pursuing our Examination along the Eastern Shore till 7 we pitched our Tents to the Northward of a Long Sandy Spit[102] & in the Mean time Mr Whidbey & myself in the Cutter pulled over to an Island[103] about 2 Miles distant for Angles & to take a further View of the Inlets before us — from this Situation we could see an Immense Distance to the NW, & as we supposed a clear and unbounded Horizon[104] — Another extensive Arm[105] appeared to Branch off to the NE, from these Circumstances we began to flatter ourselves of finding yet a [p. 215] Passage out for the Vessels to the Northward but still the Flood Came from the Southward & was of the Same Rapidity as the Ebb in fair Open Channels. On this Island I procured a piece from a Solid Rock not far from the Water Edge, which attracted the Magnet round and Round, by the Quantity of Iron it contained — Capt Cook in his last Voyage met a Similar Circumstance in Another Sound, which, by influencing his Compass 11° from what it ought to have shown

---

[99]Padilla Bay.

[100]Perhaps Hat or Saddlebag Island.

[101]Puget guessed at the existence of the Swinomish Channel.

[102]Possibly near William Point on Samish Island.

[103]Vendovi Island.

[104]They were looking along the east side of Orcas into the Strait of Georgia. From this location, the nearest "distant" land was Point Roberts at twenty-five miles.

[105]Bellingham Bay.

on a Rock where Bearings were necessary, they discovered the Error by a Disagreement of the Angles. I have no Doubt but this Country abounds with Iron — We joined the Launch about ½ p^{t} 8. We were not visited by the Natives during the Night — An animal called a Skunk was run down by one of the Marines after Dark & the intolerable stench it created absolutely awakened us in the Tent. The Smell is too bad for a Description, which I understand proceeds from an Emission of the Urine when frightened. This Man's Cloaths were afterwards so offensive that notwithstanding boiling, they still retained the Stench of the Animal & in the Next Expedition others were given him on Condition that those that retained the Smell should be thrown away & happy he was to comply with it. Among the Wood we found several Pines Stript of their Bark, which the Natives use in the fabrication of a light Yellow Garment; that New is certainly an handsome & well Manufactured piece of Workmanship; but it soon is discloured with Dirt —

Next Morning Monday June 11th we set out with the dawn of Day & after examining a Small Inlet that trended likewise to the SE & terminated in Shoal Water[106] returned to Breakfast on a Small Island that lay in our way to the Ships as by Capt Vancouvers Orders we were not to pass to the Northward of Strawberry Bay — At this Island we found a Canoe suspended to a Tree by Ropes with a Skeleton in & Bows Arrows fishing Implements &c. This I should imagine is the mode of Burial as established by these tribes, for in Port Discovery we met a Similar Circumstance. This likewise argues Strongly, that the Indians believe in a future State, or else why bury with them Eatables with their Weapons for procuring more & place the Body in a Canoe suspended in the Air, which we may reasonably suppose is to prevent its being damaged by Insects or Animals, that it may be of Service to the Deceased hereafter. However at present our knowledge of the Language is so very Imperfect that it would be impossible to form from it any Idea of their Religion or of the Deity — or do I ever think from the very Short time we remain at any Place either in the Ships or Boats, that we shall every be well acquainted with their Manners or Customs — In this Expedition we have passed Several deserted Villages in all were wooden Images crudely carved,[107] each I think contained one large & others of Smaller Dimensions the former was a very rough Imitation of the Countenance [p. 216] but the features by no Means in proportion, it bore more the Appearance of an horrid distorted Face, & whether this Image was a Representation of Deity or an Ornamental piece of Furniture is at present impossible to determine as

[106]Samish Bay.

[107]Totem poles.

either may prove fallacious. From this Island we made the best of our Way for the Vessels as the Third Opening was now to the SW of us & proved only an Island; We had left an Inlet appearing trending to the NE—The Main Branch to the NW with no Land visible in that Direction and the Flood still coming rapidly from the Southward. The Land the Westward of WSW by its broken Appearance I have no Doubt will on Examination prove a Cluster of Islands—We went to the NW of the Island[108] under which the Vessels lay to look at the Channel which appeared free from Danger & got on board by two in the Afternoon. From our Representation of the Extent of the Main Branch it was determined that the Ships should proceed to the NW & anchor in some Convenient Situation to erect our Observatories—that Mr Whidbey should proceed with the *Discovery's* Cutter & a Boat from the *Chatham* to examine the NE Arm we had left & survey to the Ships & Captain Vancouver with the Pinnace & Launch to explore to the NW, this was supposing the Situation of the Ships to be on the Continent—& there is little fear but it would prove so——But the most astonishing Circumstance attending this intricate Navigation is, that the two Vessels have pursued these Channels in Strong Tides, & have been fortunate in not having as yet touched the Ground,[109] we generally ran on without our Boats ahead Sounding. It has been frequently observed that Soundings might be looked proportionall with the height of Land, This supposition will by no means stand good in the Navigation of these Streights, for we have found the same extraordinary Depth of Water both in a low and Mountainous Country & it has occurred in a Channel not a Mile Wide with an immense Rapid Stream that no Bottom could be found with 80 fths of Line, the Water every where much Discloured & perfectly Salt.—During this last & former Expeditions we have observed The White Headed Eagle Ducks Curlews Sea Pies Gulls Terns Hawkes Spruce Partridges Humming Birds Awks Puffins Woodpeckers Redbreasted Thrush Kingfishers, Great Northern Diver Crows Ravens & Pidgeons—The Inhabitants of this vast Country—Of the Fish we have yet seen few only Whales Porpoises Salmon Bream Sculpins Trout & the English Herring.—Of Shell Fish Clams Cockles Muscles & a sort of Perrywinkle—The Animals we have seen are few but from the Skins [p. 217] worn by the Natives there are Bears Deer Rabbitts & Raccoon & before we finally quit the Streights I shall obtain from Mr Menzies an Account of the Vegetable Kingdom—There had been no Natives on board since our Absence nor had the *Chatham* recovered her Anchor——

[108]Cypress Island.

[109]Puget either forgot or ignored *Chatham's* mishap in Port Susan.

	Latitude [Puget left these entries blank]
	Longitude
Strawberry Bay	Variation
	High Water
	Rize and Fall of the Tide

2

Archibald Menzies

Archibald Menzies was born at Weims, Perthshire, Scotland, on March 15, 1754, and raised at the Castle Menzies. His older brother William assisted in securing a position for him as a gardener's assistant at the Royal Botanical Garden in Edinburgh where he began his botanical training, under the tutelage of Dr. John Hope, professor of botany at the University and superintendent of the Gardens. Dr. Hope also assisted Menzies' entry to the Edinburgh University where he studied medicine, chemistry and botany. Menzies enlisted in the Royal Navy in 1782 as an assistant surgeon first aboard H.M.S. *Nonsuch*, and served later on the *Assistance* in 1784, where he met and began a long friendship with James Johnstone, ship's master.

In 1786, he was appointed surgeon for an expedition around the world aboard the *Prince of Wales*, commanded by Captain Colnett along with the sloop *Princess Royal*. The three year voyage brought him to northwest waters for a short period of time. Colnett departed the expedition in Macao. James Johnstone assumed command and with Menzies, returned to England.

In December 1790, he received his rank of surgeon. That same year, Sir Joseph Banks was instrumental in his appointment as naturalist aboard *Discovery*. Due to ill health of Alexander Cranstoun, *Discovery's* surgeon, Vancouver appointed Menzies to that position September 1792. Among his many discoveries during the expedition was a tree which was named after him: *Arbutus menziesii*, our common Madrona. Menzies retired from the Navy in 1802 from asthma but continued his medical practice in London. He married Janet about that same time, but there were no children. He retired from his practice in 1826 and died at Notting Hill February 15, 1842.

Except for the footnotes, the following was taken from C.F. Newcombe's *Menzies' Journal of Vancouver's Voyage*.

[p. 13] At noon [April 28, 1792] our Latitude was 47° 30' N & what is calld Destruction Island was at the same time about three leagues to the Northward of us. / It is low & flat coverd only with verdure & engirdled by steep rocky cliffs. In the afternoon we had light variable wind with somewhat hazy weather & perceiving the influence of a current setting us in shore we droppd Anchor in 19 fathoms about 4 miles from the shore & the same distance to the Southward of Destruction Island where we remand the evening.

At three next morning we both weighd anchor & made Sail along the coast to the Northward with a favorable breeze gradually increasing & soon after we saw a ship nearly a head of us a little way out from the Coast which on seeing us brought to & fird a gun to leeward, in passing we edgd a little down towards her & spoke the *Columbia* of Boston commanded by Mr Gray — At the name of Gray it occurrd to us that he might be the same who commanded the Sloop *Washington* at the time she is said to have performd that remarkable interior navigation on this Coast which was so much the subject of polemic conversation in England before our departure. — We immediately brought [p. 14] to & sent a Boat to the *Columbia* in which I accompanied L[t] Puget in order to obtain what information we could, & the reader may easily conceive the eagerness with which we interrogated the Commander when we found him to be the same man which our ideas had suggested, & indeed it may appear no less curious than interesting that here at the entrance of Juan de Fuca's Streights we should meet with the very man whose Voyage up it in the Sloop *Washington* as delineated by the fertile fancy of Mr Mears gave rise to so much theoretical speculation & chimerical discussion — / I say interesting because it enables us to detect to the World a fallacy in this matter which no excuse can justify.[1]

Mr Gray informd us that in his former Voyage he had gone up the Streights of Juan de Fuca in the Sloop *Washington* about 17 leagues in an East by South direction & finding he did not meet with encouragement as a Trader to pursue it further he returnd back & came out to Sea again the very same way he had enterd — he was therefore struck with astonishment when we informd him of the sweeping tract of several degrees which Mr Mears had given him credit for in his Chart & publication.

He further informd us that in his present Voyage he had been 9

---

[1]Indeed, while Meares should properly be condemned for his lies, or as Mr. Manby called it, "imprudent humbug," his imagination is to be congratulated. In his journal, Meares published a chart which actually reflected Vancouver Island as an island, and further showed Gray's route around it. Gray of course denied this, having entered the Strait of Juan de Fuca only seventeen leagues which placed him near Port Angeles.

months on the Coast & winterd at Cloiquat a district a little to the Eastward of Nootka where he built a small sloop which was at this time employd in collecting Furs to the Northward about Queen Charlotte's Isles—That in the Winter the Natives of Cloiquat calling to their aid 3 or 4 other Tribes collected to the number of upwards of three thousand to attack his Vessel, but their premeditated schemes being discovered to him by a Native of the Sandwich Islands he had on board whom the Chiefs had attempted to sway over to their diabolic plots in solliciting him to wet the locks & priming of the Musquets & Guns before they boarded. By this means he was fortunately enabled by timely precautions to frustrate their horrid stratagems at the very moment they had assembled to execute them.

/ He likewise told us that last year the Natives to the Northward of Queen Charlotte's Isles had murdered his Chief Mate & two Seamen while they were employd fishing in a small Boat a little distance from the Ship, & that the Natives of Queen Charlotte's Isles had surprizd an American Brig the *Lady Washington* commanded by Mr Kendrick [p. 15] & kept posession of her for upwards of two hours, when the united exertions of the Master & Crew happily liberated them from the impending destruction & made the Natives quit their prize in a precipitate flight in which a vast number of them lost their lives. On this occasion the Natives had watchd an opportunity to posess themselves of the arm chests on deck while open, by which stratagen they were able to arm themselves & disarm the Ship's company, but the latter rallying on them afterwards from below with what arms they could collect, rendered their vile scheme abortive.

As soon as the Boat was hoisted in we made sail & pursued our course along shore till about noon when we entered the famous Streights of Juan de Fuca. The weather was at this time so thick & hazy that we had no observation to determine our Latitude. The whole shore we saild along this forenoon is steep & rocky & entirely lind with a vast number of elevated rocks & Islets of different forms & sizes, but the land itself is of a very moderate height coverd with Pines & stretching back with a very gradual acclivity to form an inland ridge of high mountains in which Mount Olympus claimd a just preeminence. / We saw no point worthy of particular notice in the situation Cap[t] Cook places Cape Flattery, the South point of de Fuca's entrance tho about three leagues further to the Northward agrees better with his description of it than any other on this part of the Coast.

About a Mile or two off this South point of entrance is a flat naked Island coverd with verdure & facd round with steep rocks, round the North end of which we hauld into the Streights passing between it & a small Rock[2] showing above water about a mile to the Northward of it, where we met a rippling of the Tide which at first occasiond some alarm till the cause became evident. Some Canoes came off to us from a village on this Island which was not seen till we passed it as it is situated on a chasm on the East Side of it, This is what Mr Mears called the village of Tatootche, & though we had reason to believe that we saw most of its inhabitants at this time about the Rocks upon the Beach & in their Canoes gazing on us as we passed, yet we think that we should over rate their number if we were to call it as many hundreds as that author has estimated them thousands.

[p. 16] A little after we passed this green Island we had a transient view of the Pinnacle Rock close to the shore of Cape Clanset, but at this distance it did not appear to us so very remarkable as it is represented, nor did it answer the idea we had been lead to form of its situation, for we earnestly lookd for it as we were passing on the Outside of the Cape but could not then distinguish it from the high Cliffs behind it.

/ As we kept close to the Southern Shore in passing the Village of Clanset we had light fluctuating winds which afforded several of the Natives an opportunity of visiting us but the weather being thick & rainy their stay was very short. About 5 Miles within the Streights we saw the appearance of a small Cove[3] shelterd by a little Island where the Spaniards about a Month afterwards attempted to establish a Settlement & sent a Vessel commanded by a Lieutenant for that purpose from Nootka.

The *Columbia* who bore up along shore & followd us into the Streights kept under way all night but there being little wind, & that chiefly against us we anchord a little before dark under the Southern Shore about three leagues from the Entrance.

[Half a page blank in the original]

Having now enterd on our interior examination of Juan de Fuca's Streights, we on the morning of the 30th of April both weighd Anchor & after making Sail steerd to the Eastward along the Southern shore on a firm supposition that it was the Continental shore which we had tracd thus far from a little to the Southward of Cape Mendocino. We were favord with a fine Westerly breeze which soon dispersd the Fog & brought with it fair & clear weather. In the forenoon as we went along Canoes came off to us here & there from the Shore with Sea Otter Skins for which they askd Copper or Cloth, but they were able to keep with us

---

[2]Duncan Rock.

[3]Neah Bay.

a very short time as we had a fair fresh breeze. The *Columbia* was seen again working out of the Streights, & it would now seem as if the Commander of her did not put much confidence in what we told him of our pursuit, but had probably taken us for rivals in trade and followd us into the Streights to have his share in the [p. 17] gleanings of those Villages at the entrance, & this is conformable to the general practice among traders on this Coast, which is always to mislead competitors as far as they can even at the expence of truth.

Towards noon we edged into midchannel to have the advantage of a meridian altitude which gave our Latitude 48° 18' about 12 leagues to the Eastward of the South point of entrance.

The Streights appear in general to be about 3 or 4 leagues wide, the Southern Shore / is nearly streight without forming any very striking points or bays—it rises steep into Mountains near the entrance of a very moderate height, but as we advanced to the Eastward to very high mountains coverd with impenetrable forests of Pines till near their summits, where they were capt with snow in abundance as were also some Mountains in our view on the North side.

We were not above 18 leagues from the Entrance, when the Streights widend out to 9 or 10 leagues across, we however continud our course along the southern shore & in the evening went round the point of a low sandy spit which jutted out from it in very shallow water, when we came to an anchor[4] on the East side of it in 14 fathoms fine black sand about half a mile from the spit which appeard a long ridge of sand strewd over with a good deal of drift wood & some high poles kept erect by four or five supporting poles round the bottom of each — What was meant by these we were at a loss to determine. We were now about 20 leagues inland in an East by South direction true from Cape Clanset.—The Country assumd a very different appearance, the land near the water side was low mostly coverd with Pines to the very verge of a fine stoney & sandy Beach, but in the North East quarter a very high solid ridge of Mountains was observd one of which was seen wholly coverd with Snow & with a lofty summit over topping all the others around it upwards of twenty leagues off nearly in a North East direction — This obtaind the name of Mount Baker after the Gentleman who first observd it.

Next morning being the first of May I / accompanied Cap[t] Vancouver & some of the Officers of both Vessels who set out pretty early, in two Boats from us, & one from the *Chatham* to examine the shore to the Eastward of us for a Harbour.

[p. 18] When we left the Vessels it was a little foggy & calm, but

---

[4]Dungeness Spit.

clearing up soon after it became exceedingly pleasant & serene, which added not a little to our enjoyment in this days excursion. We kept along shore to the South eastward starting in our way vast flights of water fowl such as Auks Divers Ducks & Wild Geese, which were so exceedingly shy that the sportsmen had very little opportunity of shewing their dexterity. After a row of about four leagues we came to an Island the rural appearance of which strongly invited us to stretch our limbs after our long confined situation on board & the dreary sameness of a tedious voyage. Its north west side was guarded by a high naked perpendicular cliff of reddish earth & sand quite inaccessable, but the South side presented a sloping bank covered with green turf so even & regular as if it had been artificially formed.

We found on landing that Vegetation had already made great progress, the shore was skirted with long grass & a variety of wild flowers in full bloom, but what chiefly dazzled our eyes on this occasion was a small species of wild Valerian with reddish colord flowers growing behind the beach in large thick patches.

On ascending the Bank to the summit of the Island, a rich lawn beautified with nature's, luxuriant bounties burst at once on our view & impressd us with no less pleasure than novelty — It was abundantly croppd with a variety of grass clover & wild flowers, here & there adornd by aged pines with wide spreading horizontal / boughs & well shelterd by a slip of them densely copsed with Underwood stretching along the summit of the steep sandy cliff, the whole seeming as if it had been laid out from the premeditated plan of a judicious designer.

To the Northward & North west ward the eye roved over a wide expanse of water which seemd to penetrate the distant land through various openings & windings, but a little to the South East of us appeard an Inlet[5] which promisd fair for affording good shelter for the Vessels— Its entrance presents a prospect truly inviting with gentle rising banks on both sides coverd with fine verdure & tufted with tall trees loosely scatterd, we therefore embarkd to examine it & went up about 4 miles, some walkd along shore on a fine pebbly beach, others were employd sounding in the Boats till we came to a low sandy point[6] on which we found a run of [p. 19] fresh water sufficient to answer all our purposes with good anchorage close to it & the whole well shelterd by the favourite Island we had left shortning the entrance which on that account obtaind the name of Protection Island. Here we kindled a fire & regald ourselves with some refreshment, after which we returnd on board where we arrivd about

---

[5]Discovery Bay.

[6]Contractors Point.

midnight each well satified with the success & pleasure of this days excursion.

In going into the Harbour one of the Gentlemen shot a small animal which diffusd through the air a most disagreeable & offensive smell, I was anxious to take it on board for examination & made it fast to the bow of the Cutter, but the stink it emitted was so intolerable that I was obligd to relinquish my prize. I took it to be the Skunk or Polecat.[7]

In the absence of the Boats this day the / Vessels were visited by several of the Natives from a small Village abreast of them who brought some fish to barter for trinkets.

At day light on the 2d both Vessels weighd & with a light air of wind from the Westward proceeded towards the Harbour we had visited on the preceeding day, which we enterd about 9 & with the assistance of the Boats towing a head soon after came to off the low Sandy point in 34 fathoms over a black stiff Clayey bottom. In passing within Protection Island & entring the Harbour, the right hand shore was kept close aboard which was found pretty steep & the most eligible Channel.

In the afternoon I accompanied Capt Vancouver to the head of the Harbour which we found to terminate in a muddy bank of shallow water on which the Pinnace grounded — This lead to the discovery of a species of small Oyster with which the bottom was plentifully strewd but being now out of season they were poor & ill flavord & consequently not worth collecting. We then landed on the East Side where we saw the remains of a deserted village of a few houses one of which had been pretty large & in make resembled the Nootka habitations as described by Capt Cook, but neither of them seemd to have been inhabited for some time. On a Tree close to it we found the skeleton of a child which was carefully wrapped up in some of the Cloth of the Country made from the Bark of a Tree & some Matts, but at this time it afforded tenement to a brood of young [p. 20] Mice which ran out of it as soon as we touchd it — A wooden Cup was found close to it on the same tree & a bunch of small yew Boughs fastend together, which were probably the remains / of some superstitious ceremony.

Besides a variety of Pines we here saw the Sycamore Maple — the American Aldar — a species of wild Crab & the Oriental Strawberry Tree, this last grows to a small Tree & was at this time a peculiar ornament to the Forest by its large clusters of whitish flowers & ever green leaves, but its peculiar smooth bark of a reddish brown colour will at all times attract the Notice of the most superficial observer. — We met with some

[7]For another humorous description of these events, refer to Manby, Chapter 19.

other Plants which were new to me & which shall be the subject of particular description hereafter.

On our return in the evening we found the Tents & Marquee pitchd on the low point near the Vessels together with the Observatory in which the Astronomical Quadrant was fixd for taking equal altitudes to ascertain the rate of the Time-keepers.

Next day [May 3, 1792] being remarkably serene pleasant weather part of our Powder was landed on another low point at a little distance to be aired under the care of the Gunner, & this duty was daily attended to till the whole stock was perfectly dried.—The Seamen began to repair the rigging & the Mechanics were severally occupied in their different employments, while my botanical pursuits kept me sufficiently engaged in arranging & examining the collections I had already made.

On the 4th I landed opposite to the Ship to take an excursion back into the Woods which I had hardly enterd when I met with vast abundance of that rare plant the *Cypropedium bulbosom*[8] / which was now in full bloom & grew about the roots of the Pine Trees in very spungy soil & dry situations. I likewise met here with a beautiful shrub the *Rhododendrum ponticum* & a new species of *Arbutus* with *glaucous* leaves that grew bushy & 8 or 10 feet high, besides a number of other plants which would be too tedious here to enumerate.

In this days route I saw a number of the largest trees hollowd by fire into cavities fit to admit a person into, this I conjecturd might be done by the Natives either to screen them from the sight of those animals they meant to ensnare or afford them a safe retreat from others in case of being [p. 21] pursued, or it may be the means they have of felling large trees for making their Canoes, by which they are thus partly scooped out.

Next day in the forenoon some Natives came along side in a Canoe with Fish & a few pieces of Venison for which they found a ready Market & soon after left us having nothing else to dispose of & seemingly a little curiosity to gratify, our appearance affording them no degree of novelty lead us to suppose that ours was not the first European Vessel with which they had had intercourse, tho' from the few European commodities we saw amongst them the intercourse did not appear to be very extensive. From the affinity of their dress Canoe & language they appeard to be of the same nation with the Nootka Tribe & were like them fondest of Copper & Brass Trinkets for their Ears; they also took Iron with which Metal many of their arrows were barbed.

/ In strolling about the verge of the wood with some of the officers, we saw several stumps of small trees as if they had been cut down with

[8]False Lady Slipper, an orchid.

an Axe not many months ago, from this it was thought probable that some other Vessel might have been here before us, as I never observd the Natives on any part of this Coast make use of an Axe in felling of Timber of any kind preferring always an Instrument of their own construction somewhat in the form of a small adze which hackd it in a very different manner from an Axe.[9]

The Carpenters were now employd in Caulking & on the various necessary repairs— the Blacksmiths had their Forge going on shore — a party were cutting down fire wood — Another brewing Beer from a species of Spruce — in short the weather being so favorable & vivifying every spring was set in motion to forward our refitment.

The 6th being a day of relaxation parties were formd to take the recreation of the shore & strolling through the woods in various directions saw in one place a number of human bones deposited in a thicket & coverd carefully over with Planks, others were found suspended in an old Canoe coverd with the bark of Trees & with Moss, but what much surprizd them in one place of the wood they came to was a clear Area where there had been a large fire round which they found a number of incinerated bones & about half a [p. 22] dozen human skulls scattered about the Area — This lead to various conjectures, some supposing it to be a place allotted for human sacrifices made to banquet the unnatural gormondizing appetites of the Inhabitants who in a late publication[10] are all / alledged to be Cannibals but without any rational proof that brings the least conviction to my mind. The number of human bones seen in different parts of the Harbour almost equally advanced in decay would rather lead us to suppose that Battle had been fought here at a period not very remote & that the vanquishd on that occasion sufferd by the refined cruelties of their Conquerors on the above spot, for it is the known practice of the American Tribes on the opposite Coast to burn their vanquishd enemies & it is not improbable that the same horrid custom prevails here.

The Seine was daily hauled at the Tents & with some degree of suc-

---

[9]The Quimper journal of July 13, 1790 indicated that the pilot of the *Princesa Real*, Juan Carrasco, constructed a cross at Contractors Point. It is possible Menzies observed trees cut by the Spaniards for this purpose (Blumenthal 29).

[10]Menzies perhaps referenced Meares who observed at Nootka (p. 255): "Callicum and Hanapa both declared their aversion to the practice of eating human flesh; at the same time they acknowledged it existed among them and that Maquilla was so much attached to this detestable banquet as to kill a slave every moon to gratify his unnatural appetite." Meares added (p. 256) "We were not by any means disposed to give credit to this extraordinary action and rather imagined that it was invented to injure Maquilla in our opinion...."

cess though we seldom obtaind a sufficient supply for all hands, the fish generally caught were Bream of two or three kinds, Salmon & Trout & two kind of flat fish, one of which was a new species of *Pleuronectes*, with Crabs which were found very good & palatable & we seldom faild in hauling on shore a number of Elephant Fish (*Chimæra Callorhynchus*) & Scolpings (*Cottus scorpius*) but the very appearance of these was sufficient to deter the use of them, they therefore generally remaind on the Beach.

Early on the morning of the 7th I set out with Capt Vancouver & some of the Officers in three Boats manned & armed & provided with five days provision, our object was to examine & explore the country to the eastward of us, We proceeded out of the Port with foggy weather & little wind & keeping the right hand shore close on board we rowed for about two leagues to the North East ward, where we enterd a large opening which took a Southerly direction & which afterwards obtaind the name of Admiralty Inlet, but as the weather continued still very foggy we landed on the point[11] till it should clear up a little, & took several hauls of a / small Seine we had in the Boat but without the least success.

A little before noon the Fog dispersd when we saw the opening we had enterd go to the South Eastward a considerable extent & a little distance from us another arm branching off to the Southward, we walkd along the shore to the [p. 23] point[12] of this arm which we reachd by noon when a Meridian Altitude by a quick silver horizon[13] gave our Latitude 48° 7' 30" North. In this walk I found growing in the Crevices of a small rock about mid way between the two points a new Speices of *Claytonia*, & as I met with it no where else in my journeys, it must be considered as a rare plant in this country. I namd it *Claytonia furcata* & took a rough sketch of it which may be seen in my collections of Drawings.

The shores here are sandy & pebbly—the point we came to was low & flat with some Marshy ground behind it & a pond of water surrounded with willows & tall bulrushes, behind this a green bank stretchd to the

---

[11]Point Wilson.

[12]Point Hudson.

[13]Measuring the altitude of celestial objects required a horizontal reference. When not available, for example, under cloudy conditions along the horizon, or when land was present in front of the object to be measured, an artificial horizon was used. This frequently was a pan of mercury (quick silver), heavy oil, or molasses, covered by plate glass to shelter it from the wind. To use, a navigator sat or stood in front of the artificial horizon so that the distant object was in view as well as its reflection in the artificial horizon. A sextant was used to measure the angle between the object and this reflection. The artificial horizon was used primarily on land where the ocean horizon was not in view.

Southward a little distance from the shore which was markd with the beaten paths of Deer & other Animals. While dinner was getting ready on the point I ascended this Bank with one of the Gentlemen & strolled over an extensive lawn, where solitude rich pasture & rural prospects prevaild — It presented an uneven surface with slight hollows & gentle risings interspersd with a few straddling pine trees & edged behind with a thick forest of them that coverd over a flat country of very moderate height & renderd the Western side of this arm a pleasant & desirable tract of both pasture & arable land where the Plough might enter at once without the least obstruction, & where / the Soil though light & gravelly appeard capable of yielding in this temperate climate luxuriant Crops of the European Grains or of rearing herds of Cattle who might here wander at their ease over extensive fields of fine pasture, though the only posessors of it we saw at this time were a few gigantic Cranes of between three & four feet high who strided over the Lawn with a lordly step.

To the North east of us across Admiralty Inlet which is about a league wide we had from this eminence a most delightfull & extensive landscape, a large tract of flat country coverd with fine Verdure & here & there interspersd with irregular clumps of trees whose dark hue made a beautiful contrast aided by the picturesque appearance of a rugged barrier of high mountains which at some distance terminated our prospect in lofty summits coverd with perpetual snow.

After dinner we proceeded examining this southerly arm, dividing the boats for the purpose of sounding & [p. 24] exploring & fixing on a distant point[14] as a place of meeting in the evening. Invited by the enchanting appearance of the Country & fine serene weather, I walkd with Capt Vancouver & some others along the Western shore for a considerable distance as it afforded me an opportunity of exploring for natural productions as I went along. After a long walk we met with a thick pine forest which obligd us to embark & the shore here taking an Easterly direction we rowd along it & towards evening we found the arm also winding a little to the Eastward & terminate in a small basin of shallow water being here divided only from the end of another arm by a flat muddy beach / covered with thick beds of marsh samphire. Being thus satisfied of its termination we returnd back to the place of rendezvous where we met Lt Puget with the Long Boat, but Mr Johnstone who had crossed over to the Eastern shore of the arm was lead into an armlet[15] which he supposed would join with ours a little further on & that after exploring it he would be able to meet us in the evening at the place

[14]Kala Point.

[15]Kilisut Harbor.

appointed, after pulling a long way he found his mistake & being late he took up his quarters in it all night, so that we were separated for the evening, in consequence of which this armlet obtaind the name of Johnstone's decoy, it takes nearly a South East direction & is very narrow at the entrance.

The next morning was calm & pleasant & we set off on our return back in expectation of meeting Mr Johnstone whose Swivels we heard at a considerable distance pretty early, he joind us about 9 after a fatigueing row where we were at the entrance of a small brook filling our water Cags; here we met with some detention by the long Boat getting aground upon a flat with a falling Tide, but in the mean time the Pinnace went over to the opposite shore to take Angles & prepare Breakfast, so that there was very little time lost. After the Long Boat floated they all three pulld to the Northward & while we walkd along the Eastern shore[16] & on a Beach a little to the Southward of Johnstone's decoy, not far from where we Breakfasted we saw two human heads impaled upon the points of two poles erected a few yards asunder & about twelve feet high, part of the Skin about the Chin was hanging down, but the rest of the face teeth & black long hair was entire in each—/ The poles enterd under the Chin piercd their Vertex, & in [p. 25] their formation, the poles had a degree of uniformity that requird a good deal of trouble. Having crossd over the entrance of Johnstone's decoy we enterd on a low narrow beach about a mile long, on the middle of which we found nine or ten long poles erected in a row at nearly equal distances from one another which was about ninety or a hundred yards apart, Each pole was lengthend by two pieces neatly joind together to about 90 feet high terminating with a Trident by leaving the stumps of two opposite branches & the middle piece about a foot long at the extremity of the upper Pole, The heel of each was sunk in the ground & was further shord up by four other poles each about 30 feet long which spread out round the bottom & fastend about the middle pole as supporters. What was the intention or meaning of the Natives in erecting these poles with so much pains & trouble we were at a loss to form the most distant conjecture, we saw some of the same kind erected upon other Beaches since we came into the Streights but no where so numerous & regular as here.

Having now finished our examination of the first small Arm which was namd Port Townsend,[17] we pursued our walk to the South East along

---

[16]Near Walan Point on Indian Island.

[17]It is interesting to note that Menzies' spelling is consistent with today's. I believe this error belongs to Dr. Newcombe as Menzies surely was familiar with Marquis Townshend.

the shore of Admiralty Inlet & passed some perpendicular sandy Cliffs[18] which exposed to view some thick strata of fine Fullers Earth. A white animal was also seen which we supposd to be a Dog about the size of a large Fox but it made off so quick into the Woods that those who saw it were not certain what it was. About noon we reachd a low point which was the most / distant one we saw in this direction when the fog cleard up on the forenoon of the preceeding day & from this though the arm inclind a little more to the Southward yet it was so triffling that the same general direction to the South Eastward continued for about 4 or 5 leagues further & then it appeared to be separated by a bluff point[19] into two arms one of which seemd to take a more easterly direction. The Arm was still between 2 & 3 miles wide & appeard a fine navigable Channel for Vessels of any burden.

Having dind on this point which was flat with a salt marsh & pond behind it, we embarkd in the afternoon & separated on different pursuits with the Boats, but made the bluff point we saw ahead the place of meeting again in the evening. From this Point we had a fine view of [p. 26] a very lofty round topped mountain coverd with Snow about five & twenty leagues off nearly in a South East direction which afterwards obtaind the Name of Mount Rainier in Latitude 47° 3 North & Longitude 238° 21' East.

The Weather in the afternoon was Cloudy with Showers which in the evening began to rain very hard & became foggy, we rowd hard to gain our intended place of rendezvous but our endeavours provd fruitless on account of a strong tide of Ebb which set against us, & the night was so very dark & foggy with excessive rain that the only means we had of keeping together was by frequent firing of Muskets, at last the night being far advancd all idea of reaching the intended place this evening was given up & we rowd in for the Starboard / shore & went along it for some way before we could find a landing place to pitch our Tents & kindle a fire on, the latter was found a very difficult task it being so dark & everything so wet, it was midnight before we could get under any kind of shelter & then every thing about us was completely drenchd, & in this situation the greatest part of the Boats Crews passed the night without any covering to shelter them from the inclemency of the weather.

The following day continud thick rainy weather so that we could not stir to any advantage.—As intervals of fair or clear weather permitted parties strolld along the Beach & met with some Oak Trees on which account our present situation was called Oak Cove, it stretches a little to

[18] Marrowstone Point.

[19] Foulweather Bluff.

the Westward & nearly meets the termination of Port Townsend as has been already noticed.

The morning of the 10th was fair & we set out again pretty early to explore the Southern Arm, after crossing Oak Cove we kept the Starboard Shore on board & about nine fell in with a few Canoes of Indians seemingly a fishing party as they had no women with them or any thing to traffic.—We landed soon after on the inside of the point of a Cove which was named Indian Cove to Breakfast & about eighteen of the Natives landed close to us upon the Beach, where they very quietly laid down their Bows & Quivers upon the stump of a tree & sat themselves down very peaceably. They were but indifferently cloathd with the Skins of Animals chiefly / Deer Lynx Martin & Bear [p. 27] Skins, One of them had a very large skin of the brown Tyger *Felis concolor* which was some proof of that Animal being found thus far to the Northward on this side of the Continent, but we saw very little of the Sea Otter Skins among them, which also shows that that Animal is not fond of penetrating far inland.—The rocky cliffs near the Point where we breakfasted abounded with the *Terra Ponderosa aerata* & on the Beach was found different kinds of Iron Ore & a variety of the siliceous order.

After distributing some Trinkets among the Indians who readily accepted of any thing that was offerd them, & who appeard to speak a different language from those at the entrance of the Streights, we embarkd & in crossing over the Cove saw a small village at the bottom of it, to which the Natives who were with us went after we parted.

On the opposite point[20] to where we breakfasted the Latitude observed was 47° 56' N & we went but little further when we found the tide of Ebb run so strong to the Northward together with a fresh breeze of wind that we were compelld to wait till the Flood made in our favor, & then proceeded till in the afternoon we reachd a round clump of trees which had the appearance of an Island[21] but which we found joind by a narrow beach to the Western Shore, from this the arm took a South Westerly direction which we pursued till dark, & then / stopped for the night which was serene & pleasant on a snug Beach where we were very comfortable on the Larb^{d} shore.[22] The country on both sides of the arm still preservd a very moderate height & every where coverd with pine forests close down to the Beach & this afternoon I found on the western side a good number of hazle nut Trees for the first time on this side of America.

---

[20]Perhaps Tala Point.

[21]Hood Head.

[22]I.e., the eastern side of the Canal.

Next morning at day break we set out pursuing this Arm which was nearly two Miles wide in a Southerly direction with fair weather but little or no wind. In the afternoon we found a branch going off in a North West direction which we followd to its termination & finding it only a deep Bay[23] we returnd back along the opposite shore & about dark pitchd our tents for the night near its Southern point of Entrance. At a place we landed on near the bottom of the Bay I saw vast abundance of a beautiful new species of *Vaccinium*[24] with ever green leaves in full bloom, [p. 28] it grew bushy & was of a dark green colour like Myrtles which it much resembled in its general appearance. I had seen it before in several other places since we came into the Streights but no where in such perfection as here, I therefore employd this afternoon in making a delineation of it as we went along in the Boat.

We felt it exceeding cold next morning [May 12, 1792] before the sun got up, the Mercury in a Thermometer exposed to the open Air was so low as 42° of Farenheit's scale, this was occasiond by our being close under that high ridge of Mountains with snowy summits which support the Peaks of Mount Olympus & which now lay between us / & the sea coast, but their sides were every where coverd with one continued forest of Pinery.

Soon after day break we were again in motion pursuing the Arm which still lead to the Southward & as we stopt[25] about noon to get a Meridian Altitude we were overtaken by a Canoe with two men who made signs to us that there were more before us. The Seine was hauld with indifferent success while I took a stroll about the Woods where I found three different kinds of Maple & a *Rhamnus Arbutus* & *Ceanothus* that were new to me beside several others.

After dinner we set out to continue our examination of the arm which was now hemmed in by lofty Mountains on one side & low flat country of considerable extent on the other. Abut five in the afternoon we observd smoke & some Natives on a Beach on the Starboard shore to which we pulled in with the Boats & on landing[26] found two or three families occupied in drying and smoking of Clams skewerd upon small rods— We saw but a few men, the women & Children having fled into the Woods at our approach & from all appearance their residence seemd to be a temporary one merely for the purpose of drying & collecting of fish — They told us that more Natives were on the opposite point[27] where

[23]Dabob Bay.

[24]Huckleberry.

[25]Near Lilliwaup Creek.

[26]Near the Great Bend.

[27]Apparently near Ayres Point.

the arm seemd to take an Easterly direction, we crossed over & found them more numerous living on the Beach without any kind of habitation shelter or covering whatever which leads us to conclude that they were only a foraging party in pursuit of Game collecting & drying of fish / for we procurd from them a number of Salmon & flat fish & the men purchased several Bear Skins but we saw no Sea Otter Skins among [p. 29] them. Several of them were pockmarkd—a number of them had lost an eye, & amongst them were some whose faces we recollected seeing in Indian Cove, this was better confirmd by finding in their posession some of the Trinkets we had there distributed—They had also Iron Chinese Cashes (a kind of base Money piercd with a hole) & beads which clearly showed that they had had either a direct or indirect communication with the Traders on the exterior part of the Coast.

On this point we saw some Oak but in a very dwarf state & on the opposite shore saw pretty large Trees of Maple American Aldar & several other Plants which I had not before observed on this Coast.

Having spent some little time with the Indians & satisfied ourselves with respect to the termination of the Arm, we could do nothing else but return back the way we came, & for the night which was fine & pleasant we rested at a little distance from the Indians without the least disturbance or Molestation.

At day light on the 13th we set out on our return to the Vessels & had the mortification for the first time since our departure to find a fresh Northerly breeze right in our teeth, which made our progress not only slow but exceeding laborious for the people who kept pulling on their Oars the whole day with very little intermission till nine at night / when we landed & pitchd our Tents to enjoy a little repose, These exertions became now necessary on account of the exhausted state of our provisions.

The next morning was calm & pleasant but it soon after became dark & gloomy with fluctuating airs in every direction. We set off again by the dawn of day & about three in the afternoon we reachd as far as the bluff point at the Division of the two Arms,[28] when it became very thick & foggy & began to rain very hard with Easterly wind, & as it was the intention to look into the arm leading to the South East we landed & erected our Tents upon a fine plain to the Southward of the Point in hopes that the following day would be more favorable for the pursuit. In strolling about the Beach one of the gentlemen knockd down an animal about the size of a Cat with a stone & as he was going to pick it up it ejected a fluid of the most offensive smell & impregnated the air that no

[28]Foulweather Bluff.

one could remain any [p. 30] time within some distance of where it fell. I satisfied myself however that it was the Skunk (*Viverra Putorius*).

The morning of the 15th was thick fogg with constant rain which entirely frustrated the design of any further researches, & as all our provisions were now expended we were obligd to set out pretty early for the Vessels without waiting the return of fine weather, in this we were luckily assisted by a fresh breeze from the South East which enabled us to reach the Port by three in the afternoon, wet hungry & uncomfortable.

In this excursion which carried us about [left blank] Miles in a southerly direction from the Port we saw only the few Natives / I have already mentioned, silence & solitude seemd to prevail over this fine & extensive country, even the featherd race as if unable to endure the stillness that pervaded every where had in a great measure abandoned it & were therefore very scarce — A few large Cranes that inhabited the inland pastures, some white headed eagles that hoverd over the Arms & perchd in the trees on both sides watching for fish seemingly their only prey, a few Ducks that were seen in two or three places on the ponds behind the points & a kind of small Blackbird with red Shoulders (*Oriolus phœnicius*) that hopped about amongst the Bullrushes with a few Crows that seemed to accompany the Indians comprehended our ornithological list of this extensive tract. We found every where a due depth of Water for the purposes of Navigation but fresh water was scarce, a few runs we here & there fell in with supplied our wants but many of these would no doubt be dried up in the summer months. The land on each side of us was of a moderate height & nearly level till we came to the foot of that ridge of lofty mountains between us & the sea coast which extended as far to the South ward as we went.

On the 16th the wind was light & unsettled with Rain & thick weather — We were visited by some of the Natives in a single Canoe & during our absence they frequented the Port in greater numbers, one day in particular about thirty came in four or five Canoes & they always behavd themselves quiet & harmless— They all spoke a dialect of the Nootkan language, hence it is / probable that this forms the Eastern boundary of that great & numerous nation, though I am inclind to think that its limits hardly extend so [p. 31] far & that the permanent habitations of these visitors are situated much nearer the sea coast from which foraging parties occasionally come up here in pursuit of fish & game for sustenance.

The ship being found crank 20 Tons of shingle ballast was got on board & Lieu[t] Broughton & Mr Whidbey employed themselves in making an accurate survey of the Harbour & settling its exact situation by a vast number of astronomical Observations, the result of which gave the Latitude of the Observatory 48° 2' 30" North & 237° 22' 20" East longitude from the Meridian of Greenwich. Captain Vancouver named it Port Discovery but we afterwards found that the Spaniards had named it Port Quadra the year before, & having then anchord in it, surely gives their name a prior right of continuing, to prevent that confusion of names which are but too common in new discoverd countries.

The wooding watering & every other necessary refitment being now completed, the following day was employed in getting every thing ready for leaving Port Quadra — The Tents & Observatory were struck & sent on board with the Astronomical Instruments & Time-keepers— I employd the day in getting on board some live plants which were new to me as I did not know that I should any where else meet with them, & in planting them in the frame on the Quarter Deck.

At day / light on the 18th of May we both weighd anchor & with light variable airs of wind & the assistance of the boats ahead we got out of Port Quadra by the Channel to the Eastward of Protection Island, as Captain Vancouver was going to land on that Island to take some bearing I went with him to have another short stroll on that delightfull spot & among other Plants I collected I was not a little surprizd to meet with the *Cactus opuntia* thus far to the Northward, it grew plentifully but in a very dwarf state on the Eastern point of the Island which is low flat & dry sandy soil.

About noon the Vessels were advanced between the Island & the Main when in our return we called on board the *Chatham* where Captain Vancouver left orders for a short separation of the Vessels. At this time a fresh breeze sprung up at West with which we steerd for Admiralty [p. 32] Inlet whilst the *Chatham* hauld up to the North West ward being dispatchd to look into a large opening that appeard in that direction on the other side of this large gulph, & after obtaining what information they could of the size & general direction of it & the other branches in that quarter they were directed to follow us into Admiralty Inlet pursuing the South East Arm that was left unexplored by the Boats & keeping the Starboard shore of it aboard till they fell in with us.

We soon after enterd Admiralty Inlet & passing Port Townsend on our right continued our course with a moderate breeze till about five in the afternoon when we came to an Anchor on the Larboard Shore in 28 fathoms water about 10 or 12 miles from the Entrance.[29]

About 8 in the morning we weighd & made Sail with the tide of flood in our favor to the South Eastward, Soon after we passed the bluff

[29]Near Bush Point on the west side of Whidbey Island.

Point[30] & enterd the New Arm which preservd nearly the same width & general direction & which we continued sailing up with a fine breeze from the N W.—On our left hand we passed a wide opening going off to the Northward[31] & soon after on our right a pleasant point[32] coverd with the richest verdure in Latitude 47° 38' north & Longitude 237° 46 East on which we observed a small village & some Natives, To the Southward of this the Shore inclind in to a large Bay with a round Island of it coverd with wood, after passing which we found that the arm here divided into two branches, one going to the Southward which was narrow & another to the Southwestward, on which account we hauld in for the Starboard Shore & came to an Anchor about six in the evening on the inside of the Island in 35 fathoms water close to the inner point of it. A Canoe came along side with two or three men in her & after receiving some little presents they paddled off in great haste towards the Village we passed on the Point.

Two Boats were now provided with arms ammunition & a weeks provision to go off in the morning to examine the Arm leading to the Southward, & though their mode of procedure in these surveying Cruizes was not very favorable for my pursuits as it afforded me so little time on shore at the different places we landed at, yet it was the most eligible I could at this time adopt for obtaining a general knowledge [p. 33] of the produce of the Country, I therefore embarkd next morning before day light with / Lieutenant Puget in the Launch who commanded the party together with Mr Whidbey in the Cutter who was directed to continue the survey & about the dawn we entered the Arm which lead to the Southward[33] & appeard to be about half a league wide with sandy shores low land coverd with Trees to the waters edge on both sides, after pursuing it for about three leagues we passed at noon a large opening or rather deep bay going off to the Eastward[34] & apparently ending among very low marshy land, & as we saw an opening on the North East side of this Bay, we conjecturd that it might probably join the other branch of the Arm & make the land we passed on our left hand in the forenoon an Island.[35]

Up this Bay we had a most charming prospect of Mount Rainier which now appeard close to us though at least 10 or 12 leagues off, for the low land at the head of the Bay swelled out very gradually to form a most

---

[30]Foulweather Bluff.

[31]Possession Sound.

[32]Restoration Point.

[33]Colvos Passage.

[34]Dalco Passage and Commencement Bay.

[35]Vashon Island.

beautiful & majestic Mountain of great elevation whose line of ascent appeard equally smooth & gradual on every side with a round obtuse summit coverd two thirds of its height down with perpetual Snow as were also the summits of a rugged ridge of Mountains that proceeded from it to the Northward.

We pursued our Southerly direction with a strong flood tide in our favor & about two in the afternoon we came to another arm leading off to the Westward[36] which we enterd & found a very strong tide against us. At this time we were at a loss how to account for this as it evidently appeard to be the flood tide by rising on the shore, though we afterwards found that it was occasioned by a number of Islands round which the Tide had reverted / & as it was very strong against us we disembarkd on the Point[37] to dine till it should slacken a little. While we were here two Canoes passed on the opposite shore who dodged us at a distance several times in the forenoon, they afterwards crossed over & went into a small Cove[38] close to us, where we soon followed them & on the Point of it saw a number of old deserted huts amongst the trees but saw none of the Indians till we were returning back from the end of the Cove, when we heard them hailing from the opposite shore, & as we began to pull across towards them we observd the women & children [p. 34] scudding into the woods loaded with parcels, but the Men put off from the shore in two Canoes to meet us, we made them some little presents to convince them of our amicable intentions, on which they invited us by signs to land, & the only one we found remaining on the Beach was an old woman without either hut or shelter, setting near their baskets of provision & stores, the former consisted chiefly of Clams some of which were dried & smoaked & strung up for the convenience of carrying them about their Necks, but a great number of them were still fresh in the shell which they readily parted with to our people for buttons beads & bits of Copper. After making some presents to their women whom we prevaild upon them to recall from the woods we left them & were followd by the two Canoes with some men in each till we brought up in the evening,[39] & while we were erecting a small marquee for ourselves & a tent for the people they lay off at a little distance gazing on us with astonishment & greatly surprizd no doubt at the expeditious manner in / which we erected our houses, they staid with us till it was dark & then went to the

---

[36]Hale Passage.

[37]Point Fosdick.

[38]Woolochet Bay.

[39]Behind the small hook east of Green Point in Hale Passage.

opposite shore where they kindled a fire & staid for the night.—Here I found some small trees of both the American & Mountain Ash neither of which I had before met with on this side of the Continent—The other Plants I saw in the course of this day were nearly the same as I had before examined in the other arm the former cruize.

Early the next morning we were visited by the two Canoes who after we went off rushd on shore to examine the place we had occupied where we left them & soon after ran through a narrow gut leading to the Southward & winded round into a wide deep bay which lead off N W about 4 miles,[40] this we pursued passing on our right a high sandy Cliff in which a species of Diver burrowed very numerously like Swallows, we saw more of them in the Cliffs of a small Island[41] a little further on which was also inhabited by a great number of Crows attending their young, here we landed & shot several of them which were found very good—We went but a little further on when we were convincd that the bottom of the Bay was entirely closed up by a low Beach & some naked marshy land behind it. As we were pulling across we saw some Natives before us on the western shore, three of whom put off in a Canoe [p. 35] to meet us, we made them amicable signs to come along side of the Boat, but no inducement could make them venture near us, on the contrary they with menacing signs wanted us to return back the way we came, & treated with contempt the alluring presents we held up to them. As their dispositions were thus inimical it was not / thought prudent to give them any further uneasiness by visiting their habitations, it was however necessary to convince them by some means or other that we were still inclind to be friendly & an expedient was hit upon which answerd the purpose, Some Copper Iron Medals Buttons & other Trinkets were fastened on a piece of Board & left floating on the surface of the water while we pulled away to a little distance & sufferd the Indians to take it up, this was repeated two or three times with the same success, by this method they venturd to come along side of the Boats. They were three stout fellows, two of them were much pitted with the small pox & each destitute of a right eye. As we kept pulling along shore they followd us accepting of little presents

---

[40]This description conflicted with Puget's regarding their evening's encampment. The "narrow gut" is probably the western portion of Hale Passage; this leads the reader to believe they camped more toward the middle of Hale Passage. Puget indicated the camp was "about three Leagues from the Dinner Point" (Point Fosdick) which is obviously incorrect as Hale Passage in only four miles in length (he perhaps meant miles but instead wrote Leagues). However, Puget continued with a description of the islands visible to the south from their camp. This view was not possible except near Green Point. The "deep bay" reference is to Carr Inlet.

[41]Cutts Island.

but offering no return. On the whole their disposition appeard still shy & distrustfull notwithstanding our liberality & friendly behaviour towards them. They seemd to value Copper but would not part with their Bows or Arrows in exchange for it. They frequently mentioned the Words Poo Poo pointing to the direction we came from by which we supposed they meant the report of our Muskets which they might have heard while we were amusing ourselves in shooting young Crows on Crow Island. They kept calling now & then with a vociferous noise to other Indians on the opposite shore in which we could plainly perceive ourselves distinguished by the name of Poo Poo men. As the weather was now very sultry we hauld in for a small Creek[42] on purpose to dine in the heat of the day, here we found two or three small runs of water & was going to haul a small Seine we had in the Launch, but the appearance of six Canoes with about 20 people in them which our shy followers had collected by their voiciferous noise prevented it, These strangers paddled directly into the Creek & landed close to us, but a mark was drawn on the Beach which they perfectly understood to prevent their intermixing with our party till we had dind when we could better watch their motions & pilfering dispositions.

[p. 36] The Indians being thus disposed, some in their Canoes, others setting down on the Beach close to them, we went to dinner on an elevated bank in the edge of the Woods between them & the Boats, with our fire arms loaded at hand, where we had not only the Boats in which the people were at dinner under our eye, but likewise the Natives, who were now joind by another Canoe with four men in her, & notwithstanding they had obeyd our request, we could not help conceiving that there was something suspicious & distrustfull in their behaviour, for they were all armed with Bows & Quivers well stored with Arrows, & there were no women with them. A little after they quitted the Beach & went into their Canoes where they appeard for some time in earnest consultation as if they had some deep plot in view, & we had no doubt but we were the subject of it, from their pointing sometimes to us on the Bank & then to the Boats, but as we were all armed & ready to act jointly from the Boats as well as from the Shore, we chose rather to conceal our suspicions & keep a / watchfull eye over their Motions. Soon after this we observd three Canoes stealing as it were towards the Boats, but they were called to & orderd back by expressive signs which they obeyd. In a little time another Canoe was seen coming into the Creek, & as she approachd almost all of them in a moment jumpd out from their Canoes on the Beach & were stringing their Bow with every apparent preparation for an

[42]Perhaps Von Geldern Cove.

attack. At first we thought it was to oppose the Canoe coming in but we soon perceivd that their aim was at us by seeing them advance in a body along the Beach over the line that had been drawn as a Mark & explaind to them. One man more daring than the rest jumpd up the Bank within a few yards of us with his Bow & Arrows ready in hand with intention as we thought of getting behind a tree where he could molest us with more safety. At this instant we all jumpd up with our Muskets in our hands ready to oppose them, & made them understand by menacing signs, that if they did [sic] return back again to their Canoes, we would that moment fire upon them, & they seeing the people in the Boats equally ready & armed at the same time, they sneakd reluctantly back to their places, but as for the man who jumpd up the Bank, it was actually [p. 37] necessary to point a Musket to his breast before the determind villain would recede from his purpose.

Having thus retird to their station seemingly much dissatisfied with the repulse / they met with & still in deep consultation & some of them sharpening their Arrows as if they were again preparing & had not yet given up their purposd attack. We however set down again to finish our Meal, & as we could no longer have the smallest doubt of their hostile intentions, we watchd their motions very narrowly & none of them were sufferd to approach near to us & had their temerity carried them so far as to discharge a single arrow at us the consequences would instantly be fatal to them, as it was determind to punish such an unprovkd attack with the deservd severity to deter others from aspiring at such diabolic schemes & committing such atrocious actions, by which already too many have lost their lives on this Coast, a whole Boats Crew being cut off & massacred in the year 1787 not thirty leagues from our present situation,[43] besides acts equally guilty & alarming to strangers. As they were convincd of our watchfull eye over their treacherous conduct & impressed with an idea of our readiness to oppose their hostilities, they now appeard somewhat irresolute how to act, & this was thought a good time to fire off one of our swivels from the Launch that they might see we had other resources for their destruction besides those in our hands & more powerfull ones, but they shewd less fear or astonishment at either the report of the Swivel or the distant effect of the Shot than any Indians I / ever saw so little in the way of intercourse with civilized Nations. They however now seemd to relinquish their design & on seeing our things carried down to the Boat they began to offer their Bows & Arrows for sale which was a convincing sign of their peaceable intentions & they

[43]The reference was to the massacre of six crew members of the *Imperial Eagle* commanded by Charles Barkely off the Washington coast.

were readily purchased from them, as by this means we disarmd them in a more satisfactory manner.

These people were in all about thirty in number & in general stout & resolute men — They had no women or Children with them which made us more suspicious of their designs— They had a number of skins such as Bears Lynxes Racoons Rabbets & Deers which they readily parted with for any kind of trinkets that were offerd them in exchange, [p. 38] but we saw no Otter Skins amongst them & I believe they were seldom to be met with so far inland.

When the things were got into the Boats we set off to pursue our examination along shore which now took an easterly turn, followd by all the Canoes very amicably disposed, & offering every little thing they had in the way of barter, so that whatever was the cause of their late behavior they now seemd wholly to forget it, & finding we were going out of the Bay they soon quitted us & paddled in different directions towards their habitations. In the afternoon the wind set in from the Southward with hard rain which obligd us to pitch our Tents pretty early on the western point of a narrow passage[44] leading to the Southward opposite to the narrow gut we came through in the morning.

On the morning of the 22^{d} we had fine weather again with little wind, we set out pretty early & / rowed through the narrow passage after which finding we were amongst a number of large Islands which rendered the Survey & examination more tedious & perplexing we stood to the Eastward as Mr Whidbey wishd to take up his former angular bearings in the main branch which we reachd about noon & landed on a small Island[45] close to the Eastern Shore about two leagues to the Southward of where we quitted the same reach two days ago. Here we dind after which we pursued the main arm to the Southward & as we were standing for a point on the Western Shore we had very heavy rain thunder & lightning with dark hazy weather that obligd us to land in a commodious place near the Point[46] & encamp for the night.

Here three Canoes with some men in them came to us from the Eastern shore, they had a quantity of the young shoots of rasberries & of the *Triglochin maritimum* which they gave us to understand was good to eat & freely offerd us all they had which were accepted of & though we made no use of them yet we did not leave their generosity unpaid making a small present to each which was infinitely more valuable to them. We requested them to get us some fish & they went over immediately &

[44]Pitt Passage.

[45]Ketron Island.

[46]Oro Bay, Anderson Island.

brought us some Salmon & if we understood them right they told us there were plenty up a river on the eastern shore where they came [p. 39] from — They paddled off again in the dusk of the evening so that we remaind quiet & unmolested all night.

The morning of the 23[d] was so thick & foggy that we did not quit our place of Encampment till after breakfast when it cleard up so that we could go on with our examination — We first / pulled over to the opposite shore[47] in expectation of finding agreeable to the Account of the Natives a River & procuring some more fish, we found it a large Bay so flat & shallow that we could not approach near the shore seemingly backd by a large extent of Marshy Country, but we did not see any appearance of a River though there may probably be some large streams as the water was brakish, & as we were not likely to obtain a nearer view of them or gain any advantage from them we pursued the Arm which now took a sudden turn to the North West, followd by a number of Canoes which joind us from the large Bay, & as we were pulling on our Oars without any wind they easily kept up with us for some time & behavd very peaceably, & as I found one of them very communicative I amused myself in obtaining some knowledge of their language which I found very different from that spoken at Nootka or at the entrance of De Fuca Straits.

As we were passing the Island[48] we had examined yesterday on our right we were joined by a Canoe in which was one of our one eyed acquaintance who had behavd so treacherous & was so active against us two days before, his conduct then entitled him to no favor from us & we took no further notice of him than that of neglecting him when we bestowd little presents on all the rest who were with us on which account he soon went away & the other Canoes likewise soon left us. We continued up this reach which is about three leagues in the above direction & about half a / league wide, passing about the middle of it a large opening going off to the Southward[49] & reaching an Island[50] at the further end of it about two in the afternoon where we landed to dine & on account of the heavy rain thunder & lightning which set in soon after we were obligd to pitch our Tents & remain on it all night.

On the 24th we set out pretty early to continue our examination, here the arm trended more to the Northward N N W. & after pursuing it

[47]Nisqually Flats.

[48]Anderson Island.

[49]Both Henderson Inlet, which trends to the south, and Dana Passage trending to the southwest would have been visible from the middle of Case Inlet. Menzies later refers to the large opening, clearly in reference to Dana Passage.

[50]Herron Island.

about 7 or 8 miles we found [p. 40] it terminate in shoal water & low marshy land near which we breadfasted in a small Creek & tried a haul of the Seine with very little success only one Salmon Trout — As we passed this morning a narrow arm[51] going to the Southward we put back & pursued it with very rainy weather & soon found it inclining a little to the Eastward to meet the large opening[52] we passed yesterday, making the land on the left of us a large Island,[53] on the south side of which we encampd for the night & found the country exceeding pleasant, & the Soil the richest I have seen in this Country — The Woods abound with luxuriant Ferns that grow over head.

Next morning we again pursued the arm keeping the Starboard Shore on board & passing on the other side some Islands that were divided by two or three branches leading off to the Eastward, we found the Arm which was now about a Mile wide winded round to the Southwestward & by noon we saw its termination[54] through we could not get with the Boats within two Miles of it on account of the shallowness of the water which was one continued flat, dry at every retreat / of the Tide, & on which we found abundance of small Oysters similar to those in Port Quadra. We returned back the Arm till we came to the last opening we had passed in the morning & then struck off to the Eastward about two Miles & encamped on the point[55] of another arm leading to the Southward.

We had on the morning of the 26th fine pleasant weather with which we pursued our examination in an arm leading to the Southward which we soon found divided into two branches[56] leading nearly the same general direction for about 4 or 5 miles & then terminating among low land. Near the termination of the Westermost branch we saw two Indian Villages one on each side of it inhabited by about 70 or 80 Natives each. We visited one of them & they receivd us in the most friendly manner without shewing the least signs of distrustfull behaviour or any fear or alarm when we landed amongst them, for the women remaind in their huts & some of them had pretty good features, while the Children followd us begging for presents. They seemd to be of the same Tribe as those we saw before though very different in their friendly & peaceable

[51]Pickering Passage.

[52]Dana Passage.

[53]While the reference to "large Island" was perhaps Hartstene Island, I believe they encamped on Squaxin Island.

[54]Totten Inlet, Oyster Bay.

[55]Hunter Point at the east end of Squaxin Passage.

[56]Eld and Budd Inlets.

dispositions, Their Huts were small wretched Sheds coverd with Mats made of Bullrushes & their Dresses were chiefly formd of the Skins [p. 41] of the wild animals of the forest, that which was peculiar to the Women was a dressd Deer's Skin wrapped round their waist & covering down to their knees or rather below them, & the men too generally wore some little covering before them to hide those parts / which modesty & almost the universal voice of nature require.

We made but a short stay among these people & on leaving them distributed some Beads & little ornamental Trinkets chiefly of Brass & Copper among the Women & Children of which they were very fond.

On our return back to the Northward[57] we kept the Continental shore a board & by two in the afternoon we came on our old ground by the large opening we had passed on the 23d so that we had now entirely finishd this complicated Sound which afterwards obtaind the name of Puget's Sound, & after dining on the East point of the opening a favorable breeze sprung up from the Southward which we made use of to return to the Ship by the nearest route we could take.

In the dusk of the evening as we were passing the Island[58] on which we dind on the 22d near the Eastern shore of the Main Arm we saw a fire kindled upon it which we could not suppose then to be any ones else but the Natives, till we afterwards understood that it was Capt Vancouver & his party putting up for the evening, they likewise observd our Boats & Sails but as we were at some distance they took us for Canoes & so they went on surveying & examining the very ground that we had gone over.

When we came into the Main Arm finding the breeze freshening & likely to remain steady in our favor we continued on under Sail all night & arrivd at the ship about 2 o'clock the / next morning, but as they had removd her out of the place we had left her in towards the Point where the village was on we were obligd to fire off some Swivels which they answerd from the Ship & thereby discoverd to us her situation.

[p. 42] We now found that the *Chatham* had joind two days before us, after examining the North West side of the gulph which they found to consist of a vast number of Islands with wide & extensive openings leading to the Northward & North westward.

We also learnd that Capt Vancouver & Mr Johnstone set off yesterday morning with two Boats to examine the arm leading to the South Eastward which we have already supposed to join with the one we were in.

While we were absent the Natives one day brought a deer along side

---

[57]Although Menzies doesn't reference it, Puget noted the exploration of Budd Inlet.

[58]Ketron Island.

of the ship which they had ensnard by means of a large net on the adjacent Island[59] & disposed of it for about a foot square of sheet copper. This being a day of recreation it induced a party of Officers with a number of Men from both Vessels to land on the Island to try their luck & enjoy the sport of the Chace & they were not wholly disappointed for they started two or three Deer but could not kill any of them, & as the party had spread out through the woods in different directions they ran no little danger of shooting one another among the Bushes.

That as little time as possible might be lost of the fine weather we now enjoyd in our investigation Lieutenant Broughton saild on the / forenoon of the 28th with the *Chatham* taking with him Mr Whidbey with a Boat & Boats Crew from the *Discovery*, & left word for Capt Vancouver that he would follow back the opposite shore of this arm[60] (which was presumd to be the Continent) & enter the first opening leading to the Northward which he would pursue till he met with a division of it & then he would bring to with the Vessel & send two Boats off to examine its branches.

I landed on the Point[61] near the Ship where I found a few families of Indians live in very Mean Huts or Sheds formd of slender Rafters & coverd with Mats. Several of the women were digging on the Point which excited my curiosity to know what they were digging for & found it to be a little bulbous root of a liliaceous plant which on searching about for the flower of it I discovered to be a new Genus of the *Triandria monogina*. This root with the young shoots of Rasberries & a species of Barnacle which they pickd off the Rocks along shore formd at this time the chief part of their wretched subsistance. Some of the women were employd in making Mats of the Bullrushes while the Men were lolling about in sluggish idleness.—There were about 70 Inhabitants on this point but a number of them removd with all their furniture since the Ship lay here. One day a Chief with some others visited the Ship [p. 43] from the Eastern Shore of the Arm to whom Capt Vancouver made some presents of Blue Cloth Copper Iron &c. but as soon as they got / into their Canoes they offerd every thing they got for sale to our people but the Copper which shewd they put most value on that Metal.—They were of the same Tribe & spoke the same language as those we saw in Puget's Sound.

In the edge of the wood I saw a good deal of Ash & Canadian Poplar.

---

[59]Likely Blake Island.

[60]I.e., the eastern shore.

[61]Restoration Point.

On the 29th Capt Vancouver & Mr Johnstone returnd from their Cruize when we learnd it was their fire we saw on the small Island in our return to the Ship on the evening of the 26th as already related. We further learnd that they pursued the Arm they went to examine in a South East direction for about four leagues when they found it enter that extensive Bay running up almost to the bottom of Mount Rainier which we have already described—then Steerd on a South westerly direction for about three leagues till they came into our Arm leading to the South ward, & being doubtfull of its being the same that we went up they pursued it & went over nearly the same ground that we did, with only this difference that they were more tenacious of keeping the Larboard Shore on board & we the Starboard so that they did not examine the small arm leading to the westward.

In one place in the South East Arm they saw two or three small Huts from which about ten Natives accompanied them a little way in four Canoes offering them nothing else for sale but Bows & Arrows, which we conceive was a sure sign of their peaceable intentions.

The morning of the thirtieth of May was calm & clear till eight, when a light breeze sprung up from the Southward with which we weighd & made Sail to the Northward back the arm[62] to join the *Chatham*. At noon our Latitude was 47° 42' north within three or four miles of the arm leading off to the Northward which we soon after enterd, but having calms & baffling winds alternately we were obligd to ply up the arm, & about the dusk of the evening had sight of the *Chatham* an [at] anchor close to a point[63] of the Starboard Shore, but the ebb tide setting strongly against [p. 44] us prevented our getting up with her till midnight, when we came to an Anchor close to her, & were informd that she reachd this place the evening of the day she parted with us, and next morning Mr Broughton dispatchd Mr Whidbey with two Boats to examine the openings that lay to the Northward.

The forenoon of the thirty-first I had a stroll on shore on the point under which we lay & which at noon was ascertained to be in Latitude 47° 58' north & Longitude 237° 37' East which is about 34 leagues inland from the entrance of the Straits & as the most easterly situation the vessels anchord in—Mr Broughton namd the point from the vast abundance of wild roses that grew upon it Rose Point—A large Bay[64] which went off to the Northward was the most easterly situation which our Boats explord in this Country, it terminates in / Latitude 48° North &

---

[62]Possession Sound.

[63]I.e., east of Elliot Point near Mukilteo.

[64]Menzies is likely referring to both Saratoga Passage and Port Susan.

238° 2' East Longitude. The land everywhere round us was still of a very moderate height & coverd with a thick forest of different kinds of Pine trees. In a marshy situation behind the Beach I found some Aquatic plants I had not before met with.

In the afternoon we both weighd to follow the Boats up the arm to the Northward but did not proceed far when we came to again near an inland[65] [sic] in mid-channel for the night during which it raind very heavy. Some dogs had been left on shore on this Island whose yellings were heard several times in the night.

In the morning of the first of June we weighd anchor & finding the Arm a little to the Northward of us divide into two branches, we stood up the Eastermost which soon in the afternoon we found to terminate in a large Bay[66] with very shallow water & muddy bottom, on which the *Chatham* who was about two miles ahead of us got aground owing to the inattention or unskilfulness of the leadsman, for on soundings afterwards they found they had run over a flat of near half a mile or so very level that there was not more than a foot depth of water difference, yet the leadsman passed over this space without perceiving it, till they struck, which was upon an ebb tide, & it afterwards fell about five feet—they carried out a small Anchor three hawsers length from the Vessel & after heaving tight waited the return of the flood tide which about 11 floated them without having [p. 45] receivd any injury, when they hauld out and brought to in deeper water.

Next morning we had rain & foggy weather which continued till about noon. In the forenoon we both weighd & with a light northerly air returnd down the arm till we came a little below the point of division & then anchord near the eastern shore abreast of a small Bay[67] formd between two steep sandy bluffs into which we found some small streams of fresh water empty themselves which was rather a scarce article hitherto / in our different explorings.—We also saw some of the long Poles already mentioned erected upon the Beach.

In the evening the two Boats returnd after having carried their examination to the termination of the western branch which was namd Port Gardner & which like the rest they found to end with Shoal water surrounded by low land.—In this arm they saw two Villages pretty numerously inhabited with Natives, they supposd there might be upwards for 200 in each, & they behavd very peaceably. They found Oak Timber more abundant in this arm than any we had yet explored & the

---

[65]Gedney Island.

[66]Port Susan.

[67]Tulalip Bay.

country to the westward of it they describe as a fine rich Country abounding with luxuriant lawns, cropt with the finest verdure & extensive prospects teeming with the softer beauties of nature as we have already mentioned in our view of it from Port Townsend.

We remaind here the two following days with fine pleasant weather. The latter being the King's Birth Day, Capt Vancouver landed about noon with some of the Officers on the South point of the small Bay where he took posession of the Country with the usual forms in his Majesty's name & namd it New Georgia & on hoisting the English Colours on the spot each Vessel proclaimd it aloud with a Royal Salute in honor of the Day.

We both weighd anchor early on the morning of the 5th & with a moderate breeze from the Northward made Sail back again out of the Arm after having explored its different branches. We were joind from the Western branch which the Boats last examined by several Canoes who accompanied us to near the entrance of the Arm, where a fresher breeze from the North West carried us from them & they remaind with their Canoes for some time [p. 46] motionless gazing upon us with the utmost astonishment, & as we were obliged to ply soon after against the breeze back Admiralty Inlet, our whole mechanical manœuvres in working the Vessels with so much apparent ease seemd greatly to increase their admiration, by which we were pretty certain that we were the first Vessels they ever saw traversing their / winding Channels.

In the dusk of the Evening we passed the bluff point[68] at the division of the first long arm & about midnight came to an Anchor a few Miles beyond it on the Western shore, but the *Chatham* being swept by a strong eddy into Oak Cove was obligd to come to in the entrance of it much sooner.

Next morning we had westerly wind, but being favord with a strong ebb tide we both weighd & plyd against a pretty fresh breeze till towards noon when it fell nearly calm & having got out of Admiralty Inlet we both came to an Anchor on the outside near the North point of its entrance.[69] As Capt Vancouver & Mr Broughton were at this time going off in a Boat to observe for the Latitude & take bearing on a small Island[70] about 4 or 5 miles to the Northward of us I accompanied them to examine it, at the same time for plants, but I found nothing different from what I had before met with in the Arms—About the Rocks were a number of black Sea pies of which we shot several & found them good

[68]Foulweather Bluff.

[69]Point Partridge.

[70]Smith Island.

eating—Most part of the Island was faced with a sandy cliff & coverd with Pines densely copsed with Underwood.

Mr Whidbey having receivd orders before we left the Vessel to equip two Boats with the necessary arms & provisions & to proceed to the Northward along the Eastern shore of this gulph examining the different Inlets he might fall in with till he came to a place on the North side where the *Chatham* had anchored which Mr Broughton had named Strawberry Bay, & which was pointed out as the place of rendezvous. On our return from the small Islands we found Mr Whidbey had gone off with the two Boats to execute these orders & that the Vessels had been visited by a few Natives who had nothing to dispose of but a few Water Fowls particularly a blackish colourd species of Auk with a hornlike excrescence rising from the ridge [p. 47] of its Bill, & as it appeared to be a new species I named it *Alca Rhinoceros* & describd it.

/ We cannot quit Admiralty Inlet without observing that its beautiful Canals & wandering navigable branches traverse through a low flat Country upwards of 20 leagues to the Southward of its entrance & 8 or 9 leagues to the Eastward & to the North East, thus diffusing utility & ornament to a rich Country by affording a commodious & ready communication through every part of it, to the termination of the most distant branches. Its short distance from the Ocean which is not above 26 leagues, & easy access by the streights of Juan de Fuca is likewise much in its favour should its fertile banks be hereafter settled by any civilized nation. Its shores are for the most part sandy intermixed with pebbles & a variety of small silicious stones abounding with Iron Ore in various forms, for we hardly met with a Rock or Stone that was not evidently less or more impregnated with this usefull Metal which the benevolent hand of Nature has so liberaly dispersed throughout almost every part of the world but perhaps no where so apparently abundant as along the Shores of this great Inlet.

At the angular windings of these Canals we generely found low flat points evidently formed by the deposits of the Tides & Currents embanking them round by a high beach, behind which were frequently seen ponds of Salt Water that at first no less astonishd our curiosity concerning their formation than baulked our hopes when we approachd them either to quench our thirst or fill our Water Cags. Many of these ponds were at the distance of some hundred yards from the Sea Side & appeard to us to have no other means of communication or supply than that of oozing through the beach & lose gravely soil which composed the Point.

The general appearance of the Country from this station was as follows. To the South West of us a high ridge of Mountains ran from the outer point of de Fuca's entrance in a South East direction,—gradually increasing in height to form the rugged elevated peaks of Mount Olympus in Latitude 47° 48' N / & Longitude 236° 30' East & afterwards diminishing suddenly & ending a little beyond the termination of the first long arm we examined.

[p. 48] To the South East of us down Admiralty Inlet was seen through a beautiful avenue formed by the Banks of the Inlet Mount Rainier at the distance of 26 Leagues, which did not diminish but rather apparently augmented its great elevation & huge bulky appearance; from it a compleat ridge of Mountains with rugged & picked summits covered here & there with patches of Snow & forming a solid & impassable barrier on the East Side of New Georgia, running in a due North direction to join Mount Baker about 15 leagues to the North Eastward of us & from thence proceeded in the high broken Mountains to the North Westward.

Between us & the above Ridge & to the Southward of us between the two Mountains already mentioned a fine level Country intervened chiefly covard with pine forests abounding here & there with clear spots of considerable extent & intersected with the various winding branches of Admiralty Inlet as already mentioned. These clear spots or lawns are clothed with a rich carpet of Verdure & adornd with clumps of Trees & a surrounding verge of scatterd Pines which with their advantageous situation on the Banks of these inland Arms of the Sea give them a beauty of prospect equal to the most admired Parks in England.

A Traveller wandering over these unfrequented Plains is regaled with a salubrious & vivifying air impregnated with the balsamic fragrance of the surrounding Pinery, while his mind is eagerly occupied every moment on new objects & his senses rivetted on the enchanting variety of the surrounding scenery where the softer beauties of Landscape are harmoniously blended in majestic grandeur with the wild & romantic to form an interesting / & picturesque prospect on every side.

The Climate appeared to us exceeding favorable in so high a Latitude, a gentle westerly breeze generaly set in the forenoon which died away in the Evening & the Nights were mostly calm & serene, nor do we believe that those destructive Gales which drive their furious course along the exterior edge of the Coast ever visit these interior regions but with the mildest force, as we saw no traces of their devastation that would lead us to think otherwise. The Soil tho in general light & gravely would I am confident yield most of the European fruits & grains in perfection, so that it offers a desirable situation for a new Settlement to carry on Husbandry [p. 49] in its various branches, if the scarcity of fresh water which we frequently experienced in most of our excursions through it, might not be severely felt in dry seasons, as many of the Rillets which supplied our wants, seemd to depend on Rain or the Melted Snow from the Neighbouring Mountains, which of consequence might then be dried up & cause an insurmountable difficulty in procuring that useful element so necessary to the existence of the animated creation.

The Woods here were chiefly composed of the Silver Fir — White Spruce — Norway Spruce & Hemlock Spruce together with the American Abor Vitae & Common Yew; & besides these we saw a variety of hard wood scattered along the Banks of the Arms, such as Oak — the Sycamore or great Maple — Sugar Maple — Mountain Maple & Pensylvanian Maple — the Tacamahac & Canadian Poplars — the American Ash — common Hazel — American Alder — Common Willow & the Oriental Arbute, but none of their hard wood Trees were in great abundance or acquired sufficient size to be of any great utility, except the Oak in some particular places, as at Port Gardner & Oak Cove. / We also met here pretty frequent in the Wood with that beautiful Native of the Levant the purple Rhododendron, together with the great flowered Dog wood, Common Dog-wood & Canadian Dog-wood — the Caroline Rose & Dog Rose, but most part of the Shrubs & Underwood were new & undescribed, several of them I named, as *Arbutus glauca, Vaccinium lucidum Vaccinium tetragonum, Lonicera Nootkagensis, Gaultheria fruticosa, Spiraca serrulata, Rubus Nootkagensis.* Others from particular circumstances were doubtful & could not be ascertained till they are hereafter compared with more extensive description &c. on my return to England.

The wild fruits were Goosberries, Currants, two kinds of Rasberries, two kinds of Whattleberries, small fruited Crabs & a new species of Barberry.

The Inhabitants of this extensive Country did not appear to us on making every allowance of computation from the different Villages & strolling parties that were met with to exceed one thousand in all, a number indeed too small for such a fine territory; but when we reflect that the hunting state is by no means a favorable state for [p. 50] population, & that in this Country neighbouring tribes are generaly at War with each other, which from their savage disposition & inexorable cruelties makes great havock amongst the weakest Tribes, our surprize at the fewness of Inhabitants will in some measure cease. But there is another cause which may have powerfuly co-operated to occasion this depopulation & that in the advantages & novelty which a traffic with civilized Nations has held out of late years by trading vessels along the Sea Coast, which has no doubt been a sufficient allurement to entice considerable emigrations from the interior Country, & this idea is by no means inconsistent with their roving dispositions & ways of life, for they seem to have no permanent or fixd habitations, but wander about from place to place just as the whim or necessity of the moment impells them, or as it happens to suit their conveniency for procuring subsistance either by fishing or hunting.

/ Most part of the 7th of June was calm till 4 in the afternoon when a light breeze set in from the Westward with which we both weighd & stood to the Northward near the Eastern side of the Gulph & having gone about 5 or 6 leagues we came to an Anchor again in the evening near some Islands & broken land on the North side.[71]

The forenoon of the 8th was mostly calm with a strong Tide running to the Southward, which detaind us till it changd in our favor about 3 in the afternoon, when both vessels weighd & began plying to the Northward for an opening in that direction, but it soon after fell calm, & the *Discovery* with the assistance of her Boats was able to get into Strawberry Bay on the East side of the opening near the entrance where she came to an Anchor at 6 in the evening, while the *Chatham* was impelled by a strong flood Tide into an opening a little more to the Eastward, in which situation as neither helm nor canvass had any power over her, all were alarmd for her safety & anxious to hear of her fate. Mr Broughton himself was not at this time on board he went off in the forenoon in a Boat to finish his Survey of the Islands that were to the Westward of us, on the North side of the Gulph, & as the rugged appearance of these seemd to offer a new field for my researches I accompanied him by a friendly invitation.

[p. 51] On landing we could not help noticing the great difference between these Islands & that fine Country we had so lately examined, tho not removd from it above 2 or 3 leagues. Here the land rose rugged & hilly to a moderate height & was composd of massy solid Rocks coverd with a thin layer of blackish mould which afforded nourishment to a straddling forest of small stinted pines. The Shores were almost every where steep rugged & cliffy which made Landing difficult & the woods were in many places equally difficult of access from the rocky cliffs & chasms / with which they abounded, but I was not at all displeased at the change & general ruggedness of the surface of the Country as it producd a pleasing variety in the objects of my pursuit & added Considerably to my Catalogue of Plants.

I here found another species of that new genus I discovered at Village Point[72] in Admiralty Inlet, & a small well tasted wild onion which grew in little Tufts in the crevices of the Rocks with a species of *Arenaria* both new. I also met with the *Lilium Canadense* & the *Lilium Camschat-*

[71]Near Kellett Ledge off Cape St. Mary, east side of Lopez Island.

[72]Restoration Point.

cense, the roots of the latter is the *Sarana* so much esteemed by the Kamtschadales as a favorite food. *Vide* Cook's Voyage.

We rowed through some small Channels among these Islands & on our return again in the cool of the evening which was serene & pleasant we saw several Deer browsing among the Cliffs in different places: they were no wise shy as they sufferd us to approach very near them & it happened unluckily that neither Mr. Broughton or myself had any thing with us but small shot for our pieces which could have no effect upon them, indeed the reason was we hardly expected to meet with any quadruped on these Islands so did not provide ourselves for it. As we were afterwards crossing the Channel to join the Vessels in Strawberry Bay we landed on a small flat Island where we shot a number of black sea pies & carried them on board with us together with the young of a large Crane we got upon another Island which I took to be the *Ardea Canadensis*. As it was late before we joind the Ship Mr. Broughton remaind on board the *Discovery* all Night.

Next day a Boat came to us from the *Chatham* when we were informd that she was at an Anchor in a critical situation at the entrance of an opening to the Eastward of [p. 52] us[73] where they lost their stream Anchor by the force & rapidity of the / Tide which ran at the rate of about 5 miles an hour & snappd the Cable as they were bringing up. As often as the Tide slackend they used their endeavours by every scheme they could think of to recover the lost Anchor but without success & the loss of it was more severely felt as it was the only one of the kind they had been supplied with.

We were likewise informed that early in the Morning Mr. Whidbey had called along side of the *Chatham* after having explored the first opening he was directed to enter, which it seems he found to communicate by a narrow Channel with what he had before conceived to be the termination of Port Gardner making the North East side of Admiralty Inlet a fine large Island which obtained the name of Whidbey's Island. After a short stay on board the *Chatham*, the two Boats set off again to continue their examination of the Continental shore to the North East ward. The Brewers landed from the *Discovery* with their Utensils & began to make Beer from the fresh branches of the Spruce, & another party began watering from a small run at the bottom of the Bay.

In the forenoon of the 10th the *Chatham* came into the Bay & Anchord on the inside of us & in the afternoon the two Boats returnd from the North ward having made the Land to the Eastward of us which was pretty high & hilly a group of Islands coverd with Pine Forests to

---

[73]Bellingham Channel.

their very summits & surrounded with rocky shores & rocky Channels. The bottom of this Bay was a stoney beach on which the Seine was repeatedly hauled without success & behind it was a small Pond in which was found a particular variety of Trout I had not seen before with a vermilion colourd spot near the lower angle of the Gills but differing in no other respect from the common fresh water Trout. The Bay was shelterd on the West side by an Island but the Anchorage was much exposed to the Southerly Wind.

At day light on the 11th we both weighd & made Sail to the Northward through the Inlet leaving / Strawberry Bay with a light breeze from the Southward & serene pleasant Weather. About 8 we passed an opening leading to the Eastward[74] & enterd a wide & spacious opening of an [p. 53] unbounded horizon to the North West & as we advanced on we could perceive that the South West shore was composed of a broken group of Islands intersected by numerous inlets branching in every direction while the opposite shore on our right appeard streight & formed by a tract of low land backd at some distance by a high broken ridge of snowy mountains stretching to the North west ward from Mount Baker which at Noon bore N78° E^{t} when our Latitude was 48° 50' North about 2 miles off the Eastern shore; at this place the opening was about 3 leagues wide.

In the afternoon we continued our course along the Starboard shore with a very light breeze & seemingly a Tide against us so that our progress was very slow & in the evening stood in for a large Bay where we came to an Anchor in 5 fathom over a soft bottom about half a mile from the Shore.

As this Bay was eligibly situated for the Vessels to stop at, Captain Vancouver & some of the Officers went on shore to look for a commodious place for erecting the Observatory on, & carrying on the other duties while the Boats might be absent. I accompanied this party who landed on the South side of the Bay where we saw the scite of a very large Village now overgrown with a thick crop of Nettles & bushes, we walkd along the Beach to a low point between us & the bottom of the Bay where we found a delightful clear & level spot cropt with Grass & wild flowers & divided from the forest by a winding stream of fresh water that emptied itself into the bottom of the Bay[75] & added not only to the beauty but to the conveniency of the situation for carrying on all our operations to the best advantage, it was therefore determined to remove the Vessels abreast

---

[74]The ships worked their way along the western side of Lummi Island, ultimately to anchor in Birch Bay. Menzies here is describing the opening leading to Bellingham and Samish Bays.

[75]Perhaps Terrell Creek.

of this point the next morning & dispatch two boats to examine the Star board shore of the large arm / to the northwestward.

Early on the Morning of the 12th Cap[t] Vancouver set off in the Pinnace accompanied by Lieut. Puget in the Launch to explore the Shore & openings on the North side of the great North West Arm. These Boats were well armed & equipped with every necessary for 10 days.

The Marquee Tents & Observatory were pitchd on the spot allotted for them on the preceeding evening—the Astronomical Instruments & Time-keepers were landed & the necessary observations for ascertaining the rates of the [p. 54] latter were diligently made & continued under the direction of Mr. Broughton.

The Blacksmiths Brewers & Carpenters were also on shore employd on their different occupations as the weather continued serene mild & pleasant & exceeding favorable for prosecuting every pursuit both on board & on shore.

I landed at the place where the Tents were erected & walked from thence round the bottom of the Bay to examine the natural productions of the Country & found that besides the Pines already enumerated the Woods here abounded with the white & trembling Poplars together with black Birch. In consequence of my discovery of the latter place, the place afterwards obtaind the name of Birch Bay. I also found some other Plants unknown to me, two of which had bulbous roots & grew plentifully near the Tents, one of them was a new species of *Allium* from six to ten inches high & bore a beautiful number of pink colourd flowers & appeard to be a new species of *Melanthium* of which I made a rough drawing & collected roots of both to put in the plant frame as neither of them were at this time in Seed.

In one place in the verge of the Wood I saw an old Canoe suspended five or six feet from the ground between two Trees & containing some / decayed human bones wrapped up in Mats & carefully coverd over with Boards; as something of the same kind was seen in three or four instances to the South ward of this, it would appear that this is the general mode of entombing their dead in this Country, but what gave rise to so singular a custom I am at a loss to determine, unless it is to place them out of the reach of Bears Wolves & other Animals & prevent them from digging up or offering any violence to recent bodies after interment.

On the following day [June 13] Mr. Whidbey sat out about 2 in the afternoon with two Boats one from us & another from the *Chatham* to explore the opening which we had passed on the morning of the 11th leading to the Eastward & which was supposd not to reach any great distance from the appearance of the land behind it which formd a solid ridge of high snowy Mountains. These Boats had not gone far on their intended expedition when they observd two Vessels coming from the Southward & steering towards the Bay, [p. 55] the sight of these in this remote corner so unexpectedly inducd them to return in the dusk of the evening to acquaint us with it, & as it was expected that they would Anchor near us in the course of the night, the two Boats were detaind till we should obtain some further information about them, but the night being very dark we saw nothing of them & early next morning the Boats were again dispatchd to pursue their intended examination, while Mr. Broughton who wishd to know something more of the strange Vessel went out with the *Chatham* in search of them, having his reduced Crew augmented by an Officer & ten Men from the *Discovery* & Mr. Johnstone was left behind to carry on the Astronomical Observations on Shore. Soon after they got out of the Bay they saw the two Vessels laying at Anchor under the Land in a Bay a little to the North East of us & as they soon after got under way on seeing the *Chatham* she soon joind them & found them to be Spanish Vessels belonging to his Catholic Majesty, the one a small Brig / between 40 & 50 Tons named *Sutil* & commanded by Don Dionisio Alcala Galeano Captain of a Frigate in the Spanish Navy, the other was a Schooner named *Mexicana* & commanded by Don Cayetano Valdes likewise Captain of a Frigate. They both saild from Acapulca on the 8th of March & arrivd at Nootka the 11th of April where they had remaind until the 5th of this Month when they saild for the Streights of De Fuca which they enterd on the day following to examine & survey it, in continuation they said of what had been already done by other Vessels of his Catholic Majesties, for it was now we learnd that they had Vessels employd on this examination last Year that anchord in the same Harbour we did on our first arrival & had namd it Port Quadra, These had made a Chart of the Streights & this interior Navigation considerably to the North West of our present situation but did not put off much time to examine the narrow Inlets going off on either side, & the business of these two Vessels was to prosecute the examination of the great North West Arm & settle by their Time Keepers the different head lands of what had been already surveyed by their Pilots.

They further said that they had at Nootka the Frigates *Getrudie*, *Conception*, *Aranzara* & the Brig *Activa* under the Command of Don Quadra Captain of a Man of War [p. 56] & Commander in Chief of their Navy in Mexico & California, who had come to Nootka early in the Spring to deliver up that Settlement to any person duly qualified from our Government to receive it agreeable to the Conventional Articles.

In the place where the *Chatham* met these Vessels they said that they expected to find a large River but it provd only a large deep shallow Bay surrounded by low Land.

On the morning of the 15th we had a fresh breeze of wind from the Eastward which provd squally with / very heavy Rain & dark cloudy weather so that the *Chatham* was not able to get into the Bay again till about Noon when she anchord along side of us & the Spanish Vessels followd the object of their pursuit to the North west ward.

The following day we had dry weather with a gentle breeze from the Southward which cooled the Air & made it pleasing & refreshing. I landed on the opposite side of the Bay, where I enjoyd much pleasure in Botanical researches, in wandering over a fine rich meadow cropt with grass reaching up to my middle, & now & then penetrating the verge of the Forest as the prospect of easy access or the variety of plants seems to invite. Here I found in full bloom diffusing its sweetness that beautiful Shrub the *Philadelphus Coronarius* which I had not met with before in any other part of this Country, & having collected a number of other Plants in this little excursion I returnd in the afternoon round the bottom of the Bay to have them examind & arrangd, & in this route I saw another old Canoe laying in a thicket with some human bones in it far advancd in decay which seemd to have been wrapped up & coverd in the same manner as in the other Canoe already mentioned.

We had not yet seen any of the Natives since we anchord here but in this days excursion I saw two or three recent fire places on the Beach which made it very evident that they had been lately in the Bay, & a fresh path which went back from them into the Country inducd me to follow it in expectation of reaching their village, but I found it lead only to a small well of fresh water dug in the middle of the Meadow with two or three large shells laying on the brink of it which were intended no doubt to serve as drinking Cups.

[p. 57] In the evening Mr. Whidbey returnd with the two Boats from the South East ward having entirely finishd his examination in that quarter & brought the continental shore to our present situation & the / following day being Sunday a day of recreation to all hands, some of the Officers went to the South point of the Bay to determine the Latitude of it which by the mean of several Meridian Altitudes by different Sextants places it in 48° 52' 30" North.

At day break on the 18th of June I accompanied Mr. Johnstone who set out with two Boats in order to connect their former Survey in the *Chatham* among the Islands on the South West side of the Arm with our present situation. We rowed across & landed upon the Easternmost of a group of small Islands[76] where we staid breakfast & where Mr. Johnstone took up his first bearings, after which we proceeded to the

[76]Perhaps Matia.

South Westward landing here & there as occasion required it to continue the Survey.

Nothing could be more conspicuous than the contrast that now appeard between the opposite sides of this great Arm, Here the Shores were rocky rugged & cliffy rising into hills of a moderate height composing a numerous group of Islands thinly coverd with stinted Pines, while the side we left in the Morning was fine sandly pebbly beaches backd by an extensive tract of fine flat level country coverd with a dense forest of Pinery & at some distance swelling out gradually into a high ridge of snowy Mountains stretching to the North West-Ward from Mount Baker & approaching the course of the great Arm with high & steep declivities.

On a Point where we landed to dine we found growing some trees of Red Cedar; the Plants we met with in other respects did not differ much from the Plants I had collected a few days before on the Southernmost of these Islands; a new species of the Genus *Epilobium* & another of the Genus *Polygonum* excepted. In the Cliffs of a small rocky Island I also found a species of *Saxifraga* / I had not before met with & towards evening we reachd the outermost extent of our intended excursion being a small Island which Mr. Johnstone had formerly settled & on which we encamped for the night.[77] The weather was exceeding mild pleasant & favorable for our pursuits.

Early next morning we quitted the Island on which we had encamped to return to the Vessels by a different rout, [p. 58] the weather was then hazy with gentle showers but it soon cleard up & the rest of the day was fair & pleasant with little or no wind. We had not gone far when the appearance of smoke issuing from a part of the wood on an Island before us inducd us to land at a place where we found four or five families of the Natives variously occupied in a few temporary huts formd in the slightest & most careless manner by fastening together some rough sticks & throwing over them some pieces of Mats of Bark of Trees so partially as to form but a very indifferent shelter from the inclemency of the weather.

Their food at this time was some dried fish & Clams; we also saw some fresh Halibut & purchasd two large pieces of it for an English half penny each. In one Hut some pieces of the flesh of a Porpuse were seen by some of the party who had taken it for Venison & nearly purchasd the

---

[77]It is impossible to determine Johnstone's and Menzies' route. With some speculation, they traveled around the north end of Orcas Island and south into President Channel where they camped on one of the numerous small islands in the area. It appears that they continued their circumnavigation of Orcas the following morning, entering Harney Channel via either Pole Pass or more likely, Wasp Passage.

whole of it with great eagerness at a very high price when the mistake was discovered & all importunities suddenly ceased, tho the Natives were somewhat surprizd at this turn of conduct & could not comprehend the cause, yet they were by no means displeasd at finding themselves thus freed from the temptation of parting with their favourite food.

The Women were employd in making Mats & large Baskets for holding their provisions stores & Luggage. In one place we saw them at work on a / kind of coarse Blanket made of double twisted woollen Yarn & curiously wove by their fingers with great patience & ingenuity into various figures thick Cloth that would baffle the powers of more civilizd Artists with all their implements to imitate, but from what Animal they procure the wool for making these Blankets I am at present uncertain; it is very fine & of a snowy whiteness, some conjecturd that it might be from the dogs of which the Natives kept a great number & no other use was observd to be made of them than merely as domesticated Animals. Very few of them were of a White colour & none that we saw were covered with such fine wool, so that this conjecture tho plausibly held forth appeard without any foundation. On our landing we observd that all their dogs were muzzled, a precaution which we supposd the Natives had taken to prevent their giving us any disturbance or alarm at our approach to their Village, & indeed the whole tenor of their conduct shewd them to be an harmless [p. 59] & inoffensive tribe, so after distributing some few trinkets amongst their women & children we left them apparently well satisfied with our short visit, & afterward walkd for some distance along the Sea side where we passd a low extensive Morass well cropd with Bullrushes of which large patches had been pluckd by the Natives & were now laid neatly out upon the Beach to season them for making their Mats, & it is probable that the conveniency of procuring a good supply of this Plant so necessary to their domestic comforts inducd these few families to fix their temporary residence in the vicinity.

After a walk of about two Miles we embarkd in our Boats to pursue the survey & in the afternoon having got out from amongst the Islands we crossed the great Arm to the Vessel where we arrivd about Sun set.

/ Next morning two Canoes came from the Northward & paid us a visit pretty early; Curiosity seemd to be their principal motive as they had nothing to dispose of neither fish nor furs. In the bottom of one of the Canoes I was told they had some Bodies coverd up which were supposd to be dead as they would not suffer them to be examind, but it is probable that it might be some of their women hiding themselves from strangers which is not uncommon amongst Indian Tribes.

This & the following day we had fair pleasant weather with a light breeze of wind from the South ward.

About noon on the 22^{d} the Launch returnd to the Ship having accidently parted Company with the Pinnace on the evening of the 19th as they were coming back a long Arm that had carried them among the snow Mountains to the Latitude of 50° 32' North; they had explord several Arms leading to the North ward & traced the large opening a considerable way to the North West ward which they found to preserve that direction uninterrupted by the intervention of any land as far as the eye could discern from the most distant point of it they had explord. The Weather continued remarkably serene & pleasant this & the following day.

At noon on the 23^{d} of June Capt Vancouver & Lt Puget returnd to the Ship in the Pinnace after being absent about eleven days & a half, & the latter gentleman was so [p. 60] obliging as to favor me with the following Extracts from his copious journal of this long Cruize.

Menzies' journal continued with a description of Vancouver's journey north along the British Columbia coast to the head of Jervis Inlet. Upon Vancouver's return, camp was broken on shore, and astronomical instruments stowed on board the ships. The expedition departed Birch Bay the following morning. This final day in inland Washington waters was highlighted by again meeting up with the Spanish:

[p. 63] Early in the Morning of the 24th we both weighd & with a moderate breeze from the Eastward soon passed [p. 64] Cape Roberts & stood up the great North West Arm. About two in the afternoon being joind by the Spanish Brig & Schooner & favord with a visit from the Commander they agreed to keep under Sail & stand on with us all night as the Channel was spacious & apparently free of danger—Our progress however was very slow, the evening breeze being very light & baffling with Showers of Rain & cloudy weather.

3

James Johnstone

James Johnstone was born in 1759 along the Scottish border. His first naval service was aboard the HMS *Keppel* as a clerk and steward in 1779. During the next several years, he also saw service aboard the *La Fortunée*, *Formidable*, *Queen* and in 1783, the *Assistance* along with Menzies. He was appointed Master in 1785 and discharged in 1786.

Both Johnstone and Menzies signed on with the *Prince of Wales* under Captain James Colnett for a fur trading expedition. They departed England in 1786. Johnstone assumed command in 1789 and returned to England mid year.

In early 1791, Johnstone joined the armed tender *Chatham* as master. Upon reaching Nootka in August 1792, Vancouver appointed Lieutenant Hanson to the command of the *Dædalus*, and replaced him with Johnstone. He was promoted to commander in June 1802 and post captain in June 1806. Continuing with naval service, he was appointed Commissioner of the Navy in Bombay in 1811. In 1817, he was to succeed Peter Puget at Madras but due to ill health, both he and Puget returned together to England. Johnstone moved to Paris where he died on April 1, 1823.

Johnstone's journal is available only through May 20. The balance is apparently lost.

Saturday April 28th. With a gentle breeze between WSW and SW we steered NW, NW by N & NNW 26 Miles and Cape Disappointment bore S 42° E from the Deck. Seen [symbol of full moon] a little above the Horizon, the low land within it was hid which made it appear like an Island. Further in the Coast gradually rose to mountains of a moderate height. At 7 we were about 5 Miles from the Shore and had 26 fathoms of water over a fine black sand. At 8 we hauled off to spend the night and at

2 Tacked and stood in. At 6 being at the distance of 4 or 5 miles from the shore having from 22 to 25 fathoms fine black sand — The Land had greatly lost its former height since we passed [Quick] sand bay — It was here a thick forest of wood. The trees growing close to the brink of the shore which rose steeply from the water but to a very small height. The Shore was straight and a number of elevated rocks lay along it, but at no great distance off— The land further back rose pretty high in mountains, towards the summits of, which we saw several patches of snow — The Country appeared entirely inaccessible by the thickness of the forests nor yielded that agreeable prospect which the verdant hills and interspersed woods of the Coast more to the Southward presented. At Noon we were between 4 and 5 miles from the shore, our depth of water was 15 fathoms fine black sand when we had sight of Destruction Island (by Mr Barkely) bearing N 18° W Distant 7 or 8 Miles and the Extreme of the Coast E 46° S — The Obs^{d} Lat^{d} 47° 30' — Destruction Island is of a small height and level without trees, its sides from the water bare, the tops covered with verdure.

Sunday April 29th. The wind which was very light gradually drew to west. At 1^{h} 20^{m} Cape Fear and a point further off bore S 48° E — at 2 Tacked. Cape Fear being the Extreme bore S 37° E and the other extreme N 35° W. The Island N 16° W and N 21° W. Breakers off it N 25° W from the Island three or four miles and from the shore about the same distance, after we had tacked to the Southward the wind was so very light, that we found we were setting more in shore. And at three came to an anchor in 16 fathoms over a bottom of fine black sand. The Extremes of the land from S 45° E to N 25° W. Destruction Island between N 10° and N 5° W. Dist 3 or 4 Miles and from the Shore about the Same — All the afternoon it was calm — In the night a light breeze sprung up from the Southward which at 3 AM we weighed with and made sail. The winds gradually increasing to a fresh breeze and hazy with showers. Soon after we had weighed we had sight of a Ship to the Northward, which the *Discovery* coming up with, brought to and sent her boat on board — She was the *Columbia* belonging to Boston had been here nine months and wintered on the Coast — The breeze grew very fresh and hazy with rain — At 10 Southernmost rock and the Extreme bore S 50 E off shore 3 Miles. At 10^{h}. .30^{m} A Point open a little way within Cape Classet N 3° W and the northernmost group of Islands[1] ENE dist 2 or three miles— The largest rock which lays farthest from the land or Extreme S 45° E. At 11 largest Rock S 40° E. Angle to Point within 4° that point being on with another

[1]Tatoosh Island, a grouping of six major islands, numerous smaller and a large number of rocks. Johnstone referred to it as Green Island later.

farther off. At 11^h. $.40^m$ Group rocks and a second from South S 33 E, Extreme N 40° W. At 12^h Group and large Rock to the Southward S 30° E. Cape Classet N 10° E 3 Miles—The weather was so hazy that we had no observation—Green Island now made its appearance opening with the Cape, but in this direction we could not observe any rock that had the resemblance of pinnacle rock, though the whole coast which we have run along to day and yesterday forenoon has been entirely lined with an infinite number of elevated rocks whose forms were various as well as their size. Some were pyramidical, others conical, and many were large with steep sides and flat tops—I did not decidedly observe any prominence, so as to be convicted which was the real Cape Flattery.—

Monday April 30th. The weather grew very thick with a fresh breeze and rain from the Southeastward. At 1 we hauled up for green Island and soon after passed between it and a rock above water, which lays about a mile to the northward of it. In going through there was a small rippling on the water, immediately betwixt them but that I believe was occasioned by the tide, which was now setting out very strong. As we passed two Canoes joined from the Village Situated on green Island. This Village cannot be much seen till within the Island as it is formed in a Chasm which has nearly left the whole substance in [ ] this Island is but very small nearly level at the top without any trees, and lays close off Cape Classet. Whether there is a passage for vessels between it and the Cape, we had no opportunity of determining. What we took for pinnacle rock spoke of at the entrance we saw after we got within the Island—and instead of lying in the <u>entrance of the straits</u> it is close on the Shore of Classet, by no means answering the idea which I had been led to from of its situation—many rocks of this kind lay along shore for a degree and a half to the Southward—It was very thick and rainy as we passed the Village of Classet but being under the weather shore we had but very little wind. As we passed we were visited by a good many natives who accompanied us but a little way and then returned—Our view of the Straits owing to the fog was very indistinct. We stood up till about 6 O Clock when we tacked and stood over to the South shore where we anchored a little before dark in 13 fathoms over a gravelly bottom about half a mile from the Shore. The tide running strong into the eastward and did not slack till near 9—The *Columbia* we saw coming in after us—No natives seen since we passed Classet—a little after daylight it grew fair with a light breeze from the westward which seemed to disperse the fog—When at Anchor the Island above Classet which was then the Extreme bore W 12° N. The other extreme to the northward which was at a great distance W 26 N from the Island we supposed ourselves 6 miles and to the land on the opposite shore 6 or 8 Miles—The eastern extremes were E 2° N and E 25° N. A prominence on the south shore which jutted out a little H[2] E 5° S. When at anchor the tide changed and run to the eastward about ½ past 3 AM whether or not it was flowing or ebbing we could not tell but both run pretty strong mostly between 1 and 2 knot per Hour by the log. A fine breeze from the westward continued with which we steered along the South Shore. At about a mile distant and passed **H** at the distance of a Short mile estimating the distance from the Anchorage 11 miles and from the Island 6 leagues which bore W 3° N. At the same time the north extreme of entrance measured an angle of 19° which made it bear W 22° N. A point opened with the South Extreme E 5° N. At 11 measured head **K** being E 5° N to the opposite side Extreme **L** to 26°. .E 29° N. At noon by an Observation of the sun which was rendered but very indifferent from the nearest of the South shore this Lat^d^ was 48° 18' N. We reckoned ourselves three miles from the south shore and 6 or 7 from the opposite side. The Extremes bore W 5° S and W 15° N. The other two Extremes E 35 N being **L** E 2° N of **K** E 2° S — The Shore on each side was low to the water from whence it rose steeply into mountains so thickly covered with trees that they appeared almost inaccessible — The shores were straight without any kind of bay or prominence worth notice nor Islands, or rocks lay off— here and there were some sandy beaches but tho were no depth. From some of those we were joined by some of the natives as we passed along — they brought some Sea Otter Skins for barter and asked for Copper — by Noon they had all quitted us— On the summits of the mountains on each side we saw some patches of snow but a very dense haze obscured most of the elevated country — The *Columbia* in the morning was employed in working out to Seaward.

Tuesday May 1st. With a fine steady fresh breeze from the westward we steered up E by N until 6 O Clock when we altered to the NE by E along a low sandy spit which formed from the South shore. At ½ past 7 we hauled round the end of it in 4 fathoms about half a mile from it. The shoal water was visible from the rippling of the Sea which run over it — End of the sandy spit on with the South end of a low level woody land S 4° E, and sandy spit on with the other Extreme of this level woody ground **A** and where the Sandy spit formed from S 35 W. End of sandy spit and high head **K** W 23° S. Sand spit on with the Extreme of the North shore West. This Extreme is where about I set at **M L** for ascertaining the width of the Bay, by some Angles taken before noon and closed about ½ past 2 PM I make the breadth of the Channel about 11

[2]As land masses were unnamed, Johnstone used alpha characters so that they could be distinguished later for charting purposes.

Miles which appears to be much the same or rather less than what we computed it to be at the place which we weighed from. After hauling round this low sandy spit we kept our wind in for a low level tract of land thickly covered with wood, and about half an hour after Anchored a mile from that shore in 8 fathoms over a bottom of fine black sand — The end of sandy spit bearing [left blank] the high head **K** [left blank] and a very high peaked mountain that overtopped those which rose near to us and was covered by snow. The Night remained a fresh breeze from West, the morning and forenoon was nearly calm and pleasant, when two boats from the *Discovery* and our Cutter with Capt Vancouver set out for the shore to the eastward to examine for a harbour — We were visited by a few of the Natives, who had their residence on the low shore abreast of us, their number was very inconsiderable — they brought some fish which was all they had for Barter.

Wednesday May 2nd. We had a light wind and pleasant weather — In the night the boats returned after having found a harbour six or seven leagues to the eastward of our present situation and at day light both Vessels weighed with a light air from the westward, and proceeded towards it — in running woody point **A** and high head **K** in one bore W 20° S, from the time we weighed till then we had 12 fathoms— The outer point of Redoubt Island and point **S** in one E 25° N. Inner point of redoubt Island and **K** E 35° N. Inner Pt of Redoubt and high snow mountain N 25° E. Outer Pt of Redoubt on with harbour sandy point N 55° W — After 12 fathoms we had no ground with the hand line nor with 30 and 40 fathoms (which we often tried) by the Deepsea.[3] In passing protection Island we kept close to the opposite shore, which shore was very steep. As we stood into the Harbour in a SE direction we rounded a low sandy point on the right hand which was very steep. Redoubt Island shutting up the mouth formed an excellent Harbour — To where we anchored was a good four miles— this was a spacious harbour remarkably easy of access but generally deep water. Draught of water aft 12 ft 2 In — Forward 9 ft 8 in.

Thursday May 3d. At 1 we anchored in 26 fathoms over soft bottom

---

[3]Shaped like a cylinder, the lead contained a "hollow" on the bottom where a lump of tallow was placed. When the lead struck the bottom, a bit of the sand, mud, shells or grit stuck to the tallow. Thus, the function was two-fold, to measure the depth as well as determine the type of bottom. Earliest versions weighed from ten to twelve pounds. The men measured the depth while retrieving the line based upon the span of one's arms, about six feet, and termed a fathom. As depth increased, a heavier lead (the "Deepsea") was used, from eighteen to twenty-four pounds. Because the line for this was also heavier, it was wound off a winch. Thus, it could only be used while the ship was stationary.

and steadied with the stream to the southeast (see plan of the Harbour). In the evening the *Discovery* got on shore her water Casks, Marquee and tents and the Quadrant and Observatory — and in the morning began to take equal altitudes for ascertaining the going of the watches. We landed all our water Casks and overhauled the topmast rigging. The wind west serene pleasant weather.

Friday May 4th. The weather remained serene and pleasant. The forenoon a little cloudy, having overhauled the rigging we were next employed in arranging the holds by getting the provisions and their articles to hand which were the most likely first to be wanted — we landed water Casks with the Forge and sails and the different [artificers] to work at them — Got two Caulkers from the *Discovery* who began caulking the vessels side.

Saturday May 5th. Mod^{t} and pleasant weather, wind from the westward. A party of hands were employed in culling fire-wood and the Kettles were erected on shore for brewing spruce beer.

Sunday May 6th. D^{o} Weather. After all hands were mustered clean they had permission to recreate themselves on Shore.

Monday May 7th. In the morning at daylight in the Cutter I accompanied Capt Vancouver in his pinnace with Lieu^{t} Puget in the *Discovery's* Longboat. The morning was little wind and exceeding foggy. We proceeded out of Port Discovery and afterwards to the eastward keeping the South shore close on board for about 2 Leagues when we found an opening which took a southerly direction, but as the weather continued so very foggy as to prevent us from a view of the adjacent shores, we landed[4] for the weathers clearing up and in the mean time took several hauls with the seine, but without the smallest success. Towards noon the fog dispersed, when we saw the opening which we had entered extend in a Southeast direction with an Arm which branched off by a Southerly Course. After observing the Suns meredian altitude by a quick silver horizon[5] which gave the Lat^{d} 48° 07' 30" N we proceeded in examining the Southerly Arm when I pulled over to the Larboard shore (to which I

---

[4]Point Wilson.

[5]Measuring the altitude of celestial objects, e.g., the sun, required a horizontal reference. When not available, for example, under cloudy conditions along the horizon, or when land was present in front of the object to be measured, an artificial horizon was used. This frequently was a pan of mercury, heavy oil, or molasses, covered by plate glass to shelter it from the wind. To use, a navigator sat or stood in front of the artificial horizon so that the distant object was in view as well as its reflection in the artificial horizon. A sextant was used to measure the angle between the object and this reflection. The artificial horizon was used primarily on land where the ocean horizon was not in view.

was directed). I found a long narrow beach[6] which separated two high heads nearly a mile asunder. On this beach were erected seven long poles. They were nearly at equal distance from between 80 and 100 yards apart. We estimated the tallest to be about 70 feet — the others might be 10 or 12 feet short of that. They were of two pieces being lengthened towards the top by a piece which was neatly joined and terminated as it were in three groups by their leaving two branches out at about a foot in length from the pole. The heels being sunk in the earth were supported with four shorter pieces which were fastened to them as shores about twenty feet high. At the South end of this beach was an opening about a Cables length over, which led into an arm[7] in some places half a mile across, and like the other branches took a S 30° E direction. At the mouth of the narrow entrance was a sandy flat dry at low water. On the Starb[d] shore of entrance which was a high steep bluff, was a narrow channel of 4 or 5 fathoms, and on the beach side, which was steep there was six feet at low water. The rise of spring tides we computed to be about 12 feet or more and it was high water. The moon passed the meridian — within was 4, 5, 6 and 7 fathoms and on the beach was a fine sandy shore for laying a Vessel dry. As I was in hopes of finding a communication from this arm into the one which the other two boats were examining I proceeded onward till sundown when I found it terminated by another narrow beach[8] over which the top of the tide seemed to have a connection with another extensive arm of water which extended to the South east. As it was now about half ebb I was content to wait the return of the mornings flood to seek a passage into the extensive arm which I was still in hopes had intercourse with the reach which the other boats were in. The night was favourable for our quarters which we took up on the beach.

Tuesday May 8th. Before daylight we were stirring and a little before 4 passed the bridge at the top of high water — a little more depth than the boat drew. Being now in a large branch of Sea which extended to the SE,[9] but was separated from the bay which the boats were in by the land which in one place was so very narrow a neck that it was a stone beach without any wood. Finding no passage I hastened to return by the same channel which I had passed and was just in time to get over as the tide had fallen about a foot which was ebbing strong to the NW. The morning was Calm and pleasant and a little before 7 we passed out by the narrow channel where we had first entered computing the length of this inlet to

---

[6]The sand spit forming the entrance of Kilisut Harbor.

[7]Kilisut Harbor.

[8]Scow Bay.

[9]Oak Bay.

be 7 or 9 Miles—At 9 I joined the other boats at the bottom of the Southern reach, where they had been all night and where we were some time detained owing to the Longboats having got aground with the falling tide. After having completed the part of examination which had been left unfinished, in the evening we quitted the bay and pulled to the northward. On the beach to the southward of the narrow Channel which I had entered, we found two human heads, stuck upon two poles about twelve feet in height. The teeth and long black hair were entire, part of the skin of the face was wasted off. The poles were uniform being about 14 feet apart—At noon obs[d] the Lat[d], which was on the point we had seen the preceding day,[10] making the Southern entrance of the South east arm. From this station the Arm still run to the Southeastward and about 5 leagues distant it separated when one Arm took a more easterly direction. At 3 we set forward in hopes of reaching the point which made the separation to which for distinction we gave the appellation of Long Island.[11] The wind now became very light and [flattening] and cloudy with showers—In the evening it begun and rained hard, and was very foggy. We had little or no wind using the oars in hopes of gaining the spot which we intended to rest at—The first of the night was spent in this fruitless attempt, for with all our endeavours we could not increase our distance from the land astern of us which we had when the evening begun, owing to the strong tide against us—It rained exceeding hard and was so very foggy that the only means we had of keeping together was by the frequent firing of Muskets. Towards midnight it was evident that we would be unable to reach the intended point, which we had long lost sight of, and therefore rowed back till we found a low shore, as we then (and rightly) conjectured was not far from the bridge, over which I had passed in the boat. After landing, pitching the tent and kindling a fire we found no [ ] in the midst of rain and darkness—It was 12 O Clock before we got under any kind of shelter, and then with every thing on and about us completely drenched—The major part of the boats crew had no covering till after daylight.

Wednesday, May 9th. All the day we had constant thick rainy weather so that we could not stir to any advantage, but we traversed along the beach and as often as an interval of clear permitted we took the bearings of the points in view. There we found some Oak from which the place was called Oak Cove.

Thursday May 10th. In was thick weather and rained incessantly with little wind until 6 in the morning, when we set out to explore the South-

---

[10]Marrowstone Point.

[11]Foulweather Bluff.

ernmost opening and kept the Starboard shore on board — about 9 we fell in with a few small Canoes which I believe were out fishing, we landed on a point to breakfast, when the natives to the number of twenty or more assembled on the beach with us, they had nothing for barter but a few pieces of deer skin — we made them presents of some few trinkets, and afterwards embarked, continuing our course along the west shore, but our progress was very slow, owing to the breeze which now blew strong from the Southward — we passed a deep bay at the bottom of which we saw the Village to which the natives we had just parted from belonged — At Noon the Obs^{d} Lat^{d} was 47° 56' 30" N°. The ebb tide now run so strong to the northward with a fresh of wind from the southward, that we were compelled to wait for the making of the flood, and then proceeded with the weather tide. At 4 reached what had made like an Island, and was distinguished by App^{t} Round Island[12] — This was joined by a narrow beach to the west shore, and from whence the arm took a south westerly direction which we pursued until dark and then stopped for the night, which was serene and pleasant.

Friday May 11th. At day light we again set out and soon found the arm for a little way to trend South, and then Southwesterly — The morning and forenoon was calm or little wind. At noon the Obs^{d} Lat^{d} was [left blank]. A little beyond this the Arm broke. One branch running to the Southwest[13] and the other to the Northwest.[14] We first pulled up the source of the latter, and discovering it to be a bay again run down for the former until dark when we rested for the night on the west entrance of it.

Saturday May 12th. The morning and forenoon was fine pleasant weather with very little wind. We still rowed down the arm which trended S by W and at noon Obs^{d} in the Lat^{d} of 47° 44' 15". Here we were overtaken by a Canoe with two men, who made signs, that more were before us — Hauled the Seine and had indifferent success — At 5 we saw some natives on the beach, where we landed, and found them occupied in drying clams — It appeared as if this was only a temporary residence for the convenience of collecting and drying fish — They gave us to understand that more natives were on the opposite point,[15] where the arm now took and easterly direction, we went over and found them more numerous, residing on the beach, without any kind of shelter or covering whatever, which led us to conclude that they were here merely for the

---

[12]Hood Head.

[13]The continuation of Hood Canal.

[14]Dabob Bay.

[15]Either Musqueti or Ayres Point.

time, to collect fish and dry it—some salmon which they had partly dried, we procured with some flat fish—Amongst those which we now found, some of us recollected, the faces of those which we had fallen in with, on Thursday morning, and this was the [ ] confirmed, by our seeing them in possession of those trinkets which we had bestowed on them at that time—we had now reached the head of this extensive arm, which terminated in a bay wider than almost any other part of it—After having spent some little time with the natives, we could do nothing further than return by the way we came, and for the night which was remarkably pleasant, rested a little way from the Indians.

Sunday May 13th. At Day light set out on our return, but had now the mortification for the first time since our setting out to find a fresh northerly breeze. As this was directly in our teeth our progress was not only slow, but exceeding laborious. But as our provisions were mostly expended, we were anxious to make the most of it and therefore kept pulling the whole day until 9 O Clock when we landed for the night, during which time we had a fresh breeze from the Northward.

Monday May 14th. The morning was calm and pleasant, and we were off by day light. As the day advanced it became dark and gloomy with light [flashing] airs from every direction. About 3 in the Afternoon we reached the North end of apparent long Island,[16] when it became very thick and foggy and begun to rain very hard, the wind from the eastward. As it was the intention to look into the entrance of the more easterly arm, we landed for the night, in hopes that the weather in the morning would allow us to pursue the research. It continued raining exceeding hard all night.

Tuesday May 15th. The morning was a constant deluge of rain with exceeding thick foggy weather, which utterly prevented us from setting out upon any new search, and our provision which was naturally became very short, obliged us to seek a supply without waiting the return of finer weather, and at 8 we set out for the Ships under a thick fog and heavy rain, but with a fresh breeze from the Southeast, which enabled us to reach the Vessels about 3 in the Afternoon—In this excursion, which carried nearly due South from port Discovery we saw only the few natives which are mentioned. Silence prevailed every where, the feathered race as if unable to endure the absence of man had also utterly deserted this place. Every where we found a due depth of water for navigation, but fresh water was much scarcer. We met with no river, a few runs which we fell in with, here and there supplied us—many of those from the smallness of their streams I conceive would be dried up in the

[16]Foulweather Bluff.

summer months— The Shores and most of the land about us was of a moderate height, some more elevated lay between us and the Sea coast. When near the head of the arm, the summits of which were covered with snow—Tho a regular and exact survey of this branch of De Fuca, under the time and circumstances which we had could not possibly be made, yet the plan which was made from a continuation of Angles, with the few Soundings which were taken will prove more satisfactory information, than any written description which I could give—The woods we met with were the white or Canadian Spruce, Norway spruce, hemlock spruce, Silver fir, Common Yew, American Arborvita, American Alder, Sugar maple, Mountain maple, Pensylvania Maple, American Ash, Canadian Poplar, Oak, Hazel, Willow, Oriental Strawberry tree, and small fruited Crab. The underwood are Goose-berries, Black currants, Two kinds of Rasberries, Canada an [ ], Purple Rhododendron, Great flowered Dogwood, Two kinds of Arbutus, Andromeda, and wild roses.

Wednesday May 16th. The wind continued moderate, from the South east with thick rainy weather. In the evening it was from the westward, and fair weather, but in the night it returned to its old quarter and was thick and rainy.

Thursday May 17th. We had the wind variable with shower of rain. In the forenoon we got on board the spruce beer, and some plank which the Carpenters had cut, the Forge and every person from the Shore. In the evening the wind was westerly, when we weighed and wrought out of the harbor. At dark we anchored in 26 fathoms, close over on the north shore within the sandy spits.

Friday May 18th. At Day light we weighed the anchor, being calm, with the boats ahead towed out of the harbour, all the forenoon the wind was light and fluctuating, till noon when a fresh breeze sprung up at west when broad beach point bore E 22° N dist 3 Leagues. An opening in the head of the bay at N 3° W, a Small Island N 18° W, another opening N 24° W and a third more extensive than the other two N 41° W. With this haze the *Discovery* steered for the opening which we had examined with the boats[17] to search the easterly Arm which the bad weather prevented the boats from entering whilst we hauled our wind to the northward, to examine the Coast in the direction. Half past 3 passed the west side of small Island[18] of at the distance of a quarter of a mile, and had 7 fathoms rocky bottom for a good way, afterwards it deepened.—The wind now veered to about SW and blew fresh which enabled us to fetch the middle

---

[17]Admiralty Inlet.

[18]Smith Island.

opening.[19] The water across the entrance having a suspicious appearance of shoals, I went ahead in the Cutter, whilst the Vessel followed under easy sail — Found the rippling of the water which gave the alarm to be owing to the meeting of the tides, which was exceeding intricate, caused by the number of little Islands and passages, which made off the entrance — The only perfect entrance (by which we entered) is better than a mile wide. In the left, forms a small round Island,[20] without trees, covered with grass. This we passed close in 13 fathoms. The opposite point bore N 30° W, before we had 25, 28 and 30 fathoms— when within the entrance, the place widened to the westward.[21] We stood well up to the mouth of a branch which took a NW direction. We anchored with the Stream in 9 fathoms, close to the shore. The night was calm — It was high water 5 hours after the moon had passed the meridian but the Current very irregular.

Saturday May 19th. Till 10 O Clock it was calm when with the first of the flood in the Cutter accompanied by the Long boat I set out to examine the Arm which took a NW direction[22] about 4 Leagues. In that direction it opened by another channel into the Bay. This opening is what was set as the more extensive one, bearing N 41° W to the northward the land as far as the foot of the Mountains, appeared broke into different Islands. The summits of the mountains were covered with snow. In the evening with both boats I returned to the Vessel and found she had proceeded a little way up the north arm,[23] and by a meridian Observation they made the Latd 48° 35' N. The wind was from the NW — the weather remarkably pleasant.

Sunday May 20th. At Daylight I set out in the Cutter to ascertain the position of the different rocks and Islets at the entrance by which we came in. At 8 the Vessel, finding a slack tide weighed and with the assistance of the boats towing, got a little way further up the north Arm, but at 10 she had the current against her (though flowing by the Shore), being perfectly calm, anchored with the stream in 35 fathoms— the Channel here being about a mile wide, higher up branching off into different openings, by apparent Islands towards the entrance of the reach we had a fine westerly breeze. At noon returned on board. At 3 we again weighed, and tho both boats were ahead yet we gained nothing. It continuing

[19]South entrance to San Juan Channel.

[20]Goose Island.

[21]Griffin Bay.

[22]San Juan Channel.

[23]Upright Channel

without a breath of wind, and what little current there was against us which had been the case all day — Finding we could make no hand in getting on with the Vessel. At 5 both boats were sent off to examine the upper opening — Both yesterday and to day, the seine was hauled, but had little success — nor were we better supplied with Fowl — The Ducks were plenty but very shy — On a high Island, at the upper end of the North west arm where I was yesterday were a great many [ ]. There was little wood but Oak which grew at a good distance from each other on the summit — At 9 the Launch returned. She had been about 5 miles to the left, fell in with nine Natives in two Canoes from which she purchased some deer. Soon after the Cutter returned from an arm that led in a Southerly direction, and from the conjecture of the officer communicated with the Bay.

4

William Robert Broughton

William R. Broughton was born in Gloucestershire in 1762. He enlisted in the navy in 1774 as a midshipman and initially saw service in the war for American Independence. He spent a number of years in East Indian waters and on December 28, 1790, was appointed to the command of the *Chatham*, consort to *Discovery*. Following the circumnavigation of Vancouver Island, Vancouver met with Bodega y Quadra in Nootka attempting to resolve the controversy.

Failing to reach a satisfactory agreement, *Discovery* and *Chatham* headed south on October 12, 1792, to meet again with Quadra at Monterey. Along the way Broughton explored the Columbia River, which was discovered by Gray earlier that year. Upon arriving in Monterey, Vancouver decided to transmit his dispatches home with Broughton. Upon reaching England, Broughton received a commission to command the *Providence* on October 3, 1793, and was sent back to the north Pacific. Finding that Vancouver had already departed, Broughton continued exploration of the Asiatic coast, publishing his findings in 1804.[1] On January 28, 1797, he received the rank of Captain. Broughton's career of command continued aboard several ships until he returned to England in 1812 and was made Commander of the Bath. The final years of his life were spent in Florence, Italy. He died March 12, 1821, and was buried at Pisa.

I located two journals. The first is a "rough" journal, transcribed from University of Washington microfilm, which briefly described day-to-day events and was similar in content and appearance to other journals. There

---

[1]Entitled *A Voyage of Discovery to the North Pacific Ocean: In Which the Coast of Asia, from the Lat of 35° North, the Island of Insu, (Commonly Known Under the Name of the Land of Jesso,) the North, South, and East Coasts of Japan, the Lieuchieux and the Adjacent Isles, As Well As the Coast of Corea, Have Been Examined and Surveyed.*

appeared to be page numbers in the journal but they were not frequent, and not always correct. I ignored the columnar format while the ship was at anchor and simply transcribed the remarks.

The second Broughton journal, *Proceedings of His Majesty's Brig* Chatham *from the 18th to 25th of May, 1792,* was extracted from the *Washington Historical Quarterly*, XII (January, 1930) as edited by J. Neilson Barry. Apparently, the source for this was University of Washington microfilm which I was unable to locate. While I transcribed the text directly, I did not include Barry's footnotes. Thus, the footnotes reflect my opinion. While Broughton referenced a chart in this journal, it has never been found. The journal begins May 18, 1792, and is a summary of exploration in the San Juan Islands.

After landing on Protection Island and observing the land to the northward, Vancouver "directed Mr. Broughton to use his endeavours, in the *Chatham*, to acquire some information in that line, whilst I continued my examination with the *Discovery*..." (Blumenthal, 139). At this point, the ships parted company with Broughton heading towards Middle Channel between San Juan and Lopez Islands, and Vancouver rounding Point Wilson and continuing southward through Admiralty Inlet.

ROUGH JOURNAL

[p. 51]

H	K	F	Courses	Winds	Remarks on Monday, Saturday 28th, 1792.
1	4	6	NW½N	SW	Moderate & Cloudy with Showers.
2	4				At 1 Sounded in [30] fms fine black sand.
3	4	4	NWbyN½N		
4	5	2		Wby[S]	
5	4		N½W		
6	3		North		
7	4		NNW	WSW	At 7 Sounded in 25 fms Black Sand 4 or 5 Miles
8	4	2			off shore. The Extremes of the Land from
9	3	6	NWbyW	SWbyW	North to S 40° E. In Royals & [Top g^{l}] Sails.
10	2	4	WNW	SW	
11	2				
12[2]	2	6	West	SSW	*Discovery* WSW.

[2]As noted previously, because Broughton used astronomical time which ran from noon to noon, this represents midnight of April 27.

H	K	F	Courses	Winds	Remarks on Monday, Saturday 28th, 1792.
1	2	6		SbyW	
2	1		SbyW	WNW	½ past the Wind Shifted and [ ] to WNW which
3	1	2	SE to East		took us aback—fill^{d} & stood to the North. At 2
4	2	6	NEbyE	SEbyE	[per] Signal—At ½ past 5 Sounded in 30 fms
5	3	4	NEbyN	vble	black stones. At 7 bore away along shore
6	2				—out Reefs [Sett] Stud^{g} Sails & Royals. Thick
7	5		North	ENE	Raining W^{r}.
8	4	6	WNW		At 8 the extremes of the Land from SSE to
9	3	4	NNW½W		NNW. Sounded in 25 fms Clay & black stones,
10	2	6		Vble	4 or 5 miles off shore. Employ^{d}occasionally.
11	2	4			Sailmakers as before. At Noon the Extremes
12	2	6			of the Land from S 40° E to N 28° W. Sounded
					in 13 fms fine Black Sand.
					Lat Obs^{d} 47° 32' N. Light Winds & Clear W^{r}.

H	K	F	Courses	Winds	Remarks on Sunday, April 29th, 1792.
1	4		NW½N	SWbyW	Light Airs & Clear W^{r}. At 1 Down Stud^{g} sails.
2	3		NWbyN	WbyS	At 2 Tack'd Ship—
3	1		SbyW		At 3 came to an anchor [per] Signal 16 fms
4					Black Sandy bottom. Found the Current
5					Setting NNE [½] a Knot P^{r} hour—
6					
7					
8					
9					
10					
11					
12					D^{o} W^{r}.[3]
1					
2					½ past 2 ans^{d} the Sig^{l} to weigh—4 Weigh^{d} &
3					made Sail, the *Discovery* fir'd a gun, which
4					we answer'd by firing another—At 5 [Sett
5	3	6	NW½W	EbyN	Stud^{g}] Sails & Royals—at 6 saw a strange
6	4				Sail in the NW [ ]. North Extreme of the
7	4	4			Land N 20° W^{t}. ½ past 7 spoke the *Columbia*
8	5	2	NWbyW		an American Vessel that had Winter'd on the
9	6		NWbyN		Coast—Moderate Breezes with Rains. At 11
10	6		NWbyN½N		the *Discovery* made [ ] Sig^{l} to lead into Port or
11	6	2	NNW		Places bearing that appearance. [ ]. At Noon
12	5	2	N½W		no observations. Cape Classet N [ ] 2 miles.

[3] "Ditto weather."

H	K	F	Courses	Winds	Remarks on Monday, April 30th, 1792.
1	6		North	SSE	Moderate Breezes & thick Rainy W^{r}.
2	6		ENE	vble	At 1 haul^{d} round green island passing between
3	3	6			it & a small Rock to the North of it.
4	3				
5	4		ENE	SE	½ past 5 Tack^{d} Ship. ¼ past 7 the *Discovery* made
6	4		SW		our Signal to Anchor. ½ past 7 brought up in
7	4	4	SWbyS		12 fms with the Best Bower Anchor on hard
8					stoney Bottom. The Extreme of the Land from
9					E½S to West, off shore ¼ of a mile.
10					
11					
12					Light Winds & Cloudy W^{r}.
1					
2					
3					
4					
5					½ past 6 the *Discovery* made our sig^{l} to weigh—
6					weigh^{d} made sail to the East^{d}. At the Extremes
7					of the Land from E by N to West. Employ^{d}
8	3		EbyN	West	getting provisions out of the Hold. Open'd a
9	3	4	E½N		Cask of Beef [ ] Compleat & a Cask of Pork.
10	4				Moderate Breezes & Clear W^{r}.
11	4		EbyN		At Noon the Extremes of the North Shore from
12	4		ENE		NE by E to W by N—& the South Extreme from
					East to W by S.

H	K	F	Courses	Winds	Remarks on Tuesday, May 1st, 1792.
1	5	6	EbyN	West	Moderate Breeze & Clear
2	5	6			
3	5	6	East		
4	5	6	E½N		
5	5	4			
6	4		EbyN½N		
7	4	4	NEbyE		At 7 ans^{d} the Signal to prepare to Anchor.[4] ¾
8					past anchor^{d} up in 8 fathoms Water.
9					
10					
11					
12					D^{o} W^{r}.

[4]Dungeness Spit.

H	K	F	Courses	Winds	Remarks on Tuesday, May 1st, 1792.
1					
2					
3					
4					
5					
6					Hoist out the Cutter. Wash^{d} Hammocks
7					below — the [ ] setting up Casks—
8					Sailmakers repairing the Main Sail.
9					
10					
11					
12					Light air & Clear W^{r}.

[p. 52]

H	K	F	Courses	Winds	Remarks on Wednesday, May 2nd 1792.
1				ENE	Moderate Breezes & Clear W^{r}. Employ^{d}
2					occasionally about Rigging — Sailmakers
3					as before.
4					
5					
6					
7					
8				vble	
9					Light Airs inclinable to Calms.
10					
11					
12					
1					
2					
3					
4					
5					At ½ past 5 Weigh^{d} per Signal & made Sail
6					with the *Discovery* to the Eastward into the
7					Harbour.[5]
8					
9				West	At 11 Brought up in 25 fms water. Hoisted out
10					the Launch & moor'd with Stream Anchor to
11					the South^{d} & the Best Bower to the North^{d}.
12					Moderate Breezes & Clear W^{r}.

---

[5]Discovery Bay.

H	K	F	Courses	Winds	Remarks on Thursday, May 3rd, 1792.
1				vble	Moderate & Clear. Employ^{d} [ ] Sail Room. [ ]
2					Sails Down. T G^{l} Yard & Top G^{l} Mast upon
3					Deck & [struck] lower Yards & Top Masts.
4					
5					
6					
7					
8					
9					
10					
11				Calm	
12					
1					
2					
3					
4					
5					
6					
7					Scrub^{d} Hammocks. Employed overhauling the
8					Top Mt Rigging & Top G^{l} Rigging. Sent the
9					Coopers on shore with the empty Casks.
10					Carpenters caulking the Top Sides Sailmakers
11					as before. Sway^{d} up Lower yards Top Masts &
12				WSW	Top G^{l} Masts.

Friday, May 4th. Moderate Breezes & Clear W^{r}. PM. Employ^{d} about the Rigging. Haul'd up the small Bower Cable to get [ ] from under its Sett. D^{o} W^{r}. Coil^{d} down the Small Bower Cable. Employ^{d} in the after Hold. [ ] two Caulkers from the *Discovery* who began caulking the vessels [sides].

Saturday, May 5th. D^{o} W^{r}. PM. Sent the Sailmakers on shore to repair the Fore Top Sail—[ ] a Party of them Cutting Wood & Brewing—AM. D^{o} W^{r}. Employ^{d} as before. Sent the Armourer's Forge on shore—Sailmakers, Coopers &c employ^{d} as before. Carpenters as before. Put the Ship's Company to two thirds of allowance of [Bread].

Sunday, May 6th. D^{o} W^{r}. Employ^{d} as before. The Parties on shore the same. AM. D^{o} W^{r}. Mustr'd the Ships Company. Punished Thos Townsend Quarter Master & Wm Clark [Marine] with 12 Lashes each for Insolence to their Superior Officer.

Monday May 7th. D^{o} W^{r}. PM. Employ^{d} Cutting Wood & Brewing on shore. Coopers, Carpenters &c as before. AM. D^{o} W^{r}. Employ^{d} as before. Sent the Cutter to attend Captn Vancouver in exploring.

Tuesday, May 8th. Calm & Thick Foggy Wr. Fir'd two swivels in answer to the Boats, same number heard from the Boats—Employd as before—AM. Do Wr. Parties on shore as before. Carpenters employd occasionally. Sent some Powder on shore to [air].

Wednesday, May 9th. Light Breezes with Rains. PM. The Parties on Shore employd as before. Carpenters occasionally. AM. Moderate Breezes & Clear Wr. Employd as before. Carpenters Caulking the Top Sides.

Thursday, May 10th. Moderate Breezes & Clear. PM. Employd as before. Carpenters as before. AM. Do Wr. Received [ ] of Wood. Stow'd it in the [ ] Hold.

Friday, May 11th. Do Wr. PM. The Parties on shore employd as before. AM. Received a Raft of Water and a turn of Wood. [Stored] it in the After Hold.

[p. 53] Saturday, May 12th. Moderate Breezes & Clear Wr. PM. Received a turn of Wood & Water. [ ] Launch. AM. Do Wr. The Parties on shore employd as before. Received a turn of Wood. [ ] Launch. Caulkers finished Caulking and was returned to the *Discovery*.

Sunday, May 13th. Light Winds & Cloudy. PM. Received 2 turns of Water & a Cask of Spruce Beer. [ ] Launch. AM. Do Wr. Scrubd the Tides. Received a turn of Water [ ] Launch. Muster'd the Ship's Company.

Monday, May 14th. Do Wr. PM. [ ]. AM. Do Wr. Sent some Barrels of Powder on shore to dry. Receive'd two turns of Water [ ] Launch. Coopers, Sailmakers & Brewers employd as before. Carpenters occasionally.

Tuesday, May 15th. Light airs & Cloudy Weather. PM. The Parties on shore as before. Carpenters preparing a Tree to Saw. AM. Thick Rainy Wr. Employd occasionally on board.

Wednesday, May 16th. Thick Rainy Wr. PM. The Cutters return'd. Employd occasionally. Received a turn of Wood on board. AM. Moderate Breezes & Cloudy. Employd occasionally with the Boatswain.

Thursday, May 17th. Light airs & Cloudy. Received on board 22 Casks of Spruce Beer. [ ] it upon Decks. AM. Light airs with Showers of Rain. Bent Sails [ ] Top Gl Yards. Brought off the Coopers & Brewers from the shore.

Friday, May 18th. Light & variable airs with Shower of Rains. PM. Weighd the Best Bower Anchor & hove in to half the Stream Cable. Brought off the Armourer & Forge & hoist in the Cutter. ½ past 6 Weighd & work'd nearer the mouth of the Harbour. At 8 brought up in 26 fms water with the [ ]. AM. Do Wr. At ½ past 3 Weighd & made sail out of the Harbour. Light & variable airs & Clear Wr.

H	K	F	Courses	Winds	Remarks on Saturday, May 19th, 1792.
1	6				Calm & Clear W^{r}. At 1 part'd company with
2	2	6	NNW½W	vble	the *Discovery* to Explore an opening which
3	4	2	NNW		appeared to the North^{d} & West^{d}. Moderate &
4	4	4	NWbyN		Clear. At 3 [ ] Sails—At 4 set Top Gall^{t} Sails.
5	4	4	NW½W	SWbyW	½ past 5 hove to & Sent the Cutter to Sound the
6	2	2	WNW	SW	entrance of an opening[6] which was
7					discover'd. At 6 entr'd theHarbour. Sounded
8					19 fms. At 8 Brought up in 9 fms with the
9					Stream Anchor.[7]
10					
11					
12					Light winds.
1					
2					
3					
4					
5					
6					
7					[ ]
8					At 10 Sent the Launch & Cutter to Explore the
9					West arm of the [left blank]. Weigh^{d} & made
10					sail up the East Arm. ½ past 11 Brought up in
11					24 fms with the Stream Anchor[8] about 1½
12				WSW	Mile up the arm.

H	K	F	Courses	Winds	Remarks on Sunday, May 20th, 1792.
1				WSW	Moderate & Clear.
2					
3					
4					
5					
6					
7					
8					The Launch & Cutter came on board.
9					
10					Light Winds & Clear.
11					
12					

[6]South entrance to San Juan Channel.

[7]This location is difficult to place. It is either at the south end of Shaw Island or near the entrance to Fisherman Bay on Lopez Island.

[8]Flat Point in Upright Channel.

H	K	F	Courses	Winds	Remarks on Sunday, May 20th, 1792.
1					
2					
3					
4					
5					
6					Sent the Cutter to explore the Entrance.
7					At 7 Weigh^{d} & made sail up the arm.
8					
9					½ past 10 Brought up in 25 fms ½ a cable
10					length off shore.
11					Sent the Launch further up the Arm.
12					D^{o}. W^{r}. The Cutter return^{d}.

[p. 54]

H	K	F	Courses	Winds	Remarks on Monday, May 21st, 1792.
1				Calm	Clear W^{r}. At 1 the Launch return^{d}. ½ past 9
2					Weigh^{d} but it being calm & the tide began to
3					[ ] down.
4					At 4 Brought up in 26 fms. Sent the Launch &
5					Cutter away to Explore some openings
6					in the Arm.
7					
8					
9					At 9 the Boats return^{d}.
10					
11					
12					
1					
2					
3					
4					
5					
6					
7					At 7 Weigh^{d} & made sail further up the arm.
8					
9					Clean'd below.
10				vble	Light Winds & Cloudy.
11					
12					

H	K	F	Courses	Winds	Remarks on Tuesday, May 22^{d}, 1792.
1				NE	Light Winds & Cloudy. At ½ past 1 Dropt^{d}
2					through the Narrows.

H	K	F	Courses	Winds	Remarks on Tuesday, May 22^{d}, 1792.
3					
4					
5					
6					
7					
8					
9					At 9 Brought up in 19 fms with the Stream
10					Anchor. Sent the Cutter to Explore the Bay.
11					
12				Calm	Clear.
1					
2					
3					
4					
5					
6					
7					
8					
9					At 9 Weigh^{d} & with the tide dropt^{d} towards an
10					opening into Straits.
11					
12					D^{o}. W^{r}.

H	K	F	Courses	Winds	Remarks on Wednesday, May 23rd, 1792.
1				NNW	Moderate Breezes & Clear. At 1 a Breeze Sprung
2					up. At 2 Brought up between a small Island &
3					the Main[9] in 12 fms. Sent the Launch on shore
4					& Received a turn of Water.
5					
6					
7					
8				SE	Squally with Rain
9					
10					
11					
12					
1					
2					
3					
4					
5					½ past 5 Weigh^{d} & made sail into the [Strait].
6					Tack'd occasionally passing to the East of Sandy

[9]Strawberry Bay.

H	K	F	Courses	Winds	Remarks on Wednesday, May 23rd, 1792.
7					Island.[10]
8					
9					Moderate & Clear.
10					
11					At Noon Sandy Island N 25° W 5 Miles & the opening through which the *Discovery* went open.
12					

H	K	F	Courses	Winds	Remarks on Thursday, May 24th 1792.
1				SEbyE	Moderate & Clear. At 1 Enter'd the Inlet[11] with a strong Flood Tide.
2					
3					
4					
5					½ past 5 brot up in 8 fms ¼ of a mile from the North Shore & 5 or 6 Leagues from the Mouth of the Inlet.
6					
7					
8					Squally
9					
10					
11					Moderate & Cloudy.
12					
1					
2					
3					At 3 Weigh^{d} & stood over to the South [side] with the last of the flood & at 7 Brought up 9 fms ½ a mile off shore. Sent the Launch on Shore & received a turn of Wood—[opened] a cask of flour [ ] Damaged. Sent up the Top Mast & Top G^{l} Rigging.
4					
5					
6					
7					
8					
9					
10					
11					
12					At Noon Weigh^{d} & with the Flood [went] up the Inlet.

[p. 55]

H	K	F	Courses	Winds	Remarks on Friday, May 25th 1792.
1				South	Moderate Breezes & Clear.
2					
3					

[10] Smith Island.

[11] Admiralty Inlet.

H	K	F	Courses	Winds	Remarks on Friday, May 25th 1792.
4					
5					At 5 Brot up in [19] fms Sandy Bottom —
6					
7					
8					
9					
10					
11					
12					
1					
2					
3					Do Wr. At 3 Weighd & with the Flood work'd up
4					the Inlet but finding no tide with us & gaining
5					little or no ground at 7 brot up on the East Shore
6					in [left blank] fms water Sandy bottom half a
7					Mile off Shore.
8					
9					
10					
11					Clear Wr.
12				Calm	At Noon weighed & Dropp'd up with the tide.

H	K	F	Courses	Winds	Remarks on Saturday, May 26th 1792.
1				North	Light Winds & Cloudy. A Light Breeze sprung
2					up from the Northd. made sail up the Inlet.
3					
4					At 4 saw the *Discovery* at an Anchor in a
5					harbour[12] on the West Shore. Standg for it & at
6					7 Brought up near her in 38 fms 3 Miles off
7					Shore.
8					
9					
10					Moderate Breezes.
11					
12					
1					
2					
3					
4					At 4 the Cutter was sent to accompany Captn
5					Vancouver

[12]Restoration Point.

H	K	F	Courses	Winds	Remarks on Saturday, May 26th 1792.
6					in Exploring the Inlet.
7					
8					
9					At 9 Weigh^{d} & made sail further on Shore.
10					
11					At 11 brot up in 25 fms ¾ of a Mile off Shore
12					Sandy Bottom.

H	K	F	Courses	Winds	Remarks on Sunday, May 27th 1792.
1				North	Moderate & Cldy. Sent the Empty Water Casks
2					on Shore. Carpenters Painting the Sides.
3					
4					Emp^{d} occasionally.
5					Wash^{d} hammocks below.
6					
7					
8					
9					
10				vble	
11					
12					
1					
2					
3					Calm & Cloudy
4					
5					
6					
7					
8					[Much] the same.
9					
10					
11					
12					Moderate & Thick Cloudy W^{r}.

H	K	F	Courses	Winds	Remarks on Monday, May 28th 1792.
1				SSE	Moderate & Cloudy. Received the Water Casks.
2					
3					
4					
5					
6					
7				South	
8					
9					
10					
11					
12					

H	K	F	Courses	Winds	Remarks on Monday, May 28th 1792.
1					
2					
3					
4				SEbyS	
5					
6					
7					
8					At [8] Weigh^{d} & made sail out of the Bay—
9					accompanied by the *Discoverys* Launch
10					D^{o} W^{r}.
11					At Noon Enter'd an arm trending to the North^{d}
12					& West^{d}.

[p. 56]

H	K	F	Courses	Winds	Remarks on Tuesday, May 29th 1792.
1				SEbyS	Moderate Breezes & vble, Clear W^{r}.
2					
3					
4				vble	
5					
6					
7					
8					At 8 Brot up with the Stream in 75 fms Sandy
9					Bottom 1½ Cables Length off Shore.
10					
11					
12					D^{o} W^{r}.
1					
2					
3					Sent the Launch to accompany the *Discovery's*
4					Launch in exploring the arm[13]—
5					
6					
7					At 7 Weigh^{d} & made sail up the arm in search
8				vble	of a convenient place to Anchor in.
9					
10					
11					
12					D^{o} W^{r}.

[13]According to Vancouver's Narrative, Mr. Whidbey and Lt. Hanson from the *Chatham* surveyed Port Susan. Hanson made no mention of participating in his journal.

H	K	F	Courses	Winds	Remarks on Wednesday, May 30th 1792.
1				SW	Moderate Breezes & Clear. Sent the Small Boat
2					on Shore in search of Water upon a small Island
3					but found none—
4				NW	
5					
6					
7				South	At 7 Brot up in 35 fms Muddy Bottom 1 Cable
8					length off shore. Down Top G^{l} Yards—
9					
10					
11					
12					
1					
2					
3					
4					
5					Sent Carpenters on shore to Saw Plank & the
6					Brewers to Brew Spruce. Hauld the Seine.
7					Punished Henry Barfleur Seaman With 12
8					Lashes for Insolence to his superior officer.
9					
10					
11					
12					

H	K	F	Courses	Winds	Remarks on Thursday, May 31st 1792.
1				vble	Light & Variable Winds & Clear W^{r}. Haul^{d} up
2					the Best Bower Cable to get [ ].
3					Employ^{d} as before.
4					
5					
6					
7					
8					
9					Arriv^{d} here HM Ship *Discovery* & the Cutter
10					came on board.
11					
12				vble	D^{o} W^{r}.
1					
2					
3					
4					
5					
6					

H	K	F	Courses	Winds	Remarks on Thursday, May 31st 1792.
7					
8					
9					Employ^{d} as before. Haul^{d} the Seine.
10					
11					
12					Cloudy with Showers of Rain.

H	K	F	Courses	Winds	Remarks on Friday, June 1st 1792.
1				ESE	At 1 Weigh^{d} but there being but little Wind the
2					tide Drifted us down the Inlet—
3					At 3 a Breeze sprang up from the South^{d} & East^{d}.
4					Made sail up the Inlet again.
5					
6					
7					
8					
9					At 9 Brot up in 13 fms on the Larb^{d} Shore.
10					D^{o} W^{r}.
11					
12					
1					
2					
3					
4					At 4 Weigh^{d} & in company with the *Discovery*
5					made sail up the Inlet. At 11 Enter'd a
6					Harbour.[14]
7					
8					
9					At Noon the Mouth of the Harbour from S 40
10					E to S 26 E—White Cliff Island[15] from S 29
11					E to S 34 E. The Low Land at the Bottom
12					of the Harbour from N 11 W to N 22 W.

[p. 57]

H	K	F	Courses	Winds	Remarks on Saturday, June 2^{d} 1792.
1				ESE	Moderate Breezes & Cloudy W^{r}. At 1 got
2					aground on soft muddy bottom. Fir'd two guns
3					& made the signal of Distress. the *Discovery*
4					sent her Boats to our assistance. Run out the
5					Stream Anchor with a Hawser and hove taught
6					till high water. When aground the Point of

[14]Port Susan.

[15]Gedney Island.

H	K	F	Courses	Winds	Remarks on Saturday, June 2^{d} 1792.
7					Entrance from S 32 E to S 27 E. the West End
8					of White Cliff Island S 28 E. The Low Land pt
9					the Shore of the Bay from N 19 W to N 31 W.
10					Down Top G^{l} Yards & Top G^{l} Masts. Punished
11					David Dorman Seamen with 36 Lashes for
12					Neglect of Duty. At 12 hove her off the Tide
					having flood^{d}. Took the opportunity of repairing
1					with copper a piece which had been rubbed off
2					from the Starbd bow by the back of the Anchor.
3					At 2 Warp^{d} her into 9 fms water soft bottom
4					where we brought up with the Stream Anchor.
5					
6					
7					
8					
9					At 9 Weigh^{d} per signal. Sail^{d} out of this Habour.
10					
11					At Noon Brought up in 40 fms. Extreme White
12					Cliff Island From S 27° W to S 3° E. [ ]

H	K	F	Courses	Winds	Remarks on Sunday, June 3^{d} 1792.
1				NW	Moderate Breezes & Clear W^{r}. Employ^{d} occa-
2					sionally.
3					
4					
5					
6					The Launch return^{d}.
7					
8					
9					
10					
11				vble	D^{o} W^{r}.
12					
1					
2					
3					
4					
5					Received a turn of water [ ] Launch.
6					
7					
8					
9					Sent the Launch to paint.

H	K	F	Courses	Winds	Remarks on Sunday, June 3^{d} 1792.
10					D^{o}. W^{r}.
11					
12					

H	K	F	Courses	Winds	Remarks on Monday, June 4th 1792.
1				East	Moderate & Cloudy. Employ^{d} occasionally.
2					
3					
4					
5					
6					
7					
8					
9					
10					
11					
12					D^{o}. W^{r}.
1					
2					
3					
4					
5					
6					
7					Scrub^{d} Hammocks. Receiv'd turns of Water
8					from Cutter.
9					Carpenters painting the Launch.
10					Employ^{d} occasionally
11					
12				vble	Light Variable Airs & Cloudy W^{r}.

H	K	F	Courses	Winds	Remarks on Tuesday, June 5th 1792.
1				vble	Light Winds with Showers of Rain. Employ^{d}
2					occasionally.
3					
4					
5					
6					
7					
8					
9					
10					
11					Light Winds & Cloudy.
12					

H	K	F	Courses	Winds	Remarks on Tuesday, June 5th 1792.
1					
2					
3					
4					
5				NW	Haul^{d} the Seine.
6					
7					At 7 Weigh^{d} & made sail out of the Port in com-
8					pany with the *Discovery*.
9					
10					
11					
12				NW	Moderate Breezes & [Cloudy W^{r}].

[p. 58]

H	K	F	Courses	Winds	Remarks on Wednesday, June 6th 1792.
1				NW	Moderate Breezes & Clear W^{r}. Employ^{d} occa-
2					sionally.
3					
4					
5					
6					
7					
8					
9					
10					½ past 10 brought up in 33 fms 1½ off Shore.
11					
12				vble	Light Winds
1					
2					
3					
4					
5				Calm	
6					
7					At 7 Weigh^{d} per Signal & with the tide in our
8					favour work'd down the Gulf.
9				NNW	
10					Moderate & Clear. Open^{d} a Cask of Beef [ ]
11					compleat. Carpenters painting the Launch.
12					

H	K	F	Courses	Winds	Remarks on Thursday, June 7th 1792.
1				NW	Moderate Breezes & Clear. ½ past 1 Brought up
2					in 7 fms 1½ Mile off Shore. Protection Island

H	K	F	Courses	Winds	Remarks on Thursday, June 7th 1792.
3					from S 59° W to S 48° W. Dungeness Spit [ ].
4					
5					
6					At 6 Weigh^{d} and work'd into the [ ].
7					
8					
9					
10				Calm	Clear W^{r}. ½ past 10 Brot up in 32 fms [ ] Miles
11					off Shore. [ ] & Protection Island from S 25 W
12					to [ ].
1					
2					
3					
4					Employ^{d} occasionally.
5					
6					
7					
8					
9					
10					
11					
12					

H	K	F	Courses	Winds	Remarks on Friday, June 8th 1792.
1				Calm	Clear W^{r}.
2					
3					
4				NW	Moderate Breeze
5					At 5 a Breeze sprung up. Answer^{d} the Signal to
6					Weigh. Weigh^{d} & made sail to the North side
7					of the Straits.[16]
8				vble	
9					At 10 Fir^{d} a Swivel to know where the
10					*Discovery* was. She answ^{d} it being NNW.
11					At 11 Brot up in 33 fms.
12				Calm	D^{o}. W^{r}.
1					
2					
3					½ past 3 Weigh^{d} & made sail towards the *Dis*
4					*covery*.
5					
6					

[16]Near Kellett Ledge off Cape St. Mary, east side of Lopez Island.

H	K	F	Courses	Winds	Remarks on Friday, June 8th 1792.
7					At 7 Brot up in 21 fms Sandy Island N 57° W to N 28° W in the Entrance of an [ ] running to the N^d & W^d. Employ^d work up Junk.[17] Light & Variable Winds & Clear.
8					
9					
10					
11					
12					

H	K	F	Courses	Winds	Remarks on Saturday, June 9th 1792.
1				vble	Light & Variable airs & Clear W^r. Employ^d working up Junk. Sailmakers making a New Jibb.
2					
3					
4					
5					
6					
7					
8					
9					
10					
11					
12				NNW	Light Winds. ½ past Weigh^d in company with the *Discovery* & with the tide in our favour [ ] into the [ ]. ½ past [ ] the tide [swept] us to the Back of Island[18] & finding it setting again we brot up with the Stream in [21] fms. At 3 parted the Stream Cable. Let go the Small Bower. [ ]
1					
2					
3					
4					
5					
6					
7					
8					
9					
10					
11					
12					

[p. 50 sic]

H	K	F	Courses	Winds	Remarks on Sunday, June 10th 1792.
1				vble	Light & Variable Airs & Clear. Wash^d & [ ] below.
2					
3					

[17]A term applied to converting pieces of old cable (rope) into points, mats, gaskets, sennits, etc.

[18]East side of Cypress Island.

H	K	F	Courses	Winds	Remarks on Sunday, June 10th 1792.
4					
5					
6					
7					At 7 slack water again. [ ] for the Stream Anchor
8					but did not get it.
9					
10					
11				vble	D°. W^{r}.
12					
1					
2					
3					Again [ ] for the Anchor but without success.
4					
5				SSE	Moderate Breezes & Cloudy.
6					
7					At 7 Weigh^{d} & Stood out for Strawberry Bay
8					where we found the *Discovery*.
9					At 10 brot up in 7 fms [¾] a Mile off Shore
10					anchor Island —
11					Sent the Empty Water Casks on Shore.
12				vble	D°. W^{r}.

H	K	F	Courses	Winds	Remarks on Monday, June 11th 1792.
1				North	Light Winds & variable. Employ^{d} occasionally.
2					
3					
4					
5					
6					
7					
8					
9					
10				vble	
11					
12					
1					D°. W^{r}.
2					Received the Water Casks from the Shore. Ans^{d}
3					the Sig. to Weigh.
4					
5					
6					At 6 Weigh^{d} & made sail up the Inlet.
7					
8					
9					
10				SE	At 10 Enter^{d} a very Extensive opening.
11					Employ'd working up Inlet.
12					Light Winds & Clear W^{r}.

H	K	F	Courses	Winds	Remarks on Tuesday, June 12th 1792.
1				South	Moderate Breezes & Clear W^{r}. Employ^{d} occa-
2					sionally. Sailmakers making a New Jibb.
3					
4					
5					
6					At 6 Brot up in a Bay on the Starb Shore[19] of the
7					arm in 5 fms 1½—2 miles off Shore. Received
8				Calm	a Stream Anchor & Cable from the *Discovery*.
9					
10					
11					
12					
1					
2				Calm	Clear.
3					
4					½ past 4 Weigh^{d} & tow'd further into the Bay.
5					
6					At 7 Brot up in 5½ fms with the Small Bower
7					& Moor'd with it to the NW & a Kedge to the
8					SE. Sent the Empty Water & Beer Casks &
9					Forge on shore. The Extremes of the Bay
10				vble	from N 64° W to S 20° W.
11					Received a turn of Water from Launch.
12				South	Moderate & Clear.

H	K	F	Courses	Winds	Remarks on Wednesday, June 13th 1792.
1				vble	PM Employ^{d} occasionally. Received a turn of
2					Water [ ] Launch which fill^{d} up the [ ] in the [ ]
3					Hold. Down Top G^{l} Yards. AM. Haul'd the
4					Seine. The Armouer & [brewers]
5					employ^{d} on shore.
6				South	

H	K	F	Courses	Winds	Remarks on Thursday, June 14th 1792.
1				vble	Light Winds & Clear. The [ ] on shore employ^{d}
2					as before. Sent the Cutter accompanied by one

[19] Birch Bay.

H	K	F	Courses	Winds	Remarks on Thursday, June 14th 1792.
3					of the *Discoverys* Cutters to Explore the Inlet.
4					At 10 Cutters returned having seen two Vessels
5				ESE	standing toward the Bay.
6					Moderate Breezes & Cloudy W^{r}.
7					
8					
9					
10					
11				vble	D^{o}. W^{r}.
12					
1					
2					
3					At daylight the Cutters were sent out again to
4					Explore the Inlet. At 4 [ ] and at 5 Weigh^{d} &
5					made sail to the West^{d} to speak the two
6					Vessels seen by the Boats.
7					At 10 found them to be a Spanish Brig &
8					Schooner. Hove too alongside the Brig. Sent
9					a Boat on board & found they were employ^{d}
10					surveying the Straits of [ ]. Their Names the
11					*Sutille* & *Mexicana*. At 11 the Boat return^{d} &
12					we made sail.

H	K	F	Courses	Winds	Remarks on Friday, June 15th 1792.
1				SSE	Moderate Breezes & Cloudy. Tack^{d} occasionally
2					working up to the Bay.
3					
4					
5					
6				vble	Light Winds with Rain.
7					At 7 the South Extreme of Birch Bay NE by E
8					Dist 3 or 4 Leagues.
9					
10					
11					
12				vble	Tack^{d} occasionally during the Night

H	K	F	Courses	Winds	Remarks on Friday, June 15th 1792.
1					
2					
3					
4				East	Fresh Breezes & Squally with Rain. In [ ] Reefs
5					of the Top Sails. At daylight the South Entrance
6					of Birch Bay NE 3 or 4 Leagues.
7					
8				EbyN	Employ'd occasionally.
9					
10					
11					Fresh Breezes & Squally. At Noon enter'd the
12					Bay.

Saturday 16th. PM. Fresh Breezes & Squally W^{r}. At 1 Brot up in 5 fms water with the Small Bower. Down Top Gall^{t} Yards. AM. Moderate Breezes & Cloudy. Sent the Carpenters on Shore to Cut a Tree down for Plank. A Party on Shore cutting Wood. Run a kedge & Towline out to the SE & moor'd with it. Sailmakers employ^{d} repairing the Jibb. Armourer & [ ] as before. Extreme of Bay from W 24° N to W 66° S. Snowy Mount[20] E 40° N.

Sunday 17th. Fresh Breezes & Cloudy W^{r}. Received a turn of Water onboard & a Cask of Spruce Beer. Employ^{d} occasionally. AM. Moderate Breezes & Cloudy. Employ^{d} occasionally. Must^{d} the Ships Company.

Monday 18th. PM. Moderate Breezes & Clear W^{r}. Employ^{d} occasionally. AM. D^{o}. W^{r}. Haul^{d} the Seine. Sent the Cutter & Launch to Explore the West Side of the Inlet. Employ^{d} Cutting Wood. Carpenters sawing Plank. Sailmakers Making a New Jibb. Parties on shore as before.

Tuesday 19th. PM. D^{o}. W^{r}. Employ^{d} cutting wood. Sailmakers, Carpenters &c as before. AM. D^{o}. W^{r}. Employ^{d} as before. Weigh^{d} & [ ] below the North [ ]. Received two turns of Wood.

Wednesday 20th. PM. D^{o}. W^{r}. Employ^{d} as before. The Cutter & Launch return^{d}. AM. D^{o}. W^{r}. Employ^{d} getting provisions out of the Hold. Air^{d} the [ ]. Open^{d} a Cask of Rum [ ]. Found it to be 9½ g^{l} short. Open^{d} a Cask of Island Pork.

Thursday 21st. PM. Light Winds & Cloudy W^{r}. Haul'd the Cutter up to Clean her bottom. Employ^{d} cutting Wood. Received a turn of [ ] Launch. AM. D^{o}. W^{r}. Scrubb^{d} Hammocks. Received a turn of Water [ ] Launch. Armourers, Carpenters &c employ^{d} on shore. Seamen employ^{d} occasionally on board.

Friday, 22nd. PM. D^{o}. W^{r}. Employ^{d} [ ] & cleaning the Sail Rooms. A

[20]Mount Baker.

Party on shore cutting Wood. AM. D^{o}. W^{r}. Employ^{d} as before. Parties on shore the Same.

Saturday 23^{d}. PM Moderate & Cloudy. Received a turn of Wood [ ] Launch. Sett up the Main Rigging, the Fore & Main Top Mast Rigging. AM. D^{o}. W^{r}. Employ^{d} as before. The Parties on shore the Same.

[p. 61]

H	K	F	Courses	Winds	Remarks on Sunday, June 24th 1792.
1				WNW	Moderate & Cloudy W^{r}. Launch & the Cutter
2					Brought the Forge, Water & Beer Casks from
3					the Shore.
4					
5					
6					
7					
8					
9					
10					
11				Calm	Clear W^{r}.
12					
1					
2					
3				East	At 4 Weigh^{d} the Kedge & at ½ past 5 Weigh^{d}
4					the Bower & made sail in company with the
5					*Discovery* out of the Bay. Sent the Boats to
6					bring off the Planks. ½ past 6 hove too & at
7					8 the Boats return^{d}. Hoist in the Cutter &
8					made sail to the West^{d}.
9					Moderate Breezes & Clear W^{r}.
10					[ ]. At Noon Birch Bay in with Snowy
11					Mountain EbN — Spanish Point N 56° E.
12					D^{o}. W^{r}. Lat obs^{d} 48° 59' N.

H	K	F	Courses	Winds	Remarks on Monday, June 25th 1792.
1				SSE	Moderate Breezes & Cloudy W^{r}. Employ^{d} occa-
2					sionally.
3					At 3 join'd company with the two Spanish Ves-
4					sels *Sutille* & *Mexicana*.
5					

PROCEEDINGS OF HIS MAJESTY'S BRIG CHATHAM FROM THE 18TH TO 25TH OF MAY, 1792

On Friday, the 18th of May, 1792

[p. 56] At Noon took our departure from middle or 2nd Point bearing from us East ½ a mile, with the wind at West we stood over close hauled for the North side of the Straits. At 4 having run 12 miles we weathered a small Island[21]—within half a mile to the East of it was a detach'd Sandy Spit extending some distance. An opening[22] appear'd to the North of a Point[23] over which were some Peaked Hills[24]—and another[25] bore of us N. W. for which (the Wind favouring us) we were able to fetch by ½ past 5. Some Rocky Islands lay off the entrance and the appearance of Broken Water or else a very strong Tide setting to windw'd. The Cutter went ahead to sound—and we followed her through a passage of a mile in width, carrying in—19, 13 & 12 fath^ms.^ close to the larboard Rocky Island[26] as we entered. The shore from the Starboard side of the entrance to Peaked Hill Point seem'd to be a continuation of Rocky Isles, several of them well cloath'd with wood. After stretching across the Sound[27] which was closed to the Westward, we bore up to the North side for Anchorage and opened a deep Arm of the Sea[28] in a N.N.E. direction and soon after another of greater breadth and extending to the N. W'ward.[29] We steer'd over for the N.E. Point[30] of this Arm against a Strong Ebb Tide rounding a Reef of Rocks[31] apparently covered at highwater (no soundings) within them and the shore our Boat found 17 fath^ms.^ At ½ past 8 we came too in 12 fath^ms.^ on the Starboard shore having had overfalls from 18 to 10 f^ms.^ rocky bottom.[32] In the morning the Cutter went 6 miles up the N.E. Arm—and return'd

---

21 Smith Island and the sand spit to Minor Island.

22 Entrance to Rosario Strait.

23 Point Colville.

24 Watmough Head, Chadwick Hill.

25 South entrance to San Juan Channel.

26 Goose Island.

27 Griffin Bay.

28 Entrance to Upright Channel.

29 Northern portion of San Juan Channel.

30 Southern point of Shaw Island.

31 Likely Turn Rock.

32 This anchorage is difficult to locate but is probably near the south end of Shaw. The next sentence indicates that the cutter explored six miles up the NE arm (Upright Channel). Upright Channel is only three miles in length. It is unlikely they would travel six miles without seeing any termination. Regardless, they were in a location where they could obviously see both San Juan as well as Upright Channels.

without seeing any apparent termination to it. After Breakfast, I dispatched two Boats under the direction of Mr. Johnstone (the Tide of Flood having made) up the [p. 57] N.W. Arm[33] to explore. The wind blowing down prevented the vessel's going so conveniently and I rather supposed it communicated with what we call the true N.W. passage. After their departure we weigh'd and run up the N.E. passage (which from the boat not seeing any termination of, I conceived might lead us out to the supposed opening by Peaked Point) and our situation was not the most eligible from the foulness of the ground. After running 2 or 3 miles we anchored off a Sandy Spit between which and the opposite Rocky point form'd the Narrows[34] of this passage not ½ a mile across. Our soundings were very irregular and at last we brought up in 22 fa$^{ms.}$ with a strong Ebb tide by the falling of the water on shore. Meridian observation gave the Lat. 48·35 N. Fine pleasant moderate Wea$^{r.}$—the wind from the N.W. Quarter. We frequently hauled the Seine with very indifferent success. At 8 P.M. the Boats return'd and reported the passage which they followed up communicated with an extensive Opening[35] call'd by us the N.W. passage—and two Arms branched off from it in an N. by W. & N. by E. direction—*vide* Chart.

At day light in the morning of the 20th, Mr. Johnstone went to sketch the entrance we had first entered by from the Straits and the Tide slacking at 8 we weigh'd, towing to the N.E. ward without any wind. By Noon we came to an Anchor having received very little assistance from the Tide in 27 fa$^{ms.}$ at the mouth of an Inlet which led to the N.W.—another appeared to the S.E. and the third bore of us N.N.E.[36] These different openings materially affected the Stream of the Tide—and though the rise and fall was considerable by the Shore—our progress was much impeded by their irregularity and we were necessitated to remain stationary for the day—after making another attempt in the Afternoon—No observation.

---

[33]Northern portion of San Juan Channel.

[34]Based upon the distance and description of the land features, I believe this to be off Flat Point which is the only sand spit in the neighborhood, and with Canoe Island, forms the "narrows" of Upright Channel of about 0.3 mile in width. In addition, Broughton's latitude reference to 48° 35' (which would place him center channel where Harney and Upright Channels merge) is within the degree of error of 2 minutes (2 miles) consistent with other measurements.

[35]"Extensive opening" suggests they were looking beyond Waldron Island towards the Strait of Georgia.

[36]Again, the location is difficult to determine. I believe the N.W. reference to be Harney Channel, which is really closer to west rather than NW which Broughton corrected in the subsequent sentence; that to the S.E., Lopez Sound; and to the N.N.E. could be East Sound.

By Noon the Cutter returned. After dinner the two Boats were sent to explore the passages which presented themselves on each side of the one I meant to pursue. By dark they came back. The S.E. opening Mr. Hanson went up 7 or 8 miles but saw no termination to it. The other opening took a N.W. by W. direction about 4 miles when it branched off to the N.E. and S.W.[37] About two miles up they found a Village[38]—Canoes came off and traded [p. 58] with them for Venison—A young Fawn they got alive[39]—High water by the Shore at 7 hours—The Stream of Tide very inconsiderable.

The morning of the 21st was calm—at 8 we got under way, the Boats towing us toward a narrow passage (which I suppose might carry us out to the Straits).[40] We had light breezes and cloudy weather from the N.E. quarter and by Noon we reached the 2nd Narrows having a strong tide in our favour to carry us through. Several canoes were on the beach and some paddling along shore to the Westward. Mr. Johnstone went ashore with the small boat to take the necessary Angles while we continued turning through the passage—having both boats ahead to assist us—the narrowest part was about 100fa^ms.^ across—Our soundings regular from 7 to 15 fat^ms.^ We now entered a spacious Sound[41] containing several Islands and openings in all directions—*Vide* Chart. The wind having left us, we were carried to the N.ward very rapidly by a strong Tide setting close along the Larboard shore. Unfortunately at this moment while the boats were pulling us off, they broke the Tow rope, and before we could derive any effect from another—our Head swung inshore and we drifted very gently along side the Rocks. While the Hawser was coiling away in the Long Boat to haul off by—we floated off, the Eddy tide setting us back to the South^d.^ The Boats soon towed us into the fair Tide. While alongside the rocks we had 22 fa^ms.^—without 30 fa^ms.^—The Lead got entangled and we lost it with 20 fa^ms.^ of line. At 1 P.M. we anchored in 25 fa^ms.^ there being no wind, and the Tide setting us fast towards the land. The afternoon continued calm. Mr. Johnstone went to explore the openings between the N. & E. and we tried hauling the Seine till sunset without getting any fish. The Cutter returned at dark having found the Eastern opening to lead into the Straits—to the N.E. were several Islands which apparently communicated

[37]The compass directions are confusing. West Sound branches from Harney Channel to the NW while Wasp Passage runs to the SW.

[38]Possibly near Blind Bay on the north side of Shaw.

[39]Most likely, the Indians paddled along side the fawn while it swam from one island to another.

[40]This could be either Obstruction or Peavine Pass although the narrowness of Peavine is consistent with Broughton's later observation.

[41]Rosario Strait.

in the same manner — and a third very extensive opening stretching to the N.W.ward[42] — Highwater by the Shore 6 hours.

The 22nd [May, 1792] commenced variable weather. In the morning calm — at 8 we weigh'd and towed to the E.ward — The Tide setting us fast to the South shore of this opening (which afterwards proved to be an Island).[43] An indifferent observation gave the Lat. 48·40 N.[44] The afternoon we had fresh breezes from the N.W. quarter with a strong Flood Tide against us at ½ past 2 making very little [p. 59] progress and the small boat being absent, we came too in a fine Bay on the North shore within a small Island in 11 fa^{ms}.[45] — The Straits being entirely open with Sandy Island bearing S. 5° W. — 4 or 5 leagues — Several Islands with an inlet lay to the South of us, which Mr. Johnstone went to examine — But the rapidity of the F[l]ood Tide prevented his getting over. This Inlet I imagine was the same that was before partially explored by Mr. Hanson.[46]

The Long Boat hauled the Seine with indifferent success and brought off a turn of water which lay very conveniently within the Beach. High water by the shore at ½ past 6. The Ebb made to the Eastward at 7, at which time it became squally with heavy rain from the S.E. Quarter and a great deal of thunder.

23rd. — Till 6 A.M. we had heavy rain when it clear'd up with the wind at S.S.E. the tide setting to the Eastward, we weigh'd at that time, and worked to windwards towards the Straits passing several islands on the N. side with an extensive Arm which opened in that direction.[47] By 8 we had work'd the length of the Straits — and standing over to the N. shore, perceived a small opening which took a winding direction to the Northward.[48] The Land from hence to the part now under examination of Captain Vancouver was a straight reach in an North direction[49] — we passed to the N.E. of Sandy Island in working, but had no Sounding with 16 fa$^{ms.}$ By Noon were off the entrance above mentioned and by Observa-

---

[42]Strait of Georgia.

[43]Cypress Island.

[44]And it was indifferent! This location would have placed them near Lawrence Point on the east side of Orcas.

[45]Strawberry Bay.

[46]The reference was to James and Decatur Islands, on the east side of Lopez Sound. I believe the inlet is Thatcher Pass which, with some imagination, is reflected on Vancouver's chart.

[47]Perhaps Bellingham Channel.

[48]Perhaps Deception Pass.

[49]Broughton used "north" a number of times where he clearly was referencing a different direction.

tion in the Lat. Of 48.16 N. Sandy Island, bearing N. 25 W. 5 miles and middle or 1st point on the Starboard side of entrance S.E. 3 or 4 — Off the nearest shore 2 miles.[50] The Flood tide now made strong up this opening with which we worked up very fast. It formed in several places over Falls and constant riplings, appearing like shoal water. At 4 the wind shifted to a light air from the N.W. — and at 6 the Tide having done we came to an Anchor on the Larboard shore of this Arm in 9 f^{m} off some remarkable White Cliffs forming an abrupt point at the entrance of a large Bay[51] — the night was squally wea$^{r.}$ from the Southern Quarter.

24th. — At Day light we weigh'd with the last of the Flood and turn'd to windward till 8. Our tacks were not very advantageous and we anchored on the East shore near a projecting Sandy Spit in 9 f$^{m.}$ The mouth of the entrance from the Straits still open to us bearing N.W. about 7 leagues.[52] A canoe spent the morning with us. At Noon the Tide making, we weigh'd and worked to windward having a fine turning breeze from the S.E. Quarter — after crossing a deep Bay, we opened another arm of the Sea extending [p. 60] to the N.ward.[53] By halfpast 6 we came too on the west shore in 19 fa$^{ms.}$ having increased our distance not more than 6 miles from the last Anchorage. The Tides did not run with the same rapidity we experienced yesterday which will account for our slow progress.

25th. — At 3 the next morning we again weigh'd with light breezes from the Southward and turn'd up the Arm at 8 we anchored off the East shore off a Sandy Spit, having from 3 to 25 f$^{ms.}$ close in. The forenoon continued calm. An indifferent observation made the Lat. 47.46N. At Noon again weigh'd with a light air from the N. and run up the Arm. At 6 saw the *Discovery* at an Anchor on the West Shore.[54]

W. R. Broughton.

---

[50]Near Point Partridge along the west side of Whidbey.

[51]Broughton's "rough" journal indicated this anchorage is "5 or 6 Leagues from the Mouth of the Inlet." It is somewhere along the west side of Whidbey Island ("Larboard shore"). Fifteen miles from the "mouth" would place the vessel near Double Bluff (which does form an abrupt point) and looking into Useless Bay. They were not as far south as Possession Point as several sentences later in this log, he referenced observing Possession Sound.

[52]This anchorage appears to be along the west side of Whidbey Island as they have not yet observed Possession Sound. However, Broughton's "rough" journal as well as the journal of James Hanson indicated this anchorage was on the "South shore." If they spent the previous night at Double Bluff, this location would really be on the west side of Admiralty Inlet, perhaps near Point No Point. It is unclear from either journal exactly where they were!

[53]Possession Sound.

[54]Restoration Point.

5

Joseph Baker

Joseph Baker was born in Briston, in southwest England about February 1768, the second son of James and Nancy. At the age of thirteen, on December 19, 1781, he reported for duty aboard HMS *Alert* commanded by James Vashon, as "Captain's Servant." He was promoted to able-bodied seaman within two weeks of sailing. Apparently impressed with the young man Vashon became Baker's lifelong mentor.

The French and British, at war for some years following the American Revolution, shifted the theater to the Caribbean with British forces under the command of Admiral Sir George Rodney and Admiral Sir Samuel Hood, second in command. As a result of Vashon's actions against the French there, he was promoted from Commander to Captain and reassigned to the *Prince William* on April 6, 1782. Within the week, Baker followed with the new rank of Midshipman. Two months later, he followed Vashon to the *Formidable* and then to the frigate *Sibyl*.

In 1783, Vashon was furloughed on half pay. For the following two years, Baker was assigned to the *Bombey Castle*. In 1786, Vashon was assigned to the *Europa*, Baker reported for duty on December 9 of that year. Also joining Vashon were first lieutenant George Vancouver and midshipman Peter Puget.

Because of the "Nootka problems," Vancouver was placed in charge of the *Discovery*. At the age of twenty-two, Baker, as well as Puget and Whidbey were also assigned to the *Discovery*. Because of his skills, Baker rapidly took over the tasks of charting the visited lands including a very active roll in the surveys during the Vancouver Expedition.

In early 1797, Baker married Elizabeth Weyermann, the niece of Vashon. They had seven sons and three daughters.

His next naval role was again with Vashon aboard *Pompee* until March 1, 1797, when Baker was promoted to Commander and took over the *Calypso* for three years. During this time, he and his wife became very close friends with Puget and his wife Hannah. Puget moved to Presteigne in 1801, near the Bakers. The Pugets named their fifth child Joseph Baker Puget in 1803. In 1807, the Bakers named their fourth child Peter Puget Baker.

Promoted to Captain April 26, 1802, aboard *Castor*, Baker patrolled the Scottish coast, responsible for protecting English trade vessels from attack from marauding privateers. In early 1808, he took command of *Tartar* and continued his naval activities along the coast of England and northern Europe. This same year, Vashon was promoted to Vice-Admiral and retired.

In 1811, Baker was ordered to move *Tartar* and three other frigates to the coast of Norway and Denmark to reinforce British naval strength there. He led a successful attack against the Danes and received a special commendation from Vice-Admiral Saumarez. In August 1811, Baker had the unfortunate duty of notifying the Admiralty that he struck a rock in the *Tartar* while entering a harbor on the southwest coast of Sweden. The ship was lost. Early in 1812, Baker was ordered to the command of the French prisoner-of-war camp at Stapleton, Avon. While the duty was dreary, it provided an opportunity to visit Presteigne frequently, 70 miles to the north. Losing a ship in a non-combat environment generally signaled the end of a military career. As was customary, and because of declining naval requirements, Baker was put on inactive duty in 1814, never to regain command.

In 1817, his health unexpectedly turned bad and he died on June 26 at the age of forty-nine. Admiral Vashon, Baker's mentor, died at the age of eighty-five on October 20, 1827. Elizabeth died in 1841.

Monday, April 30th, 1792. Enter'd the strait of Juan de Fuca. Fresh breezes & thick hazey Wr with Rain, several Canoes came alongside. Cape Classet is situated in the Lat of 48.23 N & Long 235.38 Et. Met with rain & thick hazey Wr. ½ past 4 Tack'd Ship, try'd for Soundings with 40 fms, no ground. At 6 Tacked. ½ past 6 made the Signal & Anchor'd in 23 fms with the Small Bower Over a bottom of Sand. Raining Wr the Land covered with a thick Haze-at 7 the Haze clear'd away. When the South entrance extreme bore N 88° E, the North entrance extreme N 68 W & the nearest Shore South ½ a Mile distant. Light Airs. ½ past 6 weigh'd & came to Sail under Top Sails, T. Galt Sail & Foresails.[1] At 8 Light Breezes & Cloudy, set Studding Sails & Royals. At noon Light Airs & clear Wr. *Chatham* in Company.

---

[1]A brief discussion of sails, masts and yards is appropriate. *Discovery* had three masts: fore (at the front of the ship), main (in the middle) and mizzen (at the back of the ship). The fore and main masts were comprised of four separate masts rather than a single tall spar, easing repair or replacement of the individual mast. (*note continued on next page*)

Tuesday, May 1st, 1792. PM: Modt breezes & Cloudy Wr. At 8 Anchor'd under a long ridge of Sand upon the South Shore in 14 fms over a bottom of fine Sand, nearest Shore South 2 Miles. Calm. Two Boats from us & one from the *Chatham* were sent to examine this part of the Shore for a Harbour. Several Canoes came alongside with the Natives who brought with them Fish. Punished Jno Munro (Seaman) with Eighteen Lashes for insolence to his superior Officer. At noon Modt Breezes & clear Wr.

Wednesday, May 2nd, 1792. Modt Breezes & fine clear Wr. At 1 A.M. the Boats returned. Succeeded in finding an excellent harbour. At 7 A.M made the Sign[1] & weighed with a light air & all sail set. At 9 entering the Mouth of the Harbour which obtained the name of Port Discovery. 2 Boats ahead towing. At 10 Modt Breezes. Anchor'd about 5 Miles from the entrance in 34 fms the bottom a stiff black Clay. Moor'd Ship with the following bearings [left blank]

Thursday, May 3rd, 1792. Modt Breezes & clear pleasant Wr. ½ past Noon the *Chatham* Anchor'd. Sent the Tents, Observatory, Timekeepers & Instruments on shore with an Officer & party of Marines. AM. Put up the astronomical Quadrant & begun to take Altitudes to determine the rate of the Timekeepers. Parties on shore cutting Wood & brewing spruce beer. Sailmakers repairing the Main T. Sails & adding Crop bands. Coopers repairing & setting up Casks. Sent the T. Galt Masts upon deck & fitted new Mast & T. Gallant Backstays.

Friday, May 4th, 1792. Modt Breezes & fine Wr. Seamen empld repairing the Rigging. Parties on shore on their various duties. AM. Sent a part of the Powder on shore to dry. Received a visit from the Natives in five Canoes who brought with them some Fish & Venison, which with their other articles of curiosity, they barter'd for small pieces of Copper, Buttons &c. Sent 2 Carpenters on board the *Chatham* to Caulk, the other empld stopping a leak in our larboard bow. Haul'd the Seine, caught some Flounder & a few Salmon Trout.

Saturday, May 5th, 1792. Modt Breezes & fine Wr. Got the new back-

---

The lower mast was at the bottom. This in turn supported a top mast which supported a topgallant mast and finally a royal mast. Running horizontally and attached to the individual masts were yards, or thick spars to which the sails were attached. Square sails were rigged on these three masts and yards and were named based upon the mast and yard from which they "flew." (E.g., the fore topsail yard carried the fore topsail.) The fore and main masts carried four sails (from bottom to top), the course (or main), top sail, topgallant and royal. The mizzen held one square sail, the top sail, as well as a fore and aft gaff-rigged sail, aft of the mast called a spanker or mizzen. Studding sails were carried on the fore and main masts. They were "flown" outboard of the "companion" sail. Thus, a fore top studding sail represented two sails on either side of the fore top sail. This brief discussion ignores up to ten triangular shaped fore and aft sails (jibs) which are rigged between the masts and at the bow of the ship.

stays overhead & sway'd aft the T. Galt Mast. Parties on shore & aboard employ'd on their various duties as before. Haul'd the Seine with indifferent success.

Sunday, May 6th, 1792. Clear pleasant Weather. P.M. blacked the yards. AM. Muster'd the Ships Company & read the Articles of War.

Monday, May 7th, 1792. Mod^{t} Breezes & fine W^{r}. AM. Capt. Vancouver in the pinnace attended by Lieut Puget in the Launch & Mr. Johnston (Master of the *Chatham*) in her cutter, set out on a surveying expedition up the Strait. Sailmakers emp^{d} on the F. T. Sail adding Crop bands to it. The other Parties on their various duties & taking on board some Pebble ballast. Receiv'd a visit from the natives in very small canoes who brought with them a few fish & various articles of curiosity.

Tuesday, May 8th, 1792. Mod^{t} Breezes & Cloudy W^{r}. Parties on shore & aboard emp^{d} on their various duties as before. Mr Whidbey (Master) surveying the Harbour. At 5 AM heard the report of a gun in the NE & another at 7 which we concluded must have come from our boats. The *Chatham* fir'd a swivel in return. Clear W^{r}.

Wednesday, May 9th, 1792. P.M. Mod^{t} Breezes & Clear pleasant W^{r}. Getting on board wood & Water. AM thick W^{r} and much Rain.

Thursday, May 10th, 1792. These 24 Hours thick hazey W^{r} and constant Rain. Parties on Shore employ'd in their various occupations. On board taking in Wood, Water & pebble Ballast.

Friday, May 11th, 1792. Light Airs & Cloudy W^{r}. Emp^{d} Wooding & Watering. Completed the Ballast having taken on board 20 Tons. Parties on shore emp^{d} on their various duties as before. AM. Clear W^{r}. Seamen emp^{d} on the Rigging. Punish'd Thos Bull (Marine) with 12 Lashes for Insolence to his superior Officer. We were this day visited by the Indians in four Canoes, who traded as usual.

Saturday, May 12th, 1792. Mod^{t} Breezes & Clear W^{r}. AM. Heard several guns in the NE. Sailmakers adding Cropbands to the Mainsail, the other Parties as before. The Master surveying the Harbour.

Sunday, May 13th, 1792. Light Winds & Clear W^{r}. People on shore emp^{d} on their Various Duties. On board getting up the Cables & cleaning the Tiers. AM. [ ] W^{r}. Muster'd the Ships Company.

Monday, May 14th, 1792. Mod^{t} & Cloudy W^{r}. Sailmakers adding Cropbands to the T. Sail. Parties on shore emp^{d} as before. AM. Black'd the bends.[2] Carpenters Return'd from the *Chatham* having finish'd Caulking her. At Noon Light Airs & gloomy W^{r}.

Tuesday, May 15th, 1792. Dark Gloomy W^{r} & Rain. Carpenters emp^{d}

[2]The bends were an extra-thick broad band of planking just above the water line. They were typically painted black. This is a nickname for "wales" or "gunwhales."

caulking the Counter. AM. Thick Hazey W^{r} & constant Rain. Emp^{d} on their various duties on shore.

Wednesday, May 16th, 1792. Light Breezes & thick Hazey W^{r} with Rain. At 3 P.M. the Boats returned with Captn Vancouver & party from their surveying expedition. AM. Calm & Rainy W^{r}. Emp^{d} preparing for Sea. Got the brewing kettles &c from the Shore. Punished Jno Henley (Seaman) with 24 Lashes for Drunkenness & Insolence to his superior Officer.

Thursday, May 17th, 1792. Cloudy W^{r} with Rain. Sailmakers emp^{d} making a new T. T. Mast, Staysails. AM. [ ] W^{r}. Bent Sails, emp^{d} getting ready for Sea, visited by one Canoe with four Indians.

Friday, May 18th, 1792. Cloudy W^{r} with Rain. Sent on board the Timekeepers & Instruments & struck the Observatory & Tents. AM. Weigh'd & came to Sail with a light air to the SE. Emp^{d} towing & Tacking occasionally with Variable Winds. The *Chatham* in Company. At Noon the East Point of the Harbour NE ½ a Mile.

This Harbour of which I have annexed the Survey (made by Mr Whidbey, Master) may be reckoned a most excellent one & is capable of being well defended. The Island in front of it, being so happily situated that if properly fortified, it might command the entrance of the Port with the greatest care & defend it from a very considerable force. The only disadvantage it has (if indeed that may be so called) is the depth of water in which you anchor, there being no less (except toward the head of it, and close to the Shore) than from 30 to 35 f^{ms}. The Land is of a Mod^{t} height & well wooded with some beautiful green banks on each side, thickly imprinted with the tracks of Deer & other animals. The Soil appears tolerably good & the Shirts of the woods are lined with gooseberry bushes &c &c. We left a small garden with a variety of seeds sown in it near to the place where our tents were pitched but as the situation did not appear to be well chosen I am apprehensive it will not be very productive. There are several runs of fresh water, that near which we anchored, is by much the largest & the best. Any sailing direction for this place will be scarcely necessary as the channel & every part of it is perfectly clear & free from any danger. The Current is hardly perceptible tho the tide rises on the full and change days to the height of ten feet perpendicular.

The Indians which we saw here are of a low stature & universally bow legged which deformity is most likely occasioned by the mode they have of siting in their canoes. They are rather ill favored than otherwise & most excessively dirty. Their dress is either the Skin of some Animal or a kind of blanket of their own Manufacture, made as it is supplied from the wool of the Mountain Sheep. Their garment is thrown loosely over the right Shoulder & made fast by the two corners under the left arm. The dress of the Women is formed of the same materials but they are much closer clad.

Their arms are bows and arrows & a short flat Club made of bone greatly resembling the Patra Patros of the New Zealanders as described in Capt Cooks voyage & they display much ingenuity in the workmanship of these warlike instruments. They parted very readily with not only their arms but even their clothes for metal buttons, small pieces of Copper &c and conducted their little traffic with much quietness and honesty. They brought no Sea-Otter skins for sale, nor do I believe they had any among them.

At the head of the harbour, we found a deserted House sufficiently large to contain at least a hundred people in the manner which they live. It must have been sometime since it was occupied as the inside was grown over with nettles & other weeds. Some human skulls were found near it & likewise in many other parts of the harbour. Not far from where our tents were pitched & a little removed from the waterside, a large Fire had been made & among the ashes were several sculls & other human bones, some burnt to a Coal & all of which had been in the fire; close to this horrid scene a Canoe was suspended between the branches of two trees & on removing a flat board which served as a cover for it, it was found to contain the Skeleton of a full grown person. On one of the trees but considerably higher up was hung a Basket, and in it was the body of a Child in a state of decay. This I conclude to be their mode of burial for many blankets with such and similar contents were found suspended in the same manner in different parts of the woods; & from the foregoing circumstances we were led to conjectures, that this place must have been at no very remote period, the scene of a battle: it however appears at present to be totally deserted; the few Indians that visited us always quitting the Harbour toward the evening, but where they retired to we knew not, for we saw none of their sheds erected near the place.

Of what nature their religion is or whether they have any at all, we could not discover. On the long ridge of Sand under which we anchored, and all along the beach to this post, there were erected several slender poles about 30 yards from each other and about 50 feet high, where the trees of which they were made happened not to be sufficiently long they were joined with much neatness & ingenuity, & on the top of all of them was placed a piece of wood carved into the resemblance of a crescent. It was conjectured that this perhaps might belong to some of their religious rites but we never could understand any thing from the Indians concerning them.

Captn Vancouver in his excursions with the Boats entered a considerable opening[3] a little to the East of this port, which took a Southerly direction and about [left blank] leagues from the entrance, branched off into two separate Arms. He followed the continental shore,[4] which led him down the western branch to the Lat^{d} of 47° 19'N & Long^{d} 237° 08' E^{t} where it concluded. His provisions being nearly exhausted, he was obliged to return to the Ships, without having it in his power to examine the other Arm. The Country where they had been appeared nearly the same as where the Ships lay. They met with but few Indians who were very civil & friendly. They found the tides regular and exceedingly strong.

Port Discovery is situated in the Lat^{d} of 48° 2' 30" N & Long^{d} 237° 22' 30" E^{t}.

Saturday, May 19th, 1792. Mod^{t} & cloudy W^{r}. At 1 the *Chatham* parted company to examine some apparent openings to the North. ½ past 2 entered a large arm taking a Southerly direction with a fresh Breeze from the West. At 4 tried for soundings with 100 F^{ms}. No ground. ½ past 4 the ebb tide beginning to make. Haul'd in for the Eastern shore and came to an anchor in 28 F^{ms} distant from it ½ a Mile. Hauled the Seine but without success. At 8 AM, Light Breezes & clear W^{r}. Weigh'd & stood up the arm with all sail set. Carried away the F.T.G^{l} Yard in the Slings, unbent the Sail & sent up another yard. At Noon fresh Breezes, standing to the South^{d}. Observed in the Lat^{d} of 47° 59' N.

Sunday, May 20th, 1792. Mod^{t} Breezes & clear W^{r}. At 4 haul'd down the Studding Sails, ½ past 6, falling little wind, & the ebb tide beginning to make, came to with the best bower, in 35 f^{ms} on the Western shore,[5] at the entrance of a small opening, apparently leading to a harbour, the Inlet at this place branching off into two separate arms. At 4 AM sent the Cutter & Launch away with an officer in each to examine the Westernmost opening. At ½ past 8 weighed & shifted our birth into a more convenient situation for wooding, watering &c. We anchor'd in 40 F^{ms} near a point on which was a small village of Indians, many of whom came along side in their canoes, behaving very honest & friendly. Washed below.

Monday, May 21st, 1792. Light Breezes & clear W^{r}. People variously emp^{d}. Sent the Carpenter on shore to cut down Spars for two new T.G^{l} Yards & sent a party on shore, with the Kettles &c to brew Spruce beer. Others to haul the Seine, several of the Natives alongside.

Tuesday, May 22nd, 1792. Light Breezes & clear W^{r}. Emp^{d} as before. AM. Small rain, at 9 fair W^{r}. Loosed sails to dry. Emp^{d} brewing, fishing & carpenters as before. Sailmakers repairing the Jibb.

---

[3]Admiralty Inlet.

[4]Hood Canal.

[5]Restoration Point.

Wednesday, May 23rd, 1792. First part Light Breezes & clear W^{r}. Furled Sails. Middle part fresh Breezes & Squally, with heavy Thunder & Lightening. Got down T. Galt. Yards. AM. Light Breezes & fair W^{r}. Punished Geo. Raybold Armourer with two dozen lashes for selling the Ships Copper & James Butters (Seaman) with three Dozen lashes for theft. Loosed sails to dry, sent the empty casks on shore. 11 Canoes canoes [sic] alongside, containing about eighty people.

Thursday, May 24th, 1792. P.M. Squally with Rain. Furled Sails, AM Light Breezes & clear W^{r}. People employed about the rigging. Parties on shore, brewing, fishing &c. Carpenters making a new T. Galt. Mast. Captn Vancouver went away in the pinnace to examine the inside of the Harbour at the Mouth of which we are lying.[6]

Friday, May 25th, 1792. Light Breezes & clear W^{r}. Emp^{d} as before. At 8 the Pinnace returned having finished the examination of the Harbour. A.M. V[ariable] W^{r}. Got up a new Main T. G^{l} Yard. Some Indians brought a Deer alongside, which was purchased.

Saturday, May 26th, 1792.[7] Light Breezes & clear W^{r}. Sent the Empty Casks on shore & filled. People emp^{d} on their various duties. At 5 we were joined by the *Chatham*. AM. V[ariable] W^{r}. At 4 Captn Vancouver in the Pinnace, attended by the *Chatham's* Cutter, went to explore the Eastern branch.[8] Emp^{d} brewing, fishing &c. Carpenters as before. At 9 Weighed & shifted our birth nearer in shore. Three Canoes alongside, the Natives peaceable & Friendly.

Sunday, May 27th, 1792. Mod^{t} & clear W^{r}. Emp^{d} occasionally. At 2 AM the Launch & Cutter returned[9] from their surveying expedition. Muster'd the Ships Company.

Monday, May 28th, 1792. Mod^{t} & cloudy W^{r}. AM the *Chatham* sailed accompanied with our Launch and an Officer to examine an Inlet upon the eastern Shore.[10] People emp^{d} on the various duties of brewing, fishing, &c.

Tuesday, May 29th, 1792. Mod^{t} & cloudy with showers of Rain. Emp^{d} occasionally. AM. V[ariable] W^{r}. Washed between Decks. Sailmakers emp^{d} repairing the Stay sails.

---

[6]According to Vancouver's journal, Mr. Baker accompanied him in the yawl to explore Rich Passage and the west side of Bainbridge Island (Port Orchard), the morning of the 24th. Baker made no note of his involvement.

[7]According to Vancouver's journal, Baker accompanied him on an expedition into Puget Sound. Baker's journal did not reference the journey.

[8]Along the east side of Vashon Island. Vancouver previously sent Puget and Whidbey to explore the western branch, Colvos Passage.

[9]Puget and Whidbey.

[10]Possession Sound.

Wednesday, May 30th, 1792. Light Breezes & Cloudy W^{r}. At 9 PM Captn Vancouver returned from his expedition, having found that the two channels were formed by a large Island which he named Vashon's Island. It is situated about the Lat^{d} 47° 28' N & Long^{d} 237° 46' E^{t}. The Inlet was found to extend to the Lat^{d} of 47° 04' N & Long^{d} 237° 18' E^{t}. The bottom of it composed of several small Islands, obtain'd the name of Pugets Sound. ½ past 8 AM weighed & made all sails to join the *Chatham* on her station. At Noon the village p^{t} bore S 3° E. Punished Wm Woodson with 24 Lashes for insolence to his superior officer. Our late anchorage was found to be situated in the Lat^{d} 47° 37' N & Long^{d} 237° 45' E^{t}. The Harbour was named Port Orchard, it affords excellent anchorage in every part of it, and the Country round it extremely pleasant and apparently capable of high cultivation; we lay in sight of two remarkable high Snowy Mountains, the North^{mt} of which bore N 3 E & was named Mount Baker, I having been the first person who saw it, the day after we enter'd the straits. The South^{mt} one on with the North p^{t} of Vashons Island bore S 53 E & obtained the Name of Mt Rainier. Mount Baker is in Lat^{d} 48° 39' N & Long^{d} 237° 19' E^{t}. Mount Rainier is in Lat^{d} 47° 03' N & Long^{d} 238° 24' E^{t}.

Thursday, May 31st, 1792. Light Breezes & Cloudy W^{r}. Working to gain an anchorage near the *Chatham*. The wind light & variable. At 10 fired some Guns as signals to the *Chatham*. Sent the boats ahead to tow. At 11 Anchor'd with the Small Bower in 44 F^{ms} about ½ a mile from the *Chatham*. A party employ'd hauling the Seine & other boats continuing the survey.

Friday, June 1st, 1792. Light air & calms. Emp^{d} occasionally. Made the Sign^{l} to Weigh but falling calm, did not get up the anchor til 7 PM when we weigh'd and stood with a light Breeze to the North^{d}. *Chatham* in company. At 11 made the Sign^{l} and anchored with the small Bower in 20 f^{ms}.[11] AM. Light Breezes, Weigh'd at ½ past 6 & stood up an arm taking a NNW direction in expectation of falling in with our Boats. At Noon Calm & clear W^{r}. The Western Shore bearing from N 17 W to S 69 E, an Island in the entrance S 36° E, nearest Eastern Shore N E b N 1 Mile, nearest Western Shore SW b W ½ a Mile.

Saturday, June 2nd, 1792. Light Breezes & clear W^{r}. At 2 P.M. fresh Breezes, standing up the arm with all Sail set. ½ past 2 the *Chatham* being about a mile ahead of us made the Sign^{l} for assistance having run aground, clued up the Sails & anchor'd with the small Bower in 20 f^{ms} upon the Eastern shore.[12] Hoisted out the Boats and sent them to the

---

[11] About half way between Gedney Island and Camano Head.

[12] About a mile northwest of Kayak Point.

assistance of the *Chatham*. Found the arm closed about 3 Miles to the North^{d} of where the *Chatham* lay aground by very low land from which the Mud bank extends itself. At 1 PM the *Chatham* floated & anchor'd about 2 Cables length from us-½ past 10 Light Breezes. Made the Sign^{l} to the *Chatham* & weighed with all sail set. Punish'd Jos Murgatroyd with 1 Dozen Lashes for Insolence to his superior officer. At Noon returning down the arm with a light Breeze.

Sunday, June 3rd, 1792. Light airs & clear W^{r}. At 2 came to with the small Bower in 50 f^{ms} in a small Bay[13] on the eastern shore intending to wait the return of the Boats-½ past 8 PM hearing some Musquets fired to the South^{d}, fired a Gun as an answer. At 9 the Boats came alongside having found the passages they had been examining not eligible for the Ships to return by. A.M. Cloudy W^{r} with light Breezes. Hauled the Seine with indifferent success. Muster'd the Ships Company and read the articles of War.

Monday, June 4th, 1792. Light Breezes & var^{ble} W^{r}. People occasionally Emp^{d}. Haul'd the Seine, caught a few flat fish & Salmon Trout.

Tuesday, June 5th, 1792. Light Breezes & clear W^{r}. This being the anniversary of His Majesty's Birth Day, we celebrated it by firing 21 Guns. At 2 PM Captain Vancouver landed, displayed the Union & took Possession of the Country (with the customary formalities) for his Majesty calling it by the name of New Georgia and the place we are lying in Possession Sound. Our situation now was found to be Lat^{d} 48° 00' N Long^{d} 238° 03' E^{t}. The Country in general of a Mod^{t} height, thickly covered with wood, and with but very few clear Spots. At 7 AM Weigh'd & made all sail to return into the large Sound by the same way we enter'd. *Chatham* in Company. In working down the arm, several Canoes came alongside, in which were some Chiefs. They are the first of any rank who have visited the Ship; some small presents were given them. Bent the Stream Cable to the Coasting Anchor. At Noon Mod^{t} & cloudy W^{r}. The Entrance P^{t} N 44 W, an opposite bluff P^{t} N 47 W. Observed in the Lat^{d} 47° 49' N.

Wednesday, June 6th, 1792. Mod^{t} & Cloudy. Tacked occasionally. Working out of the arm. At Midnight came to with the Small Bower in 22 f^{ms} upon the Western Shore.[14] Punish'd Jno Thomas (Seaman) with 36 Lashes for neglect of Duty. AM. At 7 Light Airs, the Ebb tide beginning to make. Made the Sign^{l} & Weigh'd at 8, passed the entrance points of this Inlet & came into the large Sound. We now steer'd for an opening bearing North. At Noon the East p^{t} of Port Discovery S 5 W & the East

[13]Tulalip Bay.

[14]Along Marrowstone Island.

Point of Protection Island S 15 W. The nearest Shore E b N 3 Miles. This large branch of the Sea, the examination of which we had now completed, was named by Captn Vancouver Admiralty Inlet. Its entrance is situated in the Lat^{d} 48° 11' N & Long^{d} 237° 33' E^{t}. It contains many Islands & several excellent Harbours affording a most secure Anchorage, but their remote situation from the Sea Coast renders it improbable that they will every be of much use to Navigators. The Country in most parts is thickly clothed with Wood, some beautiful lawns were observed on each side of the Inlet, but these were rare. It has very few inhabitants, their Manner & appearance, agree exactly with those we saw in Port Discovery. Pugets Sound which is the South^{n} Extremity of the Inlet is situated in the Lat^{d} 47° 04' N & Long^{d} 237° 18' E^{t}.

Thursday, June 7th, 1792. Calm & pleasant W^{r}. At 3 PM Anchor'd with the small Bower 20 f^{ms}. A low Sandy Island[15] bearing N 34° W, Protection Island S 24 W, Nearest Shore N 60 E 2 Miles. ½ past 7 AM weigh'd & stood to the North^{d} & at 10 Anchor'd in 37 f^{ms}. Emp^{d} Variously, *Chatham* in Company.

Friday, June 8th, 1792. Light Airs & clear W^{r}. At 6 Weigh'd & made all sail to the North^{d}. ½ past 8, falling Calm, came to with the small Bower in 37 f^{ms} & sent the Cutter & Launch away with an officer in each, to examine the Shore to the North^{d}. AM. Mod^{t} & Cloudy. Observed in the Lat^{d} 48° 29' N.

Saturday, June 9th, 1792. Light airs & var^{ble}. At 3 Weigh'd and stood in for a Bay to the North^{d} where at 6 we anchor'd with the small Bower in 16 f^{ms}. Sent a Party on shore to haul the Seine. A.M. Mod^{t} & Cloudy W^{r}. Sent the empty Casks on shore, employ'd making Nippers & puddening[16] the Best Bower Anchor. Carpenters sawing plank. A party on Shore brewing Spruce Beer.

Sunday, June 10th, 1792. Light Breezes & var^{ble}. Emp^{d} Watering. Lost one Puncheon which broke from the raft Rope. A.M. Mod^{t} & Clear W^{r}. The *Chatham* came in and anchor'd here. Completed our Water, haul'd the Seine with indifferent success. Punish'd Jno Monro & Walter Dillon with 12 lashes each for neglect of Duty. Emp^{d} on Various Duties.

Monday, June 11th, 1792. Light Airs, inclining to calm. Emp^{d} Variously. At 2 the Boats returned, having continued the survey to this Place, which was found to be a large group of Islands. AM Light Breezes & clear, at 7 Weigh'd & made all Sail, standing to the North^{d}. At 10 enter'd an extensive Sound, which appeared to lead to the North^{d}. At Noon the

---

[15]Smith Island.

[16]The act of wrapping short pieces of rope around the iron ring of an anchor in order to reduce chafe to the cable when bent or attached to the ring.

nearest land, N b E 2 Miles. Observed in the Lat[d] 48° 57' N. Our late anchorage was called Strawberry Bay. It lies in the Lat[d] 48° 37' N Long[d] 237° 33' E[t]. It possesses no particular advantages; this Archipelago however affords some excellent harbours.

Tuesday, June 12th, 1792. Mod[t] & Clear W[r]. At 6 P.M. stood into a small Bay[17] upon the Continental shore & anchor'd with the small Bower in 6 F[ms] over a muddy Bottom. From this station, Capt[n] Vancouver in the Pinnace, attended by the Launch, set out to continue this research to the North[d]. At 9 AM Weigh'd & stood farther into the Bay. ½ past, Anchor'd in 6 F[ms] & Moor'd Ships with ½ a Cable each way. The E[t] P[t] of the Bay bearing S b W, the W[t] P[t] N W b N, dist from the Shore ½ a Mile. Sent on shore the Tents & Observatory.

Wednesday, June 13th, 1792. Mod[t] & Clear W[r]. Sent the Time keepers on shore to the Observatory where they began to observe equal altitudes-Carpenters emp[d] cutting down timbers for [ ] new fishes[18] & for Plank. Sent all the empty Casks on shore & filled them from a Rivulet of excellent Water which ran at the back of the Observatory-sent the Cutter & *Chathams* launch away to examine an arm which had been left unexplored to the South[d]. At 9 the Boats returned and the Officer reported that he had seen two small vessels which appeared to be standing toward this Bay. A.M. the vessels not being in sight, the Boats were dispatched-and I was sent with a party of ten Men on board the *Chatham* who weighed & stood out of the Bay to look after the strange sails. At 10 oClock, she spoke them, they proved to be the Brig *Sutil* & Schooner *Mexicana* employed by the Spanish Government to survey this Part of the Coast, they were commanded by D[on] Dionisio Galiano & D[on] Cayetane Valdes, both Captains of frigates, in the Royal Navy. They arrived at Nootka Sound from Acapulco on the 11th of April of the present year; left it the 5th of June & entered the Strait of Juan de Fuca on the 6th. In Friendly Cove at Nootka Sound were lying the Frigates *Gertrudis*, *Concepcion*, *Aranzasa* & the Brig *Active*. D[on] Quadra, Commander. They pursued their course to the North[d] & the *Chatham* made sail to regain her former Anchorage in the Bay.

Thursday, June 14th, 1792. Mod[t] & Clear W[r]. Emp[d] Wooding & Watering, a party brewing Spruce beer, Carpenters cutting & sawing timber, Sailmakers repairing the Sails. At Noon the *Chatham* Anchor'd in the Bay & I return'd on board with the party.

Friday, June 15th, 1792. Light Breezes & Cloudy with Rain. People

---

[17]Birch Bay.

[18]A fish is a long piece of wood attached to the lower portion of a mast to provide additional support and strength.

employ'd on board & on shore in their various avocations. AM. Fair W^{r}. Cleaned the Ships.

Saturday, June 16th, 1792. Fresh Breezes & Cloudy. Emp^{d} stowing away the Wood & Water. AM. Loosed Sails to dry. At Noon furled Sails. Carpenters emp^{d} as before.

Sunday, June 17th, 1792. Fresh Breezes & Cloudy W^{r}. Emp^{d} stowing the Main Hold, Wooding, Watering, Brewing &c. The Carpenters having completed one fish, got it off & stowed the Booms. At 8 the Cutter & *Chathams* Launch returned having completed the service they were sent upon. AM Light Breezes & Clear. Muster'd the Ships Company.

Monday, June 18th, 1792. Light Airs & clear W^{r}. AM. The *Chathams* Cutter & Launch were dispatched to examine some apparent openings on the opposite shore. Emp^{d} airing the Sails, wooding, sawing plank & brewing.

Tuesday, June 19th, 1792. Light Air & Cloudy W^{r}. Emp^{d} Watering &c &c. Carpenters as before.

Wednesday, June 20th, 1792. Light Breezes & Clear. Emp^{d} on the various duties. PM. The *Chatham's* boats returned from their surveying expedition. A.M. Punish'd Henry Hankins (Cooper) with 12 Lashes for neglect of duty. Mod^{t} & clear W^{r}. Emp^{d} as before.

Thursday, June 21st, 1792. Mod^{t} & clear W^{r}. Emp^{d} stowing the hold. AM. Light Breezes & cloudy. Emp^{d} working up Junk, cutting brooms &c. Carpenters employ'd trimming another fish.

Friday, June 22nd, 1792. Light Airs, inclining to calm. Emp^{d} brewing Spruce Beer &c, Carpenters as before.

Saturday, June 23rd, 1792. Light Breezes & clear W^{r}. At 1 P.M. the Launch return'd on board having parted company with the pinnace in their return to the Ship. Emp^{d} as before. At 11 AM the Pinnace return'd, struck the Tents & Observatory, emp^{d} making preparations for Sailing-Captain Vancouver in this excursion, which has lasted ten Days, continued the examination of the continental shore, and determined its boundaries to the Lat^{d} 49° 41' N & Long^{d} 236° 17' E^{t}. On their return they fell in with & went on board the two Spanish vessels which we had before seen.

Sunday, June 24th, 1792. Mod^{t} & clear W^{r}. Emp^{d} getting the Observatory Tents & Instruments on board. At 4 P.M. [ ] Ship. AM made the sign^{l} & Weigh'd in Company with the *Chatham*. Set all Sails & stood to the West^{d} intending to take up the examination of the continent where it had been left off by the Boats. The Bay we have left obtain'd the name of Birch Bay from its abounding with the tree of that name. We found it an excellent station for all our purposes. The water was good & easy & expeditious in the filling. The plain on which our Observatory was fixed was of considerable extent & clear of Wood, affording a pleasant place of exercise for our people & likewise an abundance of wild fruit & vegetables of different kinds. The Latitude of the Observatory was found to be 48° 50 N & the Long^{d} by the mean of several Lunar Observations, 237° 36 E^{t}. Var^{n} of the Compass [left blank] E^{t}. We were visited by only one Canoe while we remained here. The people in it seemed to be of the same Nation as those in Admiralty Inlet. They stay'd but a short time along side and appear'd to be on their passage to a different part of the Sound. On a point to the NW of the Bay, which was named Cape Roberts, was the remains of a very large Village which must have been totally deserted a considerable time from its ruinous appearance.

Monday, June 25th, 1792. Mod^{t} & clear W^{r}. Standing to the N W through an extensive Sound. ½ past I saw the two Spanish vessels under sail. At ½ past 2 being near them, shorten'd Sail & brot to, the commander of the Spanish vessels came on board, fill'd & made Sail on a Wind & tack'd occasionally during the night. Had no Soundings with 100 f^{ms}. AM. Light Breezes & Clear. At Day light bore up & made Sail to the N.W., the *Chatham* & two Spanish vessels in Company. At Noon the nearest Shores bore NE & SW. The width of the Channel from side to side about 8 Miles. Observed in the Lat^{d} of 49° 36' N.

6

Zac. Mudge

Zachary Mudge, the son of John Mudge, M.D., was born at Plymouth in January 1770. He first shipped out on the *Foudroyant* in 1780 under Captain John Jervis. He was promoted to lieutenant in 1789 and the following year, was assigned to the *Discovery*.

Unable to resolve the Nootka controversy, Vancouver sent Mudge from Nootka in September 1792 to England with dispatches. He arrived in June 1793. He returned with Broughton to the NW coast in 1795 as a 1st lieutenant aboard the *Providence*. He was promoted to Commander in 1797 and Captain in 1800. Mudge commanded various ships until retiring in 1815. He was ultimately promoted to Admiral in 1849 and died at Plympton in October 1852.

Interestingly, his grandson, Henry Colton Mudge, was a lieutenant of marines aboard the *Thetis* in 1850 and participated in coastal surveys.

H	K	F	Courses	Winds	Remarks Saturday April 28th: 92 on NW Coast of America
1	4	2	NW	SWbW	Moderate and cloudy. Set Royals and Studding
2	4	"			sails.
3	4	"	NWbN		
4	5	"			
5	1	4	NW	SWbS	Hauld in D° and in reef in Topsails, set F T M^t
5	2	"	NEbN		Studding sails. Squally.
6	1	6	NbE		½ past 6 M° & Cloudy. Out reefs and set Main
6	2	2	NWbN		sails. Bent another Main Top sail.

H	K	F	Courses	Winds	Remarks Saturday April 28th: 92 on NW Coast of America
7	3	6			
8	3	4			At 8 shortn'd sail and hauld to Wind.On
9	2	"	WbN		Larbard Tack. Sounded 24 fms dark Brown
10	2	"			sand. The land in general fell Back. The Coast
11	1	6	West	South	appeared to be very showl with rocks laying off
12[1]	3	6			3 or 4 miles. Sounded occasionally from 9
1	2	4	WSW		oclock to 12–24 to 35 fms. Bottom as before.
2	1	"			Squally with rain. Sounded occasionally from
2	1	"	NbW		36 to 42 fathoms. At 2 Taken aback. Takd ship
3	"	"			and sounded 42 fms Stony bottom.
4	"	"	Head to Eastward	calm	Moderate & Cloudy.
5	4	"	NNE	ESE	
6	3	6	North	vble	Heavy rain. Taken aback. At 6 made all sail.
7	5	6	NbE	EbS	Moderate and Clear. Sounded 19 fms soft mud.
8	4	"	NbW½W		½ past sounded 16:17:10 fms.
9	2	4	NNW½W		At noon D° W^{r}. South extremes of Land S 53 E^{t}
10	2	"	NNW		North. D° N 36 E^{t}. Nearest shore N 69 E & 3
11	2	2			miles. Distruction Island N 14 W. Sounded 24
12	2	"	NW	D°	fms firm sand

Course	Distance	Lat: Obs^{d}	Long: Dk	Long Obs^{d}	Long Watch	Variation
		47°: 30' N°				

H	K	F	Courses	Winds	Remarks Sunday April 29th: 92 on NW Coast of America
1	3	"	NW	vble	Light Breezes and [ ]. Found a current setting
2	1	6	South		at the rate of 2 miles an hour Directly on Shore.
3	1	"	SSW		Let go the Small Bower in 19 fms Water. Veered
4	"	"			to half Cable. Extremes of the Land from N 34
5	"	"			W to S 50 E. Off shore 4 miles
6	"	"			
7	"	"			

[1]Mudge used an astronomical calendar which ran from noon to noon; this represented midnight of April 27.

H	K	F	Courses	Winds	Remarks Sunday April 29th: 92 on NW Coast of America
8	"	"			
9	"	"			
10	"	"			
11	"	"			
12	"	"			
1	"	"			D° Wr.
2	"	"			At 2 made sgl to Weigh.
3	"	"			At 3 Weighd and came to sail under T Gl sails.
4	2	4	NbW½W	ESE	Made all sail. ½ past saw a sail in NW.
5	3	"	NW½W		
6	3	"	NWbN		At 6 spoke the American Ship *Columbia*,
7	5	"	WbNE	NNE	brought Too and sent a Boat on Board her.
8	3	"	NNW		Found she was on the Fur Trade and had win-
9	3	"			tered on Coast, having lost her Mate and Two
9	2	6	NWbN		Men who were murdered by Natives. ½ past 8
10	5	6	NNW		Bore up & made all sail.
11	6	4	NbW	D°	At 11 shortnd sail and reeft Top sails. At ½ past
12	4	2			11 made [ ]*Chatham* signal and to lead in. Green Island N 15 E. Cape Classet N 39 E. Thick Hazey weather with much rain. Strong Breezes & Squally. At noon Nearest shore N 36 E & 2 miles. D° Wr. Thermometer 56.

Course	Distance	Lat Obsd	Long: Dk	Long Obsd	Long Watch	Variation
		47°: 30' N°				

H	K	F	Courses	Winds	Remarks Sunday April 30th: 92 In Juan De Fucas Straits
1	3	6	NbW	South	Fresh Breezes and Squally with Rain. ½ past
1	1	6	EbN	vble	Noon Enter'dJuan De Fucas Straits. Reeft
2	4	"	EbS		Topsails and set F Gl sails. found a strong Tide
3	4	4	EbN		setting out of Straits. Tackd occasionally Plying
4	4	"	ENE		up Straits. Several Canoes along side with Fish.
5	2	"	EbN		
5	2	"	SW		
6	4	"	SSW		At ½ past 6 made sigl and Anchord on the South
7	2	"	ENE	SE	Shore with Small Bower in 23 fms Water. Veer'd
8	"	"	vlbe		to ⅔ Cable. South Extreme of Entrance N 88 E

H	K	F	Courses	Winds	Remarks Sunday April 30th: 92 In Juan De Fucas Straits
9	"	"			to N 68 W. Nearest shore South half a mile.
10	"	"			
11	"	"			
12	"	"			More Moderate with Rain.
1	"	"			
2	"	"			
3	"	"			
4	"	"			
5	"	"			
6	"	"			Light airs. ½ past 6 weigh'd and made all sail
7	"	"			standing up Straights-keeping the South Shore
8	3	3	East	SW	on board.
9	3	4	E½S	WSW	
10	3	6	ESE	NW	
11	4	"	ENE		
12	3	6	D°	D°	At noon D° Wr.

Course	Distance	Lat Obsd	Long: Dk	Long Obsd	Long Watch	Variation
		48°: 15' N°				

H	K	F	Courses	Winds	Remarks Monday May 1st: 92 In Juan De Fucas Straits
1	4	"	East	West	Moderate & Cloudy.
2	5	"			
3	5	"	E½N		
4	3	"	ENE		
4	3	"			
5	5	"			
6	1	4			
6	1	4	NEbE		
7	5	"	ENE	D°	
8	"	"			At 8 anchored under a very sandy Beach on the South Shore in 14 fms soft ground. A distant Bluff N 35 Wt N 42 W. An Apparent Harbour S 50 E. An apparent Island N 87 Et. Nearest Shore South 2 miles. AM. D° Wr. Sent Two Boats with one from *Chatham* to examine the Coast. Several Canoes along side with Fish. Punish'd Jn° Munro with one Doz Lashes for Insolence. D° Wr.

Wednesday May 2nd, 1792. Fine clear W^{r}. 12[2] Boats return'd having found an excellent Harbour[3]—at 7 AM Weigh'd and at Nine Enter'd the Harbour. The Boats ahead Towing. At 10 anchored about 5 miles from Entrance in 34 fms Water over a bottom of Stiff Black Clay. Moor'd Ship a Cable each Way.

Thursday May 3rd. D^{o} W^{r}. Tents, observatory, Time Keeper & Instruments on shore with an officer and a Party of Marines. Emp^{d} cutting Wood, Watering and Brewing spruce Beer. Sailmakers crop banding & Repairing Sails. Sent T G^{l} Mast on Deck. [condemnd] Top Mast Back Stays (being Rotten). Got new one [ ] Head. Draught of Water 13 Foot F^{d}, 14 D^{o} Aft. Gunner on Shore drying Powder.

Friday May 4th. D^{o} W^{r}. Seamen repairing Rigging. People emp^{d} as above. AM. D^{o} W^{r}. 5 canoes along side with Fish Venison &c. Two Carpenters sent on board *Chatham* to Caulk her. Others stopping a Leak in Larboard Bow.

Saturday May 5th. D^{o} W^{r}. People emp^{d} as above. Sway'd aft T. Galt Mast. AM. D^{o} W^{r}.

Sunday May 6th. Moderate and Clear. People emp^{d} as before. Black'd yards.

Monday May 7th. Moderate and Foggy. Cap^{n} with Two Boats arm'd with one from *Chatham* set off on a surveying expedition. Emp^{d} on shore as before and taking on board 20 Tons of Pebble Ballast.

Tuesday May 8th. M^{o} & Cloudy. Emp^{d} as before and surveying Harbour. At 5 heard report of a gun Inland (NE) and another at 7. Supposing to be from our Boats.

Wednesday May 9th. Fine pleasant W^{r}. Emp^{d} as before. AM. Light airs and variable with much rain.

Thursday May 10th. These 24 Hours constant Rain. Emp^{d} receiving Wood Water & Ballast.

Friday May 11th. Light airs and clear. Completed Ballast. Ships Draft of Water 14 F Forward, Aft D 15 F having rec'd 20 Tons Pebble. Emp^{d} as before. 4 Canoes along side with various skins, fish, Roots, &c &c. Punishd Jno Bull (Marine) for insolence to his superior officer with 1 Doz Lashes.

Saturday May 12th. M^{o} & Cloudy. Heard several guns in NE. Supposed to be from Boats surveying. Emp^{d} in general as before and surveying Harbour. AM. Rain at Times.

Sunday May 13th. Moderate & Cloudy. Black'd Bends, [Round] up Cable and clean'd [Tiers] &c &c &c. AM. D^{o} W^{r}.

---

[2] I.e., midnight, May 1.

[3] Discovery Bay.

Monday May 14th. D° Wr. The Carpenters return'd from caulking *Chatham* and Empd them on our Counter. The rest of the People Empd as usual.

Tuesday May 15th. These 24 hours little Wind with constant Rain. Empd as usual.

Wednesday May 16th. D° Wr. At 3 PM the Capt returnd with Boats. Sailmakers Empd making a new F T Mt Staysail. A Canoe with Natives along side.

Thursday May 17th. Cloudy with Rain. Empd getting ready for sea. Bent Sails. D° Wr.

Friday May 18th. Cloudy with Rain. [ ] Observatory & Tents from Shore together with astronomical Instruments &c &c &c and unmoored ship. AM. Weighd with a light air. Standing out of Harbour. Boats towing. At noon East point of Harbour NE ½ a mile. Lost a Puncheon. [ ] Water East. D° Wr.

H	K	F	Courses	Winds	Remarks Saturday May 19th: 92 In Juan De Fuca Straights
1	2	4	NbE	WSW	Moderate & Cloudy.
2	2	4			
3	2	ENE			
3	2	4	SE		
4	5	"			At 4 sounded 100 fms No Ground. At ½ past
5	"	"			4 anchor'd in a Branch Leading towards Juan
6	"	"			De Fucas Straights in 28 fms off shore ½ Mile.
7	"	"			
8	"	"			
9	"	"			
10	"	"			
11	"	"			
12	"	"			D° Wr.
1	"	"			
2	"	"			
3	"	"			
4	"	"			
5	"	"			Light Breezes and Clear. In weighing carried
6	"	"			away Fore Top SailYard. Found it to be an old [
7	"	"			] Main D° and set sail as before standing up arm
8	"	"			with every Thing set. At Noon Western extreme
9	1	"	SEbS	vble	on Larboard Shore N 58 W. South Extreme S 28
10	3	2	SE		E. Western Extreme on Larboard shore in one

H	K	F	Courses	Winds	Remarks Saturday May 19th: 92 In Juan De Fuca Straights
11	4	"	SEbE		with theWestern D° on Larboard D° South
12	4	"	EbS		Extreme S 20 E. D° Wr.

Course	Distance	Lat Obsd	Long: Dk	Long Obsd	Long Watch	Variation
		47°: 59 N°				

H	K	F	Courses	Winds	Remarks Saturday May 20th: 92 In Juan De Fuca Straights
1	4	"	SbE½E	NW	Moderate & Clear.
2	4	2			
3	4	4			Shortn'd sail and hauld round an Island[4] and
4	4	"			came too in 35 fms Water with Best Bower. Off
5	"	"			shore 2 miles.
6	"	"			
7	"	"			
8	"	"			
9	"	"			
10	"	"			
11	"	"			
12	"	"			D° Wr. Sent the Launch & Cutter away to exam-
1	"	"			ine the opening to the Southward.
2	"	"			
3	"	"			
4	"	"			
5	"	"			
6	"	"			
7	"	"			At 8 Weighd and shifted our Birth nearer the
8	"	"			Northern Shore. Came too as before.
9	"	"			
10	"	"			
11	"	"			
12	"	"			D° Wr.

Course	Distance	Lat Obsd	Long: Dk	Long Obsd	Long Watch	Variation

Monday May 21th. Light Breezes and clear. Empd occasionally. Sent Carpenters on Shore to make two New Top sail yds. Empd Fishing Brewing &c. Canoes along side.

Tuesday May 22nd. D° Wr. Empd as before. AM. Light Breezes with Rain. At 9 fine Wr. Dry'd Sails. People Empd as above. Sailmakers repairing Sails. D° Wr.

---

[4]Restoration Point. The island referenced is Blake as the expedition did not recognize Bainbridge as an island.

Wednesday May 23rd. First Part Light Breezes and Clear. Middle Fresh Breezes and Squally with heavy rain attended by Thunder and Lightening. Punish'd Jno Butters & George Raybold the first with 3 Doz Lashes the sd with Two Doz for theft. AM. Light Breezes and Pleasant Wr. Dryd Sails. Sent Empty Casks on Shore. Empd as before. Several canoes along side—

Thursday May 24th. Squally with Rain. AM. Do Wr. Latter Part Mo & clear. People Empd about Rigging Fishing Brewing &c &c. Carpenters making a new T Gl Mast & T Gl yd. Sailmakers on Sails.

Friday May 25th. Light Breezes and Clear. Empd as before. AM. Do Wr. Cropt a new F Topsail yd and Bent Sail.

Saturday May 26th. Do Wr. Empd occasionally. Anchored here *Chatham*. The Capt with Two Boats went to Examine the arm to Southward. People Empd as before. At 9 weighed and shifted our Birth.

Sunday May 27th. Do Wr. Empd occasionally. AM. At 1 Launch & Cutter returned. Mustd Ships Co.

Monday May 28th. Moderate and Cloudy. AM. Saild *Chatham* accompanied by Launch and an officer on a surveying Expedition. Do Wr.

Tuesday May 29th. Moderate & Cloudy with Rain at Times. AM. Do Wr. Fired 17 guns being Anniversary of King Charles Restoration. Empd Watering, Brewing Fishing &c as before.

Wednesday May 30th. Light Breezes & Cloudy. Boats return'd at ½ past 8 Weighed and came to Sail. Made all Sail standing to Northward out of the Arm. Village Point S 32 Et. Punish'd Wm Woodson (seaman) with 2 Doz Lashes for Insolence to his superior officer—

Thursday May 31st. Light Breezes & Cloudy. Empd working up Branch. At 9 Fired 3 guns to denote our situation which was ansd by the *Chatham*. At 11 anchored in 32 fms Water a Cable Length off shore. Empd occasionally.

Friday June 1st. Light Breezes inclinable to calm. Empd occasly. At 7 Weigh'd and came to Sail standing to Northward. *Chatham* in Co. At 11 came Too with the Small Br in 26 fms. AM. Light Breezes. At ½ past 6 Weigh'd and came to Sail under Top sails & T Gl Sails standing up a Northern arm. At Noon Calm. Western Shore from N 22 W to S 20 Et. Eastern Shore from No 17 Wt to S 69 E. An Island in Entrance S 31 Et to S 41 E. Nearest Eastern Shore NEbN 1 mile. Nearest Wn Shore SWbW ½ Mile.

Saturday June 2nd. Light Breezes and Clear. Standing to the NW. At ½ past 2 came too with Small Bower in 20 fms Water. Observed [the] *Chatham* with the sigl of Distress and in want of immediate assistance. Sent all Boats to her assistance with an officer. Fresh Breezes & Squally with Rain. At 1 the *Chatham* got off having laid on shore during Tide. At

½ past 10 made sig^{l} and Weighed Standing out of the arm. Punished Jos Murgatroyd (seaman) with 12 Lashes for insolence. Fird a gun to denote our Situation to the Boats that were away. At Noon Light Airs. Standing out of arm to Southward.

Sunday June 3rd. D^{o} W^{r}. Came too with the Small Bower in 50 fms Water. At 8 fird 2 guns to denote our Situation which was answe'd by the Boats which came on Board at 9. AM. Emp^{d} occasionally. Read the Articles of War to Ships C^{o}. A Party Fishing.

Monday June 4th. Light Breezes and Cloudy. Emp^{d} occasionally. A Party Fishing-and Wooding.

Tuesday June 5th. D^{o} W^{r}. Fired 21 guns it being the anniversary of his Maj^{y} Birth Day. AM-Moderate and Cloudy. At 7 Weigh'd & came to sail under T G^{l} Sails running out of the arm-several Canoes along side. D^{o} W^{r}. At Noon Entrance Point N 44 W. Opposite Bluff N 47 W. *Chatham* in C^{o}.

Wednesday June 6th. D^{o} W^{r}. Tack'd occasionally working out of the Arm. At 12 came Too in 22 fms Water to [Stop] Tide. At 7 AM Weigh'd. [ ] Emp^{d} Working out of the arm. Bent the stream Cable and got anchor over side. Punish'd Jno Thomas with 3 Doz Lashes for Neglect of Duty. At Noon standing to Northward. E^{t} Point of Port Discovery S 3 W. East Point of Protection Island S 15 W. Dungeness Point S 54 W. Nearest shore EbN. An opening for which we were steering North.

Thursday June 7th. Calm Pleasant W^{r}. At 3 Anchored in 20 fms Water. Sandy Island N 34 W. Protection S 24 W^{t}. Nearest shore S[5] 60 E^{t} 2 miles. At ½ past 7 Weigh'd and at 10 Anchor'd in 37 fms Water. Emp^{d} occasionally. *Chatham* in C^{o}.

Friday June 8th. Light Airs and Pleasant W^{r}. At ½ past 6 Weigh'd and came to sail under T G^{l} sails standing for an opening in NW. ½ past 8 calm. Came Too with Small B^{r} in 37 fms Water. Sent 2 Boats with an officer (L^{t} P) to examine the arm to Northward. AM. D^{o} W^{r}. People Emp^{d} Working up [ ]. Carpenters cutting and sawing Plank. Lat Obs^{d} 48°:29' N^{o}.

Saturday June 9th. D^{o} W^{r}. Weigh'd and Stood in for a Bay to Northward. At 6 came too in 16 fms Water. Sent to haul the Seine. AM. M^{o} & Cloudy. Sent the empty Casks on shore. Brewers on shore brewing Spruce Beer. The rest of People Emp^{d} variously.

Sunday June 10th. Light Breezes and Variable. Emp^{d} filling and [Rafting] off Water. Lost 1 Puncheon from [ ]. M^{o} & clear. Anchor'd here the *Chatham*. [ ]. Punish'd Jno Monro and Walter Dillon with 1 Doz each for Neglect of Duty. Brewers-Carpenters-&c &c Emp^{d} as before.

---

[5] He meant N.

Monday June11th. Light airs inclinable to calm. People Emp^{d} as above. At 2 Boats returned. AM Light airs and clear. Weigh'd and came to sail under T G^{l} sails. Running up an Arm Leading to Northward. At Noon nearest Land NbE 2 miles-Lat ob^{s} 48°:51' N°.

Tuesday June 12th. Moderate and Clear. At ½ past 6 brought Too in 6 fms Water. The Capt with Two Boats went on a surveying Expedition. Sent the Tents, observatory &c &c &c on Shore with a Party of Marines-at 9 Weigh'd and came to sail under T G^{l} sails-Stood further in to the Bay. ½ past brought too with the Small Bower in 6 fms Water. Veer'd away and Moored Ship half Cable each Way. Sent the Empty Casks on Shore. Brewers &c &c.

Wednesday June 13th. D° W^{r}. Emp^{d} Wooding, Fishing and Watering. Carpenters on Shore Cutting two New [Fishes] for the Lower Mast. Sent the Cutter and *Chathams* Launch with the Master to survey an arm to Southward-at 9 the Boats returned in Consequence of seeing Two Vessels Standing out of the southern Arm they were of Explore. Sent out the Large Cutter under the Land to see which way they were standing. At 10 the Boats returned having seen nothing of the Vessels-but saw their Lights by which they had [passed]. AM. Fresh Breezes & squally-Vessels not in sight. [ ] with a Party and the *Chatham* who Weigh'd and stood after them. At 11 saw the *Chatham* [ ] a Brigg and Schooner with Spanish Colours-Flying. Sent the Master with 2 Boats to explore southern Arm. D° W^{r}.

Thursday June 14th. Moderate and Cloudy. Emp^{d} Wooding-Watering-and Brewing. Seamen Emp^{d} overhauling and repairing [ ]. Carpenters on Shore as before, Sailmakers repairing the sails.-at Noon *Chatham* returned and anchored in Bay.

Friday June 15th. Light Breezes with Rain. Emp^{d} as before. AM. M° & clear-Emp^{d} as usual.

Saturday June 16th. Fresh Breezes and Cloudy. Emp^{d} receiving and stowing away Wood, Water &c. AM. Dried sails. Carpenters Emp^{d} as before. D° W^{r}.

Sunday June 17th. D° W^{r}. People Emp^{d} as above. [ ] one Fish and Stow'd the Booms-at 8 the Boats with Master return'd. AM. D° W^{r}.

Monday Junc 18th. Light airs and Clear. Sent away the *Chathams* Launch with her Master and our Cutter to survey an Arm to the Southward. Got out and air'd all the New Sails Canvas-[ ] &c &c &c. Carpenters cutting Plank. Brewers Brewing.

Tuesday June 19th. Light airs and Cloudy. Emp^{d} Watering Cutting Wood, Brewing &c &c. AM. D° W^{r}.

Wednesday June 20th. Light Breezes and Clear. Emp^{d} as above. *Chathams* Boats returned having finish'd their survey. Punish'd Hen^{y}

Hankins (seaman) with 12 lashes for neglect of Duty. People Emp^{d} working up [ ]. AM. D^{o} W^{r}.

Thursday June 21st. Pleasant W^{r}. the People Emp^{d} at their various occupations as above. AM. D^{o} W^{r}.

Friday June 22nd. D^{o} W^{r}. The [ ] and seamen Emp^{d} occasionally. AM. M^{o} & cloudy.

Saturday June 23rd. Light Breezes and pleasant W^{r}. The Launch return'd. Emp^{d} as before. At 11 the Capt return'd from his expedition. Struck observatory-Tents &c &c.

Sunday June 24th. M^{o} & clear. The astronomical Instruments, Tents-Observatory &c &c on board-AM. D^{o} W^{r}. Unmoor'd ship, Weighed and came to sail under T G^{l} Sails. At Noon standing to Westward. *Chatham* in C^{o}. D^{o} W^{r}.

Monday June 25th. Moderate and Clear. Running up a Large NW arm. ½ past I saw the Two Spanish Vessels. ½ past 2 shortn'd sail & hove Too. At 3 Spanish Captains came on Board. Don Galiano and Don Valdez. Both Capt of Frigates in Spanish Navy. Fill'd and stood under Topsails. Made and shortn'd sail occasionally running up the Large Arm. At Noon nearest Shore NW and NE 8 Miles Over-Lat Obs^{d} 49°: 36' N^{o}

7

John A. Browne

Little is know about John Browne. According to Vancouver's muster table, he was seventeen years old when he joined the *Discovery* and hailed from London. He was promoted to midshipman during the exploration.

THE LOG OF THE PROCEEDINGS OF HIS MAJESTIES SHIP DISCOVERY GEO VANCOUVER ESQ, COMMANDER JOHN AISLEY BROWNE

April Saturday 28th 1792. Moderate & Cloudy. Set royals & studding sails. At 8 reef'd the topsails & in studding sails & royals. Hauled to the Wind & sounded 24 fm dark brown Sand. N. Extreme of the Land NWbN. S extreme S 77 E. Nearest land N 40 E. Sounded occasionally from 24 to 36 fm fine brown sand. Taken aback. At 2 made the signal & tacked. Sounded 40 fm Rocky bottom. At 4 Sounded 42 fm brown Sand. N extreme of the Land NWbN. S extreme [left blank]. At 5 heavy rain. Taken aback. Set the Main Sail out 1st reef of the topsails. Set Royals & Studding sails. Moderate & clear. Sounded 19 fm soft mud. Sounded 18 fm at Noon. S extreme S 53 E. N extreme N 36 E. Nearest shore N 69 E 3 miles. Destruction Island N 14 W. N point of D° N 17 W.

April Sunday 29th 1792. Light Breezes & hazy. Found a currant setting us on the Shore. Let go the Small bower in 19 fm & veered to ½ a cable. Extremes of the land from N 34 W to S 50 E. Off Shore 4 miles. Made the signals to Weigh. At 3 weighed & came to sail under topsails & TG sails. Made sail. Saw a sail in the NW at 6. Spoke the *Columbia* of Boston. Brought too. Hoisted out the Cutter & sent an Officer on board. Boat returned. Bore up and made sail. At 11 in studding sails & royals. On 1st reef of the topsails. At noon made the *Chatham* Signal to lead in.

Green Island from N 17 E to N 13 E. Cape Classet N 29 E. Nearest shore NEbE 2 miles.

April Monday 30th 1792. Fresh Breezes and squally with rain. Several canoes alongside. ½ past 12 in 2nd reef of the topsails. ½ past out reefs. Moderate with heavy rain. ½ past 2 tacked. Sounded 34 fm soft bottom. At 6 tacked. ½ past made the signal & Anchored in 23 fm veered to ⅔ of a cable. S extreme W 88 E. N extreme N 68 W. Nearest shore S ½ a mile. Moderate with rain. Light airs. ½ past 7 weighed & came to Sail under topsails & T G Sails. Set studding & Royals. At 8 Light breezes & cloudy. Light Breezes & clear.

May Tuesday 1st 1792. Moderate & Cloudy. At 8 anchored under a long ridge of sand on the S shore in 14 fm soft sand with these bearings. Distant low bluff N 35 W. Low point N 42 W. Flat bluff S 50 E. S point of apparent sound S 85 E. W point of app^{t} Island N 76 E. Nearest shore S 2 miles. Sent two boats & one from the *Chatham* to find a harbour. Several canoes alongside with fish. Punished Jno. Munro with 18 lashes for Insolence.

Wednesday, 2. Fine clear W^{r}. ½ past 12 the boats returned having found a good harbour. At 7 AM. Weighed & at 9 entered the harbour with a light air. At 10 anchored about 5 miles from the Entrance in 34 fm stiff black sand. Moored with the following bearings. Entrance point N 48 W. Centre of Protection Island N 50 W. W entry point N 54 W. Observatory point S 60 W one Cable distance.

Thursday, 3. Fine pleasant W^{r}. Sent the tents and Observatory on Shore with the time keepers & Instruments with an Officer and a party of Marines. Empl^{d} wooding & brewing Spruce beer. Got down T G [masts]. Draught of water Forward 13 ft aft 14 ft. Got the Powder on Shore today.

Friday, 4. D^{o} W^{r}. Emp^{d} occasionally. AM came alongside 5 Canoes with some fish & venison. Sent 2 Carpenters to assist on board the *Chatham*. The others stoping a leak in Lar^{b} bow.

Saturday, 5. Fitted new topmast Backstays and got up T G masts. Empl^{d} as before.

Sunday, 6. D^{o} W^{r}. Emp^{d} blacking the Yard.

Monday, 7. D^{o} W^{r}. AM. Capt Vancouver with two boats & one from the *Chatham* went on a surveying expedition. Sailmaker repairing the sails. Empl^{d} taking on board Pebble ballast.

Tuesday, 8. Moderate and cloudy. A boat surveying the harbour. At 5 AM heard the report of a gun from the N & E. Another at 7. Supposed to be from our boats.

Wednesday, 9. PM. Fine W^{r}. Emp^{d} wooding & watering. AM. Much rain.

Thursday, 10. The last 24 hours constant rain. Taking on board water & ballast.

Friday, 11. Light airs & cloudy. Taking on board wood & water. Compleated the ballast having taken on 20 tons. Sailmakers repairing the sails & Seamen on the rigging. 4 Canoes alongside. Punished Tomes Bull with 12 lashes for Insolence.

Saturday, 12. Moderate and cloudy. Heard the report of several guns in the SE. Emp^{d} occasionally. Much rain.

Sunday, 13. Having compleated our ballast the draught of water forward 13.10 aft 10 ft. Light winds and cloudy. Blacking the bends. Got the cables up & cleaned below.

Monday, 14. Moderate & cloudy. Carpenters return^{d} from the *Chatham*. Emp^{d} them caulking the counter.

Tuesday, 15. Light airs with constant rain. Emp^{d} wooding & watering.

Wednesday, 16. Much rain. At 3 PM the boats returned. Sailmakers emp^{d} on the sails. One canoe alongside.

Thursday, 17. Cloudy with rain. Getting ready for sea.

Friday, 18. D^{o} W^{r}. Struck the Tents & Observatory. Got them on board with the Instruments. Unmoored. AM. Weighed & came to sail with a light Breeze from the SE. Tacking occasionally. At noon the E point of the harbour NE ½ a mile. Lost a puncheon which broke from the raft rope.

[1]Moderate & Cloudy. At 4 Sounded 100 fm no ground. ½ past anchored in a branch [ ] for Juan de Fuca's streights in 28 fm off shore 2 mile. Light Breezes and Clear. 3/4 past 8 weighed & came to sail. Carried away the foretopsail yard in the slings. Unbent the sail & [swayed] up a M^{n} topsl yard in its place. Set the topsails and studding sails. At noon the W extreme Lar^{b} shore N 59 E / S / S 29 E. W extreme on Sta^{r} Shore in one with [ ].

May Sunday 20th 1792. Moderate & clear. In studding sails. ½ past 6 came too with the best bower in 35 fm. Sent the Cutter & Launch with an officer in each to explore an opening to S^{o}. ½ past 8 weighed and came to sail under stay sails. At 9 brought too in 25 fm with the best bower.

Monday, 21. Light breezes and clear. Emp^{d} occasionally. Carpenters making two new topsail yards. Several canoes alongside. Emp^{d} brewing & fishing.

Tuesday, 22. Light Breezes with rain. Emp^{d} as before. Fair W. Loosed sails to dry.

Wednesday, 23. Furled sails. Fresh breezes & squally with heavy rain thunder & lightening. AM. Light breezes & clear. Loosed sails to dry.

---

[1]The date, left blank, was Saturday, May 19.

Sent the empty water casks on Shore. Punished Ja^{s} Butters & Geo Raybold with 2 doz lashes for theft. Several canoes alongside.

Thursday, 24. Furl Sails. Squally with rain. Lost two puncheons which broke from the raft rope. AM. Fine W^{r}. Emp^{d} occasionally. Carpent on shore.

Friday, 25. Light breezes & clear. Got a fore topsail yard up & bent the sail.

Saturday, 26. D^{o} W^{r}. Anchored near the *Chatham*. AM. Capt Vancouver with a boat and one from the *Chatham* went on a surveying expedition. Emp^{d} as before. At 9 Weighed & shifted nearer in Shore. Some canoes alongside.

Sunday, 27. D^{o} W^{r}. Emp^{d} occasionally. The boats returned. Musterd ships company.

Monday, 28. Moderate & Cloudy. Sail^{d} the *Chatham* accompanied by our launch with an officer. Emp^{d} as before.

Tuesday, 29. Moderate & Cloudy with rain at times. AM. D^{o} W^{r}. Emp^{d} occas. Fired 17 guns it being the anniversary of King Charles restoration.

Wednesday, 30. D^{o} W^{r}. At 9 AM weighed & made sail standing to the North. Village point S 3 E. Punished Wm Woodson with 24 lashes for Insolence.

Thursday, 31. D^{o} W^{r}. Working up a narrow arm. Fired 3 guns as signals to the *Chatham* to denote her situation. Found the *Chatham* at 9 anchored with the small bower in 35 fm. Emp^{d} hauling the Seine.

Friday, June 1. Light Airs inclinable to calm. At 7 Weighed and came to sail with a light breeze standing to the North. At 11 made the *Chathams* signal & came to with the small bower in 20 fm. ½ past 6 AM Weighed and came to sail up a northern arm. At noon calm. The West^{rn} Shore from N 22 E[2] to S 20 E. Eastern shore N 17 W to S 69 E. An Island in the Entrance from S 31 E to S 41 E. Nearest East^{n} shore NEbN 1 mile. West^{n} D^{o} SWbW ½ a mile.

Saturday, 2. D^{o} W^{r}. Standing to the NW^{d}. ½ past 2 came two [sic] in 20 fm. The *Chatham* having run on Shore a little to N^{d} of us. Hoisted out the boats & sent them to her assistance. AM. Moderate & cloudy with rain. At 1 the *Chatham* got off. At 10 made the signal and weighed. Punished Jos Murgatroyd with 12 lashes for insolence. Fired a gun to denote our situation to the boats. Not ans^{d}. At noon standing to the West^{d}.

Sunday, 3. Inclinable to calm. At 2 came too in 50 fm. At 8 fired 2 guns to denote our situation to the boats. At 9 the boats returned. Mustered the ships company. Emp^{d} hauling the seine.

---

[2]He meant W.

Monday, 4. Light breezes & v[ble]. Emp[d] occasionally. A party hauling the Seine.

Tuesday, 5. Light breezes and Cloudy. Fired 21 guns it being the anniversary of H Majesties birth day. At 7 AM weighed standing out of the arm. Several canoes alongside. Entrance pt N 44 W. Opposite bluff N 47 W. *Chatham* in company. Lat[d] obs 47.49 N.

Wednesday, 6. Moderate & cloudy. Working out of the arm. At 12 came too in 22 fm. At 7 made the signal & weighed. Working out of the arm. Star[d] entrance West Larb[d] N 60 W. At 11 passed over a bank with 10 fm water on it. Bent the stream cable. Punished Jno Thomas with 36 lashes for neglect of duty. Standing to the north[d] with a light breeze. East point of Port Discovery S 3 W. E point of Protection Island S 15 W. Dungeness p[t] S 54 W. Nearest shore EbN. Opening for which we steered NE.

Thursday, 7. Calm & fine W[r]. At 3 anchored in 20 fm. Sandy Island N 34 West. Protection Island S 24 W. Nearest shore N 60 E 2 miles. ½ past 7 weighed. At 10 anchored in 37 fm. Emp[d] occasionally.

Friday, 8. Light airs. ½ past 7 weighed. Standing for an Inlet in the NW[d]. ½ past 2 came to in 37 fm. Sent the Cutter and launch with an officer in each to examine an opening to the N[d]. Emp[d] occasionally. Lat[d] obs[d] 48° 29' N.

Saturday, 9. Light airs and v[ble]. At 3 weighed and stood in for a Bay to the North[d]. At 6 came too in 16 fm. Sent a party on shore to haul the Seine. Sent the empty casks on shore. Emp[d] brewing Spruce Beer.

Sunday, 10. D[o] W[r]. Lost a puncheon which broke from the raft rope. Anchored here the *Chatham*. Punished Jno Monro and Walter Dillon with 12 lashes each for neglect of duty.

Monday, 11. Light breezes and clear. At 2 the boats returned. Weighed running up an arm leading to the North[d]. At noon nearest shore NbE 2 mi. Lat[d] obs 48° 51.'

Tuesday, 12. Moderate and clear. Emp[d] Wooding Watering & fishing. ½ past 6 brought too in 6 fm. AM. Capt Vancouver with the Pinnace and launch went on a surveying expedition. Sent on Shore the Tents & observatory. ½ past 9 weighed & stood farther up the bay & anchored in 6 fm. Moored ½ a cable each way.

Wednesday, 13. D[o] W[r]. Emp[d] occasionally. Sent the Cutter with the *Chathams* launch to survey an arm to the South[d]. At 9 the boats returned having seen two vessels standing towards the Ship. AM. The vessels not being in sight the *Chatham* with a party of our hands & an officer stood in search of them. At 6 sent the Boats away again.

Thursday, 14. Moderate and Cloudy. Emp[d] Watering Wooding & Brewing. At noon the *Chatham* anchored in the Bay having spoke to the Vessels which were two small Spanish Brigs.

Friday, 15. Light Breezes with rain. AM. Fair W^{r}. Emp^{d} cleaning the Ship.

Saturday, 16. D^{o} W^{r}. Emp^{d} stowing away wood & water. Dried Sails.

Sunday, 17. Fresh breezes & cloudy. At 8 the Cutter returned. AM. Mustered ships company.

Monday, 18. Light airs & Clear. AM. Sent away the *Chathams* cutter and Launch to complete the survey of arm to the Southward.

Tuesday, 19. D^{o} W^{r}. Emp^{d} Wooding &c. Carpenters cutting logs for plank.

Wednesday, 20. D^{o} W^{r}. Emp^{d} as before. The *Chathams* boats returned. AM. Punished Henry Hankins with 12 lashes for neglect of duty. Emp^{d} [ ].

Thursday, 21. Light Breezes & cloudy. Employed occasionally.

Friday, 22. Light airs. Emp^{d} brooming brewing &c. Carpenters as before.

Saturday, 23. Fine pleasant W^{r}. At 1 the launch returned. Emp^{d} as before. At [ ] the Pinnace returned. Struck the Tents & Observatory.

Sunday, 24. D^{o} W^{r}. Emp^{d} getting the Observatory & tents on board. Unmooring Ship. AM weighed. Standing to the West^{d}. *Chatham* in company.

Monday, 25. Moderate & clear. Standing up a large NW arm. ½ past 1 saw the two Spanish vessels. ½ past 2 shortened sail & the two Captains came on board. Running up an arm to the NW. At Noon the nearest shores SW & NE 8 miles.

8

Spelman Swaine

Spelman Swaine initially was a master's mate aboard *Discovery* but became and able bodied seaman in June 1791. He became master aboard *Chatham* in August 1792 and returned to *Discovery* as 3rd lieutenant the following month. Vancouver promoted him to 2nd lieutenant in November 1794. Swaine was promoted to lieutenant in 1795 and commander in 1802. That year he saw service in the Mediterranean aboard the *Raven*. He received a promotion to captain on May 1810.

Swaine continued service to the Admiralty and eventually reached the rank of Rear Admiral. He died January 14, 1848, in Wisbech St. Peters.

A LOG OF THE PROCEEDINGS OF HIS MAJESTY'S SHIP *DISCOVERY* GEORGE VANCOUVER ESQ^{R} COMMANDER COMMENCING DECEMBER 18 1790 AND ENDING THE 30TH OF AUGUST 1792 KEPT BY SPELMAN SWAINE

Saturday, April 28th, 1792. Moderate Breezes and Cloudy. Made Sail. Unbent the Main topsail and bent another. Shortn'd Sail and haul'd our Wind. Sounded in 24 f^{m} brown Sand. North Extreme of the Land NWbN South. D^{o} S 77° E. Nearest land N 40° E. Sounded during the Night from 24 to 42 f^{ms}. Taken aback at 2. Made the Signal and tack'd. Heavy Rain. Taken aback. Made Sail. Moderate and Clear. Sounded in 17 f^{m} soft mud. At Noon South Extreme S 53° E North D^{o} N 36° E. Nearest shore N 69° E 3 Miles. Destruction Island N 14° W.

Saturday [sic], April 29th, 1792. Light Breezes and Hazey. Found a Current setting us in shore. Let go the small Bower Anchor in 19 f^{m} and veer'd to ½ a Cable. Extremes of the Land from N 34° W to S 30° E. Off Shore 4 Miles. Light Breezes and Cloudy. At 3 made the Signal and weigh'd and made sail. Saw a Sail in the NW. At 6 spoke the *Columbia*, of Boston. Brought too. Hoist the Cutter out and sent an Officer on Board. At 8 the Cutter returned. Bore up and made Sail. At 11 shortn'd Sail and in first reef Topsails. At Noon Green Island from N 17° E to N 13° E. Cape Classet N 39° E. nearest shore NEbE 2 Miles.

Saturday [sic], April 30th, 1792. Fresh and Squally with rain. ½ past 12 in 2nd reef Topsails and haul'd into Juan De Fuca's St. Moderate with rain. Out 2nd reef and set top gallant Sails. ½ past 5 tack'd. Sounded in 34 f^{m} soft bottom. At 6 tack'd. ½ past made the Signal and anchor'd with the small Bower in 23 f^{m}. South Entrance N 88° E. North D^{o} N 68° W. Nearest Shore South ½ a Mile. Light airs and Clear. At 7 weigh'd and made sail.

Tuesday May 1st, 1792. Moderate and Cloudy. At 8 anchor'd under a long ridge of Sand on the South Shore in 14 f^{m} soft sandy Bottom. Distant low bluff N 35° W. Low p^{t} N 42° W. Nearest Shore South 2 Miles. AM. Sent two Boats and one from the *Chatham* to examine the Coast for a Harbor. Several Canoes alongside. Punished John Munroe with 18 Lashes for Insolence.

Wednesday 2nd. Fine Clear Weather. At 12 the Boats return'd having found a Harbor. At 7 AM weigh'd and at 9 entered the Harbor. Boats ahead towing. At 10 anch^{d} about 5 Miles from the Entrance in 34 f^{m} stiff black Clay. Moor'd Ship.

Thursday 3rd. Light Breeses and Clear. Sent the Tents Observatory Time Keepers and Instruments on Shore with an Officer and party of Marines. Employ'd wooding & Brewing Spruce Beer. Sailmakers repairing the Main Topsail and adding Crossbands to it. Got down the Top gallant Masts. Cut out a new set of Main and Fore Topmast Backstays. Draught of Water Forward 13 feet. Aft 14 feet.

Friday 4th. Light Breeses and pleasant Weather. Seamen repairing the Rigging. AM. Came alongside five Canoes with Fish and Venison. Sent two Carpenters on board the *Chatham* to assist in Caulking. The others employ'd stopping a leak in the Larboard Bow. Gunners drying Powder.

Saturday 5th. D^{o}. Weather. Got the new Backstays overhead and sway'd up the Top gallant Masts. People on shore employ'd as before.

Sunday 6th. D^{o}. Weather. Employ'd blacking the Yards and overhauling the rigging.

Monday 7th. Light Breeses and Cloudy. AM. Captain Vancouver with two Boats and one from the *Chatham* left the Ship on a surveying Expedition. Sailmakers repairing the Fore topsail and adding crossbands to it. Employ'd taking on board Pebble Ballast.

Tuesday 8th. D^{o}. Weather. Employ'd as before and surveying the Harbor. At 5 AM heard the report of a Gun to the NE and another at 7. Supposed from our Boats.

Wednesday 9th. Light Breeses and variable. Employ'd wooding and Watering.

Thursday 10th. Light airs with heavy rain. Sailmakers employ'd as before. Employ'd taking in Water and Ballast.

Friday 11th. Light airs and Cloudy. Completed the Ballast to 20 Ton. Employ'd Wooding and Watering. Seamen employ'd about the rigging. Sailmakers upon the Main topsail. Came alongside four Canoes. Punish'd John Bull with 12 lashes for Insolence.

Saturday 12th. Moderate and Cloudy with frequent showers of Rain. Employ'd as before. Sailmakers repairing the Mainsail and adding Crossbands to it.

Sunday 13th. Light airs and Cloudy. Black'd the Bends. Haul'd up the Cables and wash'd the Tiers with Vinegar.

Monday 14th. Moderate and Cloudy. Sailmakers adding Crossbands to the Foresail and repairing it. Came on board the Caulkers from the *Chatham* and began to Caulk our Counter.

Tuesday 15th. Light Airs and Variable with rain. Employ'd Wooding and Watering.

Wednesday 16th. Little Wind with rain. At 3 the Boats returned. Sailmakers making a new fore Topmast Staysail. One Canoe alongside.

Thursday 17th. Cloudy with rain. Employ'd getting ready for Sea. AM. Bent Sails.

Friday 18th. Light Airs and Cloudy with rain. Struck the Tents and Observatory and sent them on board with the Instruments. Unmoor'd Ship. AM. Weigh'd and came to Sail with a light air from the SE. Sent the Boats ahead. Tack'd occasionally. *Chatham* in Company. At Noon the East Pt of the Harbor NE ½ a Mile. Lost a Punchoen which broke from the Raft Rope in rafting off the Water.

Saturday 19th. Moderate and Cloudy. At 4 try'd for Soundings. No Bottom at 100 fm. ½ past anchor'd in [28] fm off Shore ½ a Mile. AM. At 8 weigh'd with a light Breese. Carried away the Fore topsail yard in the Slings. Got it down and sent up another. Made sail. At Noon Western Extreme on the larbd Shore N 59° W. South Extreme S 28° E. Western Extreme on the Starbd Shore in one with the western Extreme on the Larbd Shore.

Sunday 20th. Moderate and Clear. Shortn'd sail. ½ past 6 came too with the best Bower in 32 fm. AM. Sent the Cutter and Launch away with an officer in each to examine an opening to the Southward.

Monday 21st. Light Breeses and Clear. AM. Sent the Carpenters on Shore to cut two new Topsail yards. Empd brewing Spruce Beer Fishing &c. Several canoes alongside.

Tuesday 22nd. Light Breeses and pleasant Weather. Employ'd as before. Sailmakers repairing the Jib and fore topmast Staysail.

Wednesday 23rd. Light Breeses and Variable with showers of rain. Punish'd James Butters and George Raybold the first with 3 dozen and the other with two dozen for Theft. AM. Light Breezes and pleasant. Loos'd Sails to dry. Sent the empty Casks on Shore. Several Canoes alongside.

Thursday 24th. Squally with rain. Furl'd Sails. Lost two Puncheons which broke from the Raft Rope. AM. Light Airs and Clear. Loos'd Sails to dry. Emp^{d} about the rigging fishing and brewing. Carpenters making a new Top gallant Mast and yard. Sailmakers repairing the Main top gall^{t} Sail and Staysails.

Friday 25th. Light Breeses and Clear. Employ'd as before. Furl'd Sails.

Saturday 26th. Light Breeses and Clear. Employ'd at watering. Anchor'd here the *Chatham*. AM. Captain Vancouver with two Boats left the Ship upon a Surveying Expedition. Employ'd as before.

Sunday 27th. D^{o}. Weather. Employ'd occasionally. AM. At 1 the Cutter and Launch return'd. Muster'd the Ships Company.

Monday 28th. Moderate and Cloudy. AM. The *Chatham* sail'd out of the Bay accompanied by our Launch with an officer. Emp^{d} Brewing Fishing &c.

Tuesday 29th. Moderate and Cloudy with rain. Employ'd as before. Wash'd between Decks. Sailmakers repairing the Staysails. Fir'd 17 Guns it being the anniversary of King Charles Restoration.

Wednesday 30th. D^{o}. Weather. At 9 the Boats return'd. AM. ½ past 8 weigh'd and made Sail standing to the Northward. At Noon Village p^{t} S 3° E. Punished Wm Woodson with 24 Lashes for Insolence.

Thursday May 31st, 1792. Light Breeses and Cloudy. Employ'd work^{g} up a Northern Branch. At 11 anchor'd with the Small Bower in 32 f^{m}. Fir'd 3 Guns as Signals to the *Chatham* to designate her Situation. AM. Light Breeses and Clear. Employ'd about the rigging. A party hauling the Seine.

Friday June 1st. Light Airs inclinble to Calm. At 7 weigh'd with a Light Breese standing to the Northward. At 11 came too with the Small Bower in 20 f^{m}. ½ past 6 AM weigh'd with a light Breese standing up a Northern Arm. At Noon Calm. Western Shore from N 22° W to S 20° E. Eastern Shore from N 17° W to S 69° E.

Saturday 2nd. Light Breeses and Clear. ½ past 2 came too with the Small Bower in 20 fm. The *Chatham* having run on shore a little to the Northward of us. Hoisted the Boats out and sent them with an officer to her assistance. AM. Moderate and Cloudy with rain. At 1 the *Chatham* got off. ½ past 10 made the Signal and weigh'd. Fir'd one Gun to denote our Situation to the boats. Punish'd Jos Murgatroyd with 12 Lashes for Insolence. At Noon standing to the Southward with a light Brese.

Sunday 3rd. Light Airs inclinable to Calm. At 2 came too with the small Bower in 50 fm. ½ past 8 fir'd two Guns as Signals to the Boats to denote our Situation. At 9 they return'd. Muster'd the Ships Company and read the articles of War to them. A party hauling the Seine.

Monday 4th. Light Breeses and Variable. Employ'd fishing.

Tuesday 5th. Light Breeses and Cloudy. Fir'd 21 Guns it being the Anniverary of his Majestys Birth day. At 7 weigh'd with a light Breese running out of the Arm. Several Canoes alongside. At Noon Entrance Pt N 44 ½ W. Opposite Bluff N 47 W.

Wednesday June 6th 1792. Moderate and Cloudy. Tack'd occasionally workg out of the Arm. At 12 came too with the Small Bower in 22 fm. At 7 made the Signal and weigh'd working out of the Arm. At 11 pass'd over a Bank with 10 fm water on it. Bent the Stream Cable. Punish'd John Thomas with 3 Dozen Lashes for Neglect of Duty. At Noon standing to the Northward with a light Breese. East Point of Port Discovery S 3° W. East Pt of Protection Island S 15° W. Dungeness Point S 54° W. Nearest Shore EbN. Entrance for which we steer N 1° E.

Thursday 7th. Calm and pleasant Weather. At 3 anchor'd with the small Bower in 20 fm. Sandy Island N 34° W. Nearest Shore N 60° E 2 Miles. Employ'd occasionally. *Chatham* in Company.

Friday 8th. Light Airs and pleasant. ½ past 6 weigh'd standing for an Inlet to the NW. ½ past 8 Calm. Come too with the Small Bower in 37 fm. Sent the Cutter and Launch with an Officer to examine an Opening to the Northward. AM. Moderate and Cloudy. Empd making Nippers. Carpenters sawing Plank.

Saturday 9th. Light Airs and Variable. At 3 weigh'd and stood for a Bay to the Northward. At 6 came too with the Small Bower in 16 fm. Sent a party to haul the Seine. AM. Moderate and Cloudy. Employ'd watering, making Nippers and Puddening the best Bower Anchor. Carpenters sawing Plank.

Sunday 10th. Light Breeses and Cloudy. Employ'd watering. Lost a Puncheon which broke from the Raft Rope. AM. Moderate and Clear. The *Chatham* join'd us. Completed the Water. A party hauling the Seine. Punish'd Jno Munroe and Walter Dillon with 12 Lashes each for Neglect of Duty. Employ'd puddening the Stream anchor and brewing Spruce Beer.

Monday 11th. Light airs. At 2 the Boats return'd. AM. Weigh'd with a light Breese running up an arm leading to the Northward. At Noon nearest land NbE 2 Miles.

Tuesday June 12th 1792. Moderate and Clear. ½ past 6 brought too with the Small Bower in 6 fm. AM. Captain Vancouver with two Boats left the Ship on a Surveying Party. Sent the Tents and Observatory on

Shore with an Officer and a party of Marines. Moor'd Ship ½ Cable each way. Sent the Empty Casks on shore.

Wednesday 13th. Moderate and Clear. Employ'd wooding watering and fishing. Carpenters cutting a fish. Sent the Cutter and *Chathams* Launch away with an Officer to survey an Arm to the South. At 9 the Boats return'd having seen two vessels standing towards the Ship. AM. The vessels not being in Sight the *Chatham* weigh'd and stood out of the Bay to look for them. Sent a party of Men with an Officer on board of her. At 6 Sent the Boats away again.

Thursday 14th. Moderate and Cloudy. Empd wooding watering brewing &c. Carpenters cutting a Fish and sawing Plank. Sailmakers altering the [ ]. At Noon the *Chatham* anchor'd in the Bay.

Friday 15th. Light Breeses and Cloudy with rain. Employ'd as before. AM. Fair Weather. employ'd cleaning the Ship.

Saturday 16th. Fresh Breeses and Cloudy. Employ'd in the Main Hold. AM. Loos'd Sails to dry. Carpenters employ'd as before. At Noon furl'd Sails.

Sunday 17th. Fresh Breeses and Cloudy. Empd wooding watering and Brewing. Got off the Fish and tow'd the Booms. At 8 the Cutter return'd. AM. Light Breeses and Clear. Muster'd the Ships Company.

Monday 18th. Light Airs and Clear. AM. Sent away the *Chatham* Cutter and Launch with an Officer to compleat the Survey of an Arm to the Southd. Employ'd airing the Sails wooding sawing Plank and Brewing.

Tuesday 19th. Light Airs and Cloudy. Employ'd as before. Carpenters cutting Logs for Plank. Light Breeses and Clear. Employ'd as before. The *Chathams* Boats return'd. Punish'd Henry Hankins with 12 Lashes for neglect of Duty.

Wednesday 20th. Fine pleasant Weather. Employ'd Brooming Brewing &c. Carpenters cutting another Fish. Seamen working up Junk.

Thursday 21st. Light Airs inclinable to Calm. Empd as before.

Friday 22nd. Light Breeses and Clear Weather. At 1 the Launch return'd. AM. Employ'd watering. Carpenters cutting the Fish. At 11 the Pinnace return'd. Struck the Tents and Observatory.

Saturday 23rd. Moderate and Clear. Employ'd getting the Tents Observatory and Instruments on board. Unmoor'd Ship. AM. Weigh'd with a light Breese standing to the Westward. *Chatham* in Company.

Sunday 24th. Moderate and Clear. Standing up a large NW Arm. ½ past 1 saw the two Spanish vessels. ½ past 2 shortn'd Sail and hove too. At 3 the Commanders came on board. Fill'd and made Sail. Tack'd Ship occasionally. At 9 the Spanish Officers left the Ship. AM. Light Breeses and Clear. Made and shortn'd Sail occasionally running up an Arm leading to the NWward. At Noon nearest Shore SW and NE 8 Miles over.

9

Thomas Manby

Thomas Manby, born in 1766 in Lincolnshire, England, was initially a master's mate aboard *Discovery*. As his skills progressed, Vancouver ultimately promoted him to 3rd lieutenant. His father was Matthew Pepper Manby, aide de camp to Viscount Townshend, Lord Lieutenant of Ireland, who was instrumental in Thomas' billet aboard the ship. Manby spent his entire life at sea, seeing service first aboard *Hyaena* in 1783. In 1800 he married a Miss Hammond and together they had two daughters. He retired as a Rear Admiral in May 1825 because of poor health and died June 18, 1834, at the George Hotel in South Hampton, England, from an overdose of opium.

Manby provided two journals. The first was his official "ship's journal," provided to Vancouver for his text at the end of the voyage. The source for this was the Public Record Office in London. The second was a "private journal" evidently written while underway to a friend or friends. This latter journal was not given to Vancouver. The original is owned by the Yale Collection of Western Americana, Beineke Rare Book and Manuscript Library. Differences between the two journals are interesting inasmuch as Manby was indeed involved in the several small boat explorations, but one would not know that from the ship's journal. In addition, the private journal provides much more detail. The private journal used a conventional calendar running from midnight to midnight. Thus, for a specific date, A.M. and P.M. entries actually occur on that date.

Ship's Journal

Saturday April 28th. Modt Breeze and Cloudy. At Sun set N^{d} extreme NW b N. S^{h} extreme S 77 E. Nearest land N 40 E 4 miles. Regular soundings from 25 to 30 fms. Soundings from 20 to 16 fms brown Sand. Lat^{d} Obs^{d} 47. .30° N^{h}.

Sunday April 29th. Light Breezes and Hazy. Found a current setting in shore, let go the small Bower in 19 fms. Extreme of the Land from N 34 W to S 30 E, off shore 4 Miles. At 2 AM made the sig^{l} and Weighed and came to sail under Top sails, Top Gall^{t} sails and Fore Sail with a Light breeze from the ESE. At 4 Saw a Sail in the NW. At 6 Spoke the *Columbia* of Boston-Grey commander-Out Cutter and sent an officer on board. At 7 Fill^{d} and made sail. At noon enter'd the streights and made the *Chatham* Sig^{l} to Lead. Green Island N 17 E^{t} to N 13 E. Cape Classet N 39 E^{t}. Nearest shore NE b E 2 Miles. Fresh Breezes and Hazy with Rain. [ ] obs^{d} Classet Lat^{d} 40° 23N Long^{d} 235 [ ] E^{t}.

Monday April 30th. Fresh Breezes and Squally with Rain. Tack'd occasionally turning up the straight. ½ past 6 came too with the small Bower in 23 fms soft mudd. S^{h} extreme N 88 E^{t}; N^{h} D^{o} N 68 W. Nearest shore S^{h} [ ] Miles. Observed on the Southern entrance a large Village well inhabited on Green Island. A.M. At 6 Light Airs and Clear. Weighed and came to Sail with a clear horizon to the Eastward. Several Canoes came along side and sold some halibut. At Noon, Mod^{t} Breezes and Clear. Lat^{d} Obs^{d} 40.18 N.

Tuesday May 1st. Modt Breezes and Cloudy. At 8 came too under [ ] long spit of Sand on the south shore in 14 fms. Dis^{t} low bluff N 35 W^{t} Low point N 42 W^{t}. [ ] Harbor bluff S 50 E^{t}. Nearest shore S^{h} 2 Miles. A.M. At 8 sent two Boats and one from the *Chatham* to search for an Harbor. Some Canoes came off with Fish. Punished John Munro with 1 Dozen & a half Lashes for insolence.

Wednesday May 2nd. Wind NW. Light Breezes and Clear. At 11 the Boats returned having met with a good and convenient Harbor. At 7 A.M. weighed and came to Sail. ½ p^{t} 9 enter'd the Harbor. Sent the boats to tow. At 11 Anchor'd 5 miles up from the entrance. Veered away and moored ship in 34 fms stiff black clay opposite a fine run of fresh water. Lat^{d} Obs^{d} 40° 02N.

Thursday 3d. NW. Fine and pleasant weather. Sent the Tents, observatory, Time keepers and instruments on shore with an officer and party of Marines. A.M. Employed cutting wood, brewing spruce beer. Coopers repairing the Casks, Sailmakers overhauling and repairing the sails and cross banding the square sails. Hauling the Seine and Gunners drying the powder. Struck the Top Gall^{t} Masts and fitted new Fore and Main Top mast backstays. Draught of water 13 feet forward and 14 feet abaft. From the 4th to 6th Light airs and clear. Employed on shore as before. Sent all the empty Casks on shore to be fill^{d} with water. Sent a carpenter to assist in caulking the *Chatham*, others employ'd stopping a leak in the Larboard bow. Black^{d} the Yards.

Monday May 7. Calm and foggy. A.M. The Captain left the Ship with the Launch, pinnace and *Chathams* cutter on a surveying expedition.[1] Got on board a few tons of pebble ballast. Some Canoes came to the ship with fish and Venison. Employed on shore as before.

from the 8th to the 10th. Moderate breezes and Clear. Employ'd as before. Completed the Ballast and $fill^{d}$ the ground tier. Ships draught 13F.10I forward and 14F.[10I] abaft. The report of a gun being heard from the Northward. Answer'd it by another.

Friday 11th to Tuesday 16th. Variable weather. Got on board wood and water and spruce beer. Party on shore employ'd as before. Carpenters Caulking the counters. Seamen reeving new running rigging. Some Canoes came frequently to the Ship bringing Fish.

Wednesday 16th. Light airs with rain. At 3 PM the Captain returned with the Boats having proceeded up an Arm being to the SW in a winding direction and ending in Latitude 47. .27 where they found a considerable Village whose inhabitants [behaved] very friendly and barter'd fish and Clams for various trinkets. Sailmakers employ'd making new fore top mast stay sails. First part SE. Latter part NW with fine weather.

17th. Cloudy with Rain. Getting ready for Sea. Bent the Sails and got wood and water from the shore. Wind SE.

Friday May 18th. Cloudy with light Rain. Struck the Tents and observatory and sent them on board with the Instruments. Got off the remainder of wood, water and spruce beer. A.M. Unmoored and weighed and came to Sail in company with the *Chatham* with a Light air from [ ] SE. At Noon the East point of the Harbor NE 1½ a mile.

Saturday May 19th. Moderate Breezes and Cloudy. Try'd frequently for soundings with 100 fms no ground. At 4 came too under the Northern shore with 28 fms. Off shore ½ a Mile. Calm. Sent a boat on shore to haul the seine. A.M. Light air and Clear. ½ past 8 weighed and came to Sail. Carried away the Fore Top sail yard in the slings. Unbent the Sail and sway'd up a spare main Top sail Yard. Bent and set the sail. At Noon the western extreme on Lar^{d} shore N 59 W^{t}. S^{h} extreme S 50 E. W^{tn} extreme on $Starb^{d}$ shore in [ ] with the western extreme on the $Larb^{d}$. S^{h} extreme S 20 E. Lat^{d} Obs^{d} 47. .59.

Sunday May 20th, 1792. Moderate Breezes and Clear. At 6 came too under the Lee of an Island with the Best Bower in 35 fms. A.M. Sent away the Launch and Cutter with an officer in each to examine an opening to the southward. At 8 Weighed and came to Sail under stay sails and stood in for the Main and came too in 40 fms with the best bower. Wash-

[1]While the ship's journal leads one to believe Manby remained on-board, he actually accompanied Vancouver in this small-boat exploration as well as later explorations.

ing between Decks. Several Canoes came along side from a Village 1 Mile distant.

Monday May 21st. Light Breezes and Clear. A.M. Sent the Carpenters on shore to cut two Top Sails Yards. Employ'd Brewing spruce beer and sent a party to haul the seine.

Tuesday. Light airs and clear. Loosed and dryed the sails. Employ'd as before. Sailmakers repairing the Jib. Wind southerly.

23d. First part fine weather. Latter part squally with heavy rain. Thunder and Lightning from the SE. Punished James Butters with 3 Dozen for Theft and John Raybold with 2 Dozen for Insolence. Several Canoes came along side with Fish.

from 24 to 25. Moderate Breezes and Cloudy. Employed Brewing spruce Beer and watering. In rafting off the Casks lost a puncheon. Carpenters brought on board the new fore top sail yard. Got it up and bent the sail. Wind SSE.

Saturday 26th. Light breezes and clear. Anchored here the *Chatham*. A.M. The Capt with the Pinnace and *Chathams* Cutter with an officer set out to survey an arm leading to the eastward. At 9 weighed and shifted our Birth nearer in shore.

Sunday 27th. Fine weather. Employ'd as before. Carpenters completed their work on shore. A.M. At 1 the Launch and Cutter returned. Muster'd the ships company. Wind from SSE to SSW.

Monday. Moderate and Cloudy. A.M. Sailed the *Chatham* with our Launch and an officer to examine an opening left unsurveyed to the westward. Employ'd brewing spruce beer.

Tuesday 29th. Moderate with Rain at times. Employ'd as before.

30th. Light Breezes and Cloudy. At 9 the Capt returned. A.M. ½ past 8 Weighed and came to sail and stood for the opening where the *Chatham* was exploring. At Noon standing to the northward. Village point bearing S 3 Et. Punished Wm Woodson with 2 Dozen for Insolence.

Thursday 31st. Light Breezes and Cloudy. Employ'd turning up the northern Branch. At 11 Came too with the Small Bower in 32 fms near the *Chatham*. A.M. Employ'd hauling the seine.

Friday June 1st, 1792. Light airs and inclinable to Calm. At 7 Light breezes. Weighed and came to sail and stood to the northward. At 11 came too with the small Bower in 20 fms. A.M. ½ pt 6 weighed and came to sail and stood to the Northward. At Noon calm. Western shore from N 22 W to S 20 Et. Eastern shore from N 17 W to S 69 E. An Island in the entrance S 31 Et to S 41 Wt. Off shore 1 Mile.

Saturday. Light Breezes and clear. Standing to the NWrd up the arm. ½ pt came too with the small Bower in 20 fms. The *Chatham* having run on shore a little ahead of us. Hoist out the Boats and sent them with an officer to her assistance. A.M. Moderate and Cloudy with rain. At 1 the *Chatham* gott off. ½ p[t] 10 weighed and stood back. Punished Joseph [ ] with 1 Dozen for insolence. Wind [ ] SSE. A.M. N[h].

Sunday 3[d]. Light airs and Calm. At 2 came too with the small Bower in 50 fms. Fired two guns to denote our situation to the Boats. At 9 the Boats returned. A.M. Light Breezes and clear. Read the articles of war and mustered the ship's company.

Monday 4th. Light Breezes and clear. Sent a party to haul the seine.

Tuesday June 5th. Light airs and clear. Fired 21 guns it being the anniversary of his Maj[y] Birthday. At 7 weighed and came to sail. At Noon running out of the Arm. Several Canoes along side. Entrance point N 44½ W. Opposite Bluff N 47½ W. Lat[d] Obs[d] 47. .49N.

Wednesday June 6th, 1792. Moderate Breezes and Cloudy. Tack'd occasionally working out of the arm. At 12 came too with the small Bower in 22 fms. At 7 A.M. made the sig[l] and weighed. At 8 working out of the arm. Starb[d] entrance W[t]. Larb[d] entrance N 60 W[t]. At 11 passed a Bank with 10 fms water on it. Punished John Thomas with 3 Dozen for neglect of duty. At Noon standing [ ] to the northward with a Light Breeze from the southward. E[t] point of Port Discovery S 3 W[t]. E[t] point of Protection Island S 15 W. Dungeness point [ ].

Thursday. Calm and clear. At 4 came too with the small Bower in 20 fms. Sandy [Island] N 34 W. Protection Island S 24 W. Nearest shore N 60 E[t] 2 Miles. ½ past 7 weighed. At 10 came too in 37 fms. Wind NW.

Friday. Light airs and clear. Wind from the NW. ½ past 6 weighed and stood for an inlet to the northward. ½ past 8 calm. Came too with the small Bower in 37 fms. Sent the Cutter & Launch with an officer in each to examine an opening to the Northward. Lat[d] Obs[d] 48. .29N.

Saturday 9th. Light airs and variable. At 3 weighed and stood for a Bay to the northward. At 6 came too with the small Bower in 16 fms. Sent a party on shore to haul the seine. A.M. Mod[t] and cloudy. Sent the empty casks on shore. Carpenters sawing up Plank. Employ'd making Nippers and Puddening the Best Bower anchor. Sent the Coppers on shore and began brewing spruce beer. Latter part wind NW.

Sunday. Light Breezes and clear. Employ'd watering. Lost a puncheon it breaking from the raft. A.M. Mod[t] & Clear. Anchored here the *Chatham*. Punished John Munro and Walter Dillon with 12 Lashes each for neglect of Duty. Wind southerly.

June 11th. Light airs from the southward with clear weather. At 2 the Boats returned. A.M. At 10 weighed and came to sail and stood for an arm leading to the northward. At Noon nearest land N 6 E 2 Miles. Lat[d] Obs[d] 48. .51N.

Tuesday 12th. Moderate and Clear. ½ past 6 came too with the small

Bower in 6 fms off shore 1 mile. A.M. At 6 the Capt with the Pinnace and Launch left the ship to survey an arm trending to the NW. Sent the observatory and Tents on shore with an officer and party. ½ past 9 weighed and stood further up the Bay. ½ past [6] came too and moored ½ a cable each way. Sent the empty casks on shore.

From the 13th to the 22d. Light southerly breezes. Sent on shore the Instruments, Carpenters employed sawing up Plank. The 13th at Noon observed two vessels standing to the NW. The *Chatham* weighed and made sail after them. Sent the Cutter with an officer and a party on board her. Found them to be a Brig and Schooner belonging to His Catholic Majesty, last from Nootka, to survey the streights. The *Chatham* came too and moored near us. Carpenters cutting a new fish. Parties on shore wooding, watering and hauling the seine. Sailmakers repairing the sails. Brewing spruce beer and making booms.

Saturday June 23d. Light Breezes and clear. At 1 the Launch returned. Employ'd as before. A.M. At 11 the Pinnace returned. Struck the Tents and observatory and sent on board the instruments.

Sunday. Modt and Clear. Got on board the remainder of the Beer and water, Tents and Observatory. Unmoored and hove short on the small Bower. A.M. Weighed and came to sail and stood to the WNW. Muster'd the Ships company. Wind ENE.

Monday 25th. Moderate Breezes and Clear. Standing up the Large NW arm. ½ past [1] saw the two Spanish Vessels standing up the arm. ½ past 2 Brought too. The Spanish commanders came on board. Filld and made sail. Tack'd occasionally. A.M. Light Breezes and Clear. Standing to the NW. At Noon nearest shores SW & NE 8 Miles over. Latd Obsd 49. .36 N.

Private Journal

[p. 4] [April 29, 1792] At 2 A.M. We weighed with the *Chatham* and at 4 saw a strange Sail in the N.W. Our anxiety at meeting a sight so new created much satisfaction. By 8 we spoke her and found her the *Columbia* of Boston-Grey Master, trading on this coast for peltries of the Sea Otter. Scarce any event could be more gratifying than meeting with this man, as a well known character, who had lately given a voluminous work to the World, (Captain Meares) has affirmed that Mr Grey, while Commanding the Sloop *Washington*, had discovered a passage, which brought him again into the Pacific, in the Latitude 54 Nh. having a spacious Sea, and unbounded Horizon to the Eastward, which their fertile imaginations pronounced the long looked for North West passage.

An Officer was instantly sent on board the American, to make every enquiry respecting the straits of Juan de Fuga which by the Book alluded too, we were led to suppose would give a speedy termination to the object of our Voyage.

The return of our Officer made known the whole to be an egregious falsehood as Mr Grey had never penetrated ten leagues up the strait. This Gentleman related many other absurdities practiced by Mr Meares, and candidly made known what most likely produced this imprudent humbug. These two Navigators both engaged in the same pursuit, met by accident in Nootka Sound. The Jealousies of trade, taught them to play off their artful deceptions, and as Quissing was the order of the Day, Captain Meares boasted of ideal successes in having procured many Hundred Sea Otter skins. The cunning Yanky, in retaliation, knowing the North West passage to be the Hobby horse of his [p. 5] opponent in Commerce, reports his discovery of it-which is believed with greedy avidity and given to the deluded public factum factorum, dressed up in language with a Chart annexed to it, of this imaginary Ocean that points out the tracks of the Vessel with fanciful precision.

Was it worth my while I could give you many proofs how erroneously this inventive traveller has deceived his readers, and more particularly us poor fellows, who leave our friends and native Land in search of his Phantoms. I will only mention one circumstance wherein he says, he sent his Boats so far up the straits, that they left a clear unbounded Horizon, Thirty Leagues up. In confutation to this assertion, had his Boats been there or half the distance, Land would have been sufficiently conspicuous. 'Tis true his Boats entered the straits but were obliged to make a speedy retreat to his Vessel, as a ferocious tribe of Indians attacked them, wounded some of his people, desperately with Arrows and had nearly put the whole to death.[2]

After passing two hours with the *Columbia* we made sail in hopes of soon reaching the celebrated straits just spoke of. We likewise gained some information respecting the Coast we had passed, and that the opening we observed in lat. 46. .19 North was an extensive River, with a dangerous bar laying across its entrance, which at times is free from surf.[3]

---

[2]See footnote 8 in Chapter 1 for further explanation regarding Robert Duffin.

[3]This statement is confusing as Gray did not discover the Columbia River until two weeks after this meeting. It may be that Gray believed it to be there (there was previous speculation by the Spanish as well as Meares) but had not yet taken the opportunity to confirm it. However, according to John Boit's log aboard the *Columbia* for May 12, 1792: "This day saw an appearance of a spacious harbour abrest the ship, haul'd our wind for itt, observ'd two sand bars making off, with a passage between them to a fine river. Out pinnace and sent her in ahead and followed with the Ship under short sail, carried in from ½ three to 7 fm, and when over the bar had 10 fm Water quite fresh." (Howay, 396) Boit's comments and the fact that the statement was not mentioned in either Vancouver's, Puget's or Menzies' journals leaves me at a loss to explain Manby's. The latitude referenced by Manby is close to the mouth of the Columbia.

At noon we arrived in the straits of Juan de Fuga and were visited by a Dozen Canoes, that came from a Village built on a small Island near the South point of entrance. The Indian name is Classet. It lays in latitude 48. .23 N^h and Longitude 235°. .6 East.

From the number of Indians around the Ship and what we observed at the Village, we consider this tribe to consist of two or three hundred. They offered a few Skins to barter, and some fish, Copper and Metal Buttons, were given in exchange. Several of them came on board cloathed in skins of Bears and Deer. The Chiefs had their garments of Sea Otter. They sew two of them together which wraps nearly round them, and has [p. 6] a beautiful and rich appearance, from the jetty gloss of the fur. Implements for War and Hunting were seen in each Canoe, consisting of Bows, Arrows and Lances, barbed with stone Bone and Muscle shell. Some of the men were of large size, and very well proportioned, with sprightly countenances. They use train Oil Grease and Ocre to paint themselves with. Train Oil is a favorite drink with them, as they were continually passing round bladders filled with it while sitting in their Canoes alongside. The Canoes are made from one solid Pine Tree some of them sufficiently large to contain Thirty people, very sharp at the stem and stern, and well adapted for going fast. The paddles are neatly constructed, being light long and slender.

With our Glasses we observed the female inhabitants of the Village, all thronged together gazing at the Ship. A great many children and an immense quantities of Dogs. The Houses from our distant view appeared open on one side and formed by very broad plank placed on large Rafters.

April 30th-Our anxiety to proceed hurried us from our visitors. We made sail, having the wind right against us. A few tacks were made without much gain. At 4 P.M. the weather appearing unsettled with rain we stood close in to the North Shore, and Anchored in 23 fathoms in order to pass the night, being at this time advanced six Miles up the strait.

April 30th 1792. It blew hard during the night with rain. We had just reason to congratulate ourselves on being snug at anchor, as had we been at sea its violence must have forced us many Leagues from the Coast. In the Morning the Wind shifted to the N.W. and brought with it settled, and fine weather. At 8 A.M. We got underway with a light Breeze and strong flood tide.

The prospect in every view was truly pleasing. The Strait [p. 7] extended in a E.S.E. direction as far as the Eye could reach with a clear Easterly horizon. On each side the Land is rather high than otherwise covered thickly with wood from base to summit. Some distant mountains reared their stupendous heads capp'd with eternal snow, embellished the scene past all description. Its entrance is about five leagues in breadth and its bottom unfathomable unless close to the Shore.

A few Indians came to us, and bartered fine Halibut for buttons or other trinkets. They catch their fish with large hooks made of tough wood, whilst a strong kind of sea weed knotted together serves them for excellent lines.

Never was contrast greater on this days sailing than with what we had long been accustomed too. It had more the aspect of enchantment than reality. With silent admiration each discerned the beauties of Nature, and nought was heard on board but expressions of delight murmured from every tongue. Imperceptibly our Bark skimmed over the glassy surface of the deep, about three Miles an hour. A gentle Breeze swelled the lofty Canvas whilst all was calm below. The shore on either side glow'd with luxurious foilage, pleasingly variegated with every shade, a cheerful spring can give the forest. By Noon we were advanced twenty Miles and obs^d^ the Latitude 48. .18 N.

May 1st—We had not proceeded much further before we saw Land rising to the Eastward, which we imagined would soon put an end to our career. The strait at the same time became something narrower and by 6 a long sandy spit was visible from the Mast head that stretched out a considerable distance from the Land. By the dusk of the Evening being up with it, both Vessels anchored to wait the return of day-having run six and thirty Miles.

In the Morning curiosity had roused every body up to look round them. On the dawn of day, Land was seen in every direction, but in the Canal we had passed up. To the Northward it formed an extensive Sound with some small openings, which most likely [p. 8] will prove, Harbours or Channels.

A Boat was sent away with the Master to find a more convenient situation for the Ship. I attended him, and killed a few Birds of the aquatic kind. Observing two Canoes on the Beach, we stood towards them. As we approached the shore, four Indians came from the woods, armed with spears, beckoning to us not to land, but depart. We held up some trifles to them. These they rejected with disdain, spoke loud to us, in a gutteral kind of lingo and used threatening gestures. Poor souls, it would have been cruel so soon to commence hostilities, therefore we left them, in hopes time would make us better friends-and returned on board to report what we had seen. After breakfast Captain Vancouver, an Officer and myself left the Ship with three Boats, following the direction of the Continental shore, in order to find a spot well adapted for receiving the Vessels. Our success far exceeded our expectations by finding a most excellent harbour a league in circumference, well supplied with Fresh

Water and abounding in Wood. Captain Vancouver named it Port Discovery in Honor of the Ship, resolving to bring in the Vessels the following day. We did not get on board till twelve at Night, much fatigued and very hungry, having imprudently gone without provisions.

At low water we dug some Clams from the Land. A fire made them very palatable and in addition we had two Ducks I shot-but bread and Salt being wanting, they made but a shabby relish amongst a large party. In this excursion I killed a remarkable animal about the size of a Cat, of a brown color, with a large white bushy tail, that spread over his back. After firing I approached him with all speed and was saluted, by a discharge from him the most nauseous and fetid, my sense of smelling ever experienced. My gun and cloaths were so impregnated with the stench that tho' boiled in many waters, the cursed effusive could never be eradicated. A skunk is the name of this diabolical animal, and I find by consulting the History of Quadrupeds-Bounteous Nature has bestowed this mode of protection as his only defense. He lives undisturbed both by Man and Beast and for my part, I promise faithfully never to disturb another on any consideration.

In the morning of the 2nd both Vessels weighed and stood for Port Discovery [p. 9] with a day peculiarly fine and clear. By noon we arrived at our intended situation and Moored in 34 fathoms, about two Cables length from a murmuring transparent stream, with a clear spot of ground about one hundred yards long directly abreast us.

Without loss of time two Tents were Landed and Pitched and the observatory erected. My fondness for employment procured me the charge of a party to carry on various operations. I took up my abode in one of the Tents and set the artificers to work, the carpenters felling Timber for Plank, Armourers, Sailmakers and Coopers in their respective stations. Every Morning and Evening the Seine was hauled with pretty good success. It brought in large Flounders, Bream, Crabs and very fine Trout. The Boilers were hung under the branches of the spruce Tree, whose boughs soon yielded us most excellent beer. In my leisure moments I traversed the Woods in quest of game to the destruction of Squirrels and all kinds of the Feathered tribe, that came in my way, which enabled me to supply my own Table as well as that of my friends. These moments of recreation were not only satisfactory but tended in a great measure to drive unpleasing ideas from the mind.

May 1792. Every thing being in fair training for supplying our wants Captain Vancouver directed their Boats to be fitted out with Arms, Ammunition and a Week's provisions, in order to pursue the Continental shore, which could not so practicably be effected by the Vessel in this interior navigation. At 4 A.M. on the 7th the captain left the Ship in the

Pinnace, attended by an officer from the *Chatham,* in his Cutter and Lieut. Pugett and myself in the launch. We pursued every turning of the Shore stopping at each conspicuous point, for the purpose of taking the necessary angles for the Survey of the unknown part of America.

After rowing about twenty Miles, we arrived at an opening about two Miles broad. A very rapid Tide was rushing in, which pronounced it of some extent. It branched off in two arms, one of them trending Easterly the other to the Northward. The Starboard shore being our route, it was pursued, which brought us by two P.M. into a Harbor that none can excel in excellence, surrounded by Land beautifully decorated by the hand of chance. [p. 10] On a green, fertile bank we landed to dine, where Captain Vancouver named it Port Townshend in honor of the Noble Marquis, my sincere and long known friend. Few parks can boast of superior prospects that what we observed in this uninhabited spot. The lawn on which we eat our repast show the fertility of the soil, by a rich carpeting of Grass and Clover. An extensive pool of fresh Water lay at the back of it, well stored with different kinds of Wild Fowl. A hill of rather steep ascent lay beyond this which carried you to a plain some miles long, with a few clumps of Trees on it, backed by a Woody Country.

The track of Deer were very evident in many places. The face of the Hill leading to the lawn had been so repeatedly traversed that it was destitute of verdure and had more the appearance and smell of a Cow yard than any thing I ever experienced. Near the borders of the pool shew their footsteps to perfection, principally Deer. Many of them were full as large as the hoof of an Ox. These no doubt were the Moose Deer and Elk. I regretted much not passing a night in this situation, as to a certainty they wander to the low Ground on every night to feed, and might be easily shot by laying in ambush. Bears and some smaller animals come frequently to the Pond to drink. We saw the print of their feet very distant. On the upper plain I saw a good many Bustards not exactly like those found in England, being all of a light dun color, but equal in size to any I ever saw. They were very shy, not permitting me to come sufficiently near to kill one, altho' I fired several times with small shot. A good many foxes were prowling on the plain and one larger animal, I took to be a Wolf. The report of my Gun occasioned their running to the woods, but before they entered it they would stop some minutes and gaze at me.

The next visitor to this remote region should be by accident saunter to the plain, may have his curiosity attracted by the same object that drew mine: a clump formed by five prodigious Cypress Trees. On one, the most stately of the number, I carved with my Knife Ann Marie Townshend and under it T.M.-1792 and whoever thou art, Traveller, know that she possesses every beauty as a Woman, this unequalled Cypress does as a Tree, without fault or blemish, a pattern to the World for goodness and a virtuous Life. On joining my party I found them all [p. 11] preparing to depart. I therefore only waited a moment to mix a [ ] of Grog, which I passed round with some honest fellows to the health of all my Dear and respected Townshend friends. With a favorable Breeze, we embarked and bid adieu to a place I shall think of with pleasure. By sun set we had got some distance from Port Townshend, pursuing our object in a South Easterly direction. As the Evening advanced, we kept an eager look out for a comfortable situation to pass the night on. The shore being steep and rocky, it was dark before we attained the desired spot. On a level Beach we pitched a small Tent and struck up a roaring Fire beneath the Branches of a spreading Tree, round which we eat our Suppers, talked of our Friends, chose some soft root for a pillow and sunk in the arms of sleep, dividing our party one half as a watch to those wrapt in their slumbers.

It would be too tedious to give you a diary of our daily progress, whilst exploring this inland navigation in our open Boats. A Service so new and scenes so various will I trust be recounted and given to the World by some able pen on the Ships return.

Therefore, I shall only make known that we continued following the Winding of this extraordinary Inlet for six days before we arrived at its end, stopping at certain times to Cook and Eat our Meals and pass the Hours of Rest, with the Earth our Bed, the Heaven our covering.

The breadth of this Canal seldom exceeded two Miles and never less than half a Mile. Its depth near the Middle, we could never ascertain, as bottom could not be found with one Hundred fathom of line.[4] A good deal of regularity was observed in the tides. The common Tides rise to about eleven feet perpendicular height, the springs about three feet higher.

When we had approached within twenty Miles of its termination we often saw a Canoe and sometimes two or three. All our endeavours could not bring them nearer, as they paddled away with all possible speed. When first seen they were generally Fishing or Hunting the seal. In rowing along shore we pass'd on a small party digging clams at low Water. The whole flew to the Woods and would not return whilst we remained there. To convince them of our amicable intentions, their Clams and property were left untouched and a few Buttons, Hawkes Bells and other trinkets deposited in their Canoe, which was constructed in a similar way

[4]A confusing statement. The northern portion of Hood Canal rarely exceeds fifty fathoms while the southern extremity varies from sixty to ninety.

to those we saw on [p. 12] entering the straits. About six miles from the head we stopped at a small Village. Every inhabitant expressed their consternation by an immediate flight. We could plainly hear them in the interior part of the forest, shrieking loud and their Dogs yelling to a very great degree. The Hutts were constructed by [ ] plank resting on rafters. A large Fire was burning in the middle. A number of Salmon were extended on sticks and hung in the smoak for the purpose of drying and some Clams were roasting, most likely for present use. Two buckets full of these testacious fish, with part of a seal fresh killed, lay by the fire and bladders of oil were suspended round the habitation.

Two elderly men came and peeped at us. Observing them, we made every friendly salutation for them to advance. With cautious fear they did, sufficiently near to see their dwellings stand undispoiled. This gave them confidence. They came to us without fear, perfectly naked. By signs we asked them for Salmon and Clams. Our request was instantly understood and granted. In return, they were presented with a piece of Copper and each a pair of brass bracelets. On obtaining this finery their countenances brightened up. Our dress a good deal excited their attention. They inspected into each article, and expressed by signs the soles of their feet were as hard as our shoes. We plainly heard the fugitives talking in the Woods. One of our new friends went to them, subsided their fears, and made them desirous of metal decorations. A good many men and some boys, instantly came out and placed themselves near us without any apprehensions. Buttons were distributed among them, which they ornamented their Ears with. The poor Females were prohibited from seeing us, as the Men on being pressed to bring them shook their Heads and signified they were retired far inland.

They made known to us by signs we should soon be at the termination of the Branch, and that a Village lay near its End. An intelligent fellow took the following means to convince us of his meaning. By bending his arm nearly double, then making us understand his thumb was our present station, from it he traced round the inside of his Arm, which was narrow, untill he came to the part opposite his thumb, which he pointed out was the shore then abreast us. On finding himself understood he laughed heartily and became a very merry companion.

Three hours after leaving these people we came to what had been so accurately described, found its ending, and a Village situated on the Banks of a [p. 13] fresh water River. Two of our old acquaintances joined our party, and by the swiftness of their Canoes, gained the Village half an hour before us. It had this good effect in quieting the minds of the Indians, many of whom came down to the beach to receive us unarmed at landing.

Most of the men were naked; some few had the skin of an animal hung round the shoulders. The Women did not leave their habitations, but continued their occupations of smoaking Salmon and attending their culinary pursuits. Few of them possessed very engaging features, and the profusion of train oil that lay on their skins prevented my making those minute examinations I would otherwise have wished to have done. Black Eyes universally prevailed, but being destitute of animal fire, were scarce worth looking at. They wore the skin of Deer or Beaver round their middle and another on their shoulders. The Ears of all were perforated and pieces of glittering shells were placed in them. Fish they bartered with us and readily disposed of their Bows, Arrows and Spears for our trinkets.

This Village contains about two hundred of every description. The people were in general of small size and ill made, wore the Hair long and very filthy. The Country round varied not the least from what we had passed through during the last weeks, consisting of a rising Land of moderate height, overgrown with Timber, principally of the Pine kind. Where ever we landed we always saw the tracks of herds of Deer and now and then we got a sight of one grazing on the borders of the Forest. Bear must be very numerous from the number of their skins we saw with the Indians. Only two made their appearance to us, and then out of Gun shot, both of them very large and black. Now and then I got a chance shot at Ducks or some kind of Water Fowl. When this supply failed, an Eagle was easily procured. They are much larger than any I ever before saw in America. It was always necessary to steep them a few hours in Salt water to take off the cadaverous smell previous to cooking, and then junked up with Salt Beef and Pork they made a most excellent Mess.

Almost every Indian had a Dog. They do not resemble any of our European ones. The feet and head has every appearance of a Bear. Their other parts bear a great likeness to those of a Wolf. They scarce ever bark, but howl most dismally.

We did not observe any Sea Otters in this island Cruize, nor did we see any of their skins in the possession of the Indians. [p. 14] Beavers are plentiful if we may Judge from the furs seen at the Village. Many of those were Brought and one very fine Panther skin, that had not long been taken from the animal. We had now and then an opportunity of tracing this Beast in the sand, but never had the good luck to get a sight at one. Beads, buttons and other things being given to the Villagers, we left them in order to make the best of our way to the Ship. The head of this remarkable arm of the Sea lays in the Latitude and Long. [left blank]. After a good deal of toil and much pinched for Provisions, we had the satisfaction of getting to the *Discovery* on the 16th of May. Three cheers welcomed us on board, as the most gloomy apprehensions had existed in every breast for the last three Days, all imagining some fatal accident had befallen us.

The Wood and Water being compleat, our wants and defects supplied, orders were issued to embark every thing from the shore and prepare for sailing. The officer attending the observatory found its place to be in the Latitude 48°. .2.' .30" N^h^ and longitude 237°. .22.' .19' east of Greenwich.

Some Indians visited the Vessel during our absence, brought fish to traffic and a very fine Deer they had killed with an Arrow.

May the 18th 1792. In the morning both Vessels got under way and left this Harbor, which is commodiously situated for any Vessel requiring a place of safety to recruit her Crew after a long Voyage. On the North side of the Harbor many clear and beautiful spots are to be found, the rest is chiefly composed of thick woods. An Island half a mile long, lays athwart its entrance. This was named Protection Island and must break off any swell from disturbing a Vessel at anchor. I forgot before to mention that not far from where the Ship lay we found a Canoe hauled up in the woods that contained the Bodies of five Indians, regularly placed in it, all wrap'd up in many folds of Bear and Deer skins. The flesh was consumed from their bones, which prevented our ascertaining whether they had Died the death of Nature, or fell by the hand of destructive war. I frequently met with human bones during my rambles and always observed them scorched by fire, the large bones of the Thigh and Leg were always broke in two, as if for the purpose of taking out the marrow. However this may [p. 15] be the mode of disposing of their dead. If so, I think it ungenerous in those Navigators that pronounce the Inhabitants of this part of America cannibals. A strong tide and favourable breeze brought us within the arm by 2 P.M. Soon after the flood being expended, we anchored in order to pass the night. This branch was about two miles in breadth, trended to the North Eastward and had the same appearance with the Land in general seen within the Straits. Our Boats were sent to haul the Seine, and returned with some Trout and flatfish. Whilst the party were hauling in the net, a fine Buck jumped from a clump of over grown bushes and ran through our fishery. In the morning we broke from our anchorage, and proceeded up that Arm. The breeze being faint, the Boats were towing the whole day. Several beautiful scenes were passed. The dissolving snow from the back mountains made numerous gullys for its course, which burst over lofty precipices, forming the grandest Cascades ever beheld. By Sun set we had advanced twenty five Miles. We hauled into a snug situation, not far distant from a small Village and anchored.

General alarm was spread through the Village on observing the

Ship. We tried every means to pacify their fears and at length succeeded, so far that two Canoes came alongside the Ship. We got from them Clams, Mussels and a little fish-rewarded them with our articles of commerce, but could not prevail on them to come on board.

At daylight on the 20th Lieut Pugett and myself were dispatched with two Boats to explore to the end of this opening, which we attained on the 25th and found its termination much like the other, ending with a shallow fresh water River on whose banks a party of Indians had taken up their residence. As they appeared numerous, we did not go very near it but lay on our oars about two miles from it. Three Canoes with two Men in each came from the Village as if to reconnoiter, as they would not approach nearer than a quarter of a mile. Various things were held out to them, in hopes of drawing them nearer, but without effect. A Man stood up in one of the Canoes and harangued the other in a very loud tone, and used frequent gestures expressive of anger. Having waited a considerable time without accomplishing our purpose, we made fast some pieces of copper and buttons to a stick and threw it toward them. They evidently understood our intentions, but would not paddle towards it untill we retired. On [p. 16] obtaining this treasure, it was handed round to each Canoe with joyful satisfaction. The orator, who most likely was a Chief, hung the bauble to his Ears and returned to his residence.

On their leaving us we bent our course to the Vessel and soon after entered a convenient little Cove to dine about eight miles from the Village. Whilst our cooks were providing our humble fare consisting of stewed Raisins and nettle tops, two Canoes with six Indians paddled briskly up to us and landed near our Boat without the least signs of fear. We gave them some Biscuit and received a piece of Porpoise in return.

We had not long taken our places around our luxurious repast before four more Canoes came in. One of them had nine Indians in her and all the rest three or four. Amongst them was the old fellow that we had seen in the morning who would not then come to us in spite of all our persuasion. His proceedings soon convinced us of his consequence, as all the others were obedient to his command. He ordered a fish out of every Canoe and presented them to us and of course was rewarded for his civility.

Altho' their number amounted to near thirty and ours only to sixteen, we considered ourselves equal to them, even should they be ill disposed, and continued our Dinner. In the course of ten minutes twelve more Canoes dropped in, two and three at a time. This hinted to us the necessity of taking some precaution. We therefore drew a line on the Beach about twenty yards from the spot we occupied and got all to retire to it but our first visitors and the old Chief, who a good deal attracted our notice by his savage countenance and robust form. His body was deeply scarred in many places and his left eye entirely beat out.

The conduct of this treacherous old Chief soon convinced us he had some deep design in agitation by his repeatedly going from us to his collected party on the other side of the boundary and speaking to them very seriously. They all listened with attention and then called some of our first visitors, whom they likewise conversed with. Canoes kept coming in, which the Indians observed with great satisfaction, altho' their numbers exceeded ours five to one. Relying on our superiority of Arms, we set their intentions at defiance, prohibited every one from crossing the line, buckled on our pistols, examined our priming [p. 17] and prepared for action.

The tribe of savages eyed our preparations with serious attention. They had been for some time slyly slipping on their quivers and placing their spears so as to be grasped in a moment. Old one Eye gave a signal which occasioned every Indian to string his bow and rise up. A party of twenty then attempted to gain our rear by flying off to the Woods. These we stopped, forced them to set down, tho' much against the will of the diabolical old Chief. I had shown the chief the external destructive Beauties of my double barreled Gun, filled with a sliding Bayonet and fortunately got an opportunity of shewing its effect in the midst of our party by bringing down a Crow that was flying above my head. In an instant wonder and silent astonishment ensued. I advanced to them with the dead bird and evidently saw their confused surprise. Some shook with fear and terror hung on every visage. To continue the alarm this event had occasioned, we fired a Swivel loaded with bullets. Its report and the distant skipping balls completely cooled their courage. Some dropped on the ground and others jumped to their Canoes and paddled in haste from the Cove.

As soon as half the numbers of Canoes were decamped, we again assembled and finished our Dinners, highly gratified in having frustrated the wicked intentions of these ferocious people without putting any of them to Death. Before we left this place, which we called alarm Cove, we distributed some trifling things amongst the Indians and purchased many of the arrows which but an hour before were intended for our destruction. The old Chief left us in haste with disappointment and chagrin. At the time he hovered around our Boats in the morning he was naked, but on his second visit he was accoutre'd in his War dress, which is made of very thick Leather, reaching from the Shoulders to the Knees. An arrow will not pierce them, tho' a Musket ball would penetrate with ease, had hostilities commenced. I had marked him for my Bird, resolving to have seen him lifeless before I dropped myself.

On quitting Alarm Cove, we pursued our route untill very late that night before we took up our sleeping station and then kept a very diligent watch for fear of surprise. We remained undisturbed, and again pushed forward at the approach of day. At noon we stopped to refresh our people, who had been many hours labouring at the oar. As usual, I penetrated the Woods in quest of game, followed a path made by the [p. 18] Beasts of the forest. An uncommon rustling in the bushes brought me on my guard. I dropped a ball in each barrel and had only jammed it half down when out jumped a large brown Bear. Eager in the attack, I fired and had the mortification of bursting my valuable Gun. Bruin marched off and I saw no more of him. I regretted the loss of my Gun to a great degree, as it had been of essential service the day before and on many other occasions, and to add to its estimation, I had received as a present from my great friend and well wisher the Marquis Townshend.

On the 27th of May at 1 A.M. we got on board the Ship and passed a comfortable night in our Hammocs after sleeping under Trees and bushes.

Captain Vancouver had left the ship the day prevous to our arrival with two Boats to examine an opening that trended to the N.E.[5] Orders were left by him that an officer and myself should proceed on the *Chatham* brig attended by our Launch to search along the continental shore to the Northward for any openings that might run into the interior part of the Country. Early on the 28th Captain Broughton ran us to our destined situation. We left the Vessel with our Launch and a Boat from the *Chatham*, victualled for a Week, performed our service and returned to the ship on the 3rd of June.

During this Expedition we saw a great many deserted Villages. Some of them a very great extent, and capable of holding many hundred Inhabitants. The Planks were taken away, but all the Rafters stood perfect. The size of many a good deal surprized us, being much larger in girth than the *Discovery* Main Mast. A Human face was cut on most of them, and some were carved to resemble the Head of a Bear or Wolf. The largest of the Villages I should imagine had not been inhabited for five or six years, as brambles and bushes were growing up a considerable height.

We fell in with a very large tribe of Indians, consisting of four or five hundred. Necessity obliged us to pass within half a Mile of their Residence. Many Canoes were launched from the Beach and paddled toward us with Men, Women and Children. The two latter being of the party, our fears subsided. We only permitted one Canoe to approach us at a

---

[5]He meant S.E.

time and kept the others in most excellent order by our Warlike appearance, the Broadside of our Boat forming a most complete battery of two Swivels, two Musquetoons and every man his Musquet, Pistol and Cutlass. An hour or two was passed in Bartering with these people who exchanged their commodities with honesty. The major part of the Men and Boys were [p. 19] naked and the skins of animals was the general cloathing of the Ladies. Oil or paint was daubed on the faces of both sexes. Upon the whole they were by no means a bad looking race of people. The Females willingly parted with their native finery, consisting of shells and whale bone bracelets for our beads and buttons.

The country was every where Woody with innumerable Islands. On each of these we found the traces of Deer who no doubt swim from Island to Island. The rapid tides must often destroy them, as we frequently met with dead ones floating on the surface or thrown up on the Shore. In size these animals exceed those bred in England and are all of a deep red Colour. During this Expedition we rounded out several Branches. In one of them we found some well grown Oaks and many other Trees besides the Pine and Cypress. I met with some good shooting near this place; killed some Ducks, Curlews and a brace of spruce Partridges. They more resemble the [ ] than Partridge, the legs being feathered and are fond of sitting in Trees.

Where ever the land was low, Gooseberry and Rasberry bushes were not uncommon. The fruit that had received the benefit of the Sun was well grown and not ill tasted. On getting on board, we found great preparation for keeping His Majestys Birth day. The *Discovery* had followed the *Chatham* to the rendevous and Capt Vancouver on his return from his last excursion had the good fortune to bring home a remarkable large Buck, killed by one of his party.

June the 4th: 92. This day was dedicated to ease and recreation. The Seine gave all hands a fresh dinner and double allowance of Grog was served out that each might drink the health of our good and gracious sovereign. In the morning the Captain and Officers landed and took possession in due form of this Inland country by the name of New Georgia. The British Colours being hoist, both Vessels fired a Royal salute and three cheers were given by all hands.

The 5th. Both vessels weighed and stood up an extensive opening. At noon Lieut. Pugett and myself were dispatched with two Boats to examine a break in the Continental shore. It ran in a N.E. direction. We rounded it out and returned on board on the 9th. The Ship had anchored in a convenient Bay with some clear ground near her. This spot abounded with wild Strawberrys. One of our carpenters employed in the Woods had a visit from a Bear. The Animal rear'd up to look at him, which so alarmed the fellow that he dropped his axe and ran with speed to his Companions, frightened out of his senses. The latitude of this place 48°.51' N^{h}.[6] The few days the Ship passed at this place called Strawberry Bay. The Brewery was erected on shore, which furnished us with twenty Puncheons of Beer. To this Beverage we attributed the good health of our Ships Company, not a sick man being on board either Vessel since our first landing in the straits of Juan de Fuga. Now and then the shores supplied us with Samphire Nettles and a Weed known in the Garden in home by the name of [Faschin]. This part of Vegetation, altho' dispised in the land of plenty, were to us the greatest delicacies of the Table. It was a plan with us never to [ ] at our lot. Our fare, tho' often times scanty and course, was always received with contentment and Jollity.

On the 11th of June-Our little Squadron again came to Sail and on the following day anchored in a Bay well calculated as a station to forward a surveying party from, and the shore promised us every other convenience we could wish for. A small river of fresh Water filled our Empty Casks and an extant of clear Ground afforded an advantageous spot to fix our Tents and Observatory on. Capt. Vancouver left the Ship in the Pinnace, accompanied by the Launch with Lieut. Pugett and myself. Armed and victualled as usual, to pursue an extensive Channel we could plainly discern run in a northern direction.

[6]Vancouver placed the latitude at 48° 36½.'

10

James Hanson

Vancouver's muster table does not show a place of birth or age for James Hanson. At the start of the cruise, he was 2nd lieutenant aboard *Chatham*. At Nootka in late August, Vancouver appointed Hanson to the command of the *Dædalus* because of the untimely death of its commander, Richard Hergest. Hanson was promoted to commander in July 1795. In 1800 he commanded the HMS *Brazen*, operating in the English Channel. On January 26, 1800, gale force winds drove the *Brazen* onto the Ave Rocks near Newhaven. All but one hand were lost.

REMARKS &C ON BOARD
HIS MAJESTYS
ARM'D TENDER CHATHAM

Sunday April 29th 1792. Light airs and clear weather much the appearance of a Calm. The Current setting at the rate of ½ a mile to the NNE direction. At 3 Came too in 16 fathoms water fine black Sand off Destruction Island, it continued Calm till 2 AM when a breese sprung up from the Eastward. Weigh'd and made Sail. At 5 Saw a Ship in the NW Quarter standing to the Northward. ½ past 7 spoke her. Found she was the *Columbia* an American Ship Command^{d} by Capt Grey who had Wintered on the Coast. The Extreme of the Land N 20° W. At 7 Saw Cape Flattery. The Wind having veer'd to the SE with dirty weather the *Discovery* made our Signal to lead into Port or places bearing that appearance. At Noon fresh breese. Single Reef the Topsails. Cape Classet N 20° E Distance 2 Miles. Longitude B^{r} Match 235° 5' 19" East of Greenwich.

Monday 30th. Fresh breeses with thick drizling rain. At 1 haul'd round Green Island leaving a reef of rocks to the Northward. Saw a Village on the Island. One canoe came off with 12 men Cloathed with Skins. Some otter the rest Deer and Bear Skins. Some presents were given them. In the Evening brought up the Tide being against us. During the night it rain'd. At 4 AM Weigh'd and stood up the Straits with a fine Westerly Wind. Several Canoes following the Vessels—

Tuesday May 1st. Modt with fine clear weather. Standing up the Strait nearly in Mid Channel being about 3 or 4 Leagues across. The Land on both Sides trending East and West. Not the least Signs of a Harbour. A few Sandy spots. The Mountains very high cover'd with Snow. At 7 the *Discovery* made the Signal to Anchor. ¾ past brought up in 2 fathom.[1] In the morning were visited by two Canoes. They had nothing with them. Soon after another came with some fish. Hoisted out the Cutter. Unbent the Steering Sails. At 9 the Cutter attended Capt. Vancouver to look for a Harbour. People empd occasionally.

Wednesday 2nd. Fine clear Weather. Several Canoes alongside. At 12 the Cutter retd having found an exceeding fine Harbour about 12 Miles up the arm. At Daylight Weigh'd and made Sail for it with a light breese from the Westward. At 12 brought up in 26 fathoms water abreast the Watering Place.

Thursday 3rd. Fine Clear pleasant. After mooring the Vessel got the Sails upon Deck to air and [air'd] the Sailroom. Unbent the Sails. The *Discovery* Landed the Observatory & Tents. Sailmakers repairing the Sails. In the Morning Scrubb'd Hammocks. Sent the Cooper with the Packs of Staves to Set up. Seamen empd overhauling the Topmast & Top Gallant rigging and Lower yards. Caulkers Calking the Sides. Sway'd up the Topmasts. At noon the Lattitude was 48° 00' N. The Wind from the Northward and Westward with Serene weather.

Friday May 4th 1792. Fine Clear Weather. Sent all the Water Casks on Shore. The Armourer with his forge on Shore. People Empd refitting the Vessel. Some on Shore brewing Spruce Beer and Watering.

Saturday 5th. The Weather much the same. Some of the Natives alongside. People empd as yesterday.

Sunday 6th. Fine Clear Weather. Sailmakers on Shore repairing the Sails on Shore. Sent the Launch to haul the Seine. Read the Articles of War and Punish'd Thomas Townsend and William Clark with 12 Lashes for Insolence. Afterwds the People had permission to go on Shore—

Monday 7th. DWr. The People empd as before. AM. Mr. Johnstone in the Cutter accompanied Capt Vancouver with a Weeks Provisions a Surveying. Caulkers Empd on board—

---

[1]The ship would have been aground in two fathoms. The other journals indicated fourteen fathoms of water.

Tuesday 8th. Fine Pleasant Weather. The Wind from the Westward. People emp^d^ as yesterday. Sent the Powder on Shore to air. The different [ ] emp^d^ as before—

Wednesday 9th. The Wind having veer'd to the Southward & Eastward. Thick gloomy weather. People emp^d^ as usual. At noon rain which prevented Caulking.

Thursday 10th. Cloudy with Rain. The Wind at S^d^. Some People Cutting Wood. During the night it rained hard. Towards noon it clear'd up. Sent the People on Shore.

Friday 11th. Fresh breeses and Cloudy weather. The air sharp. Some Canoes. Got some fish from them. People emp^d^ as yesterday in refitting the Vessels.

Saturday 12th. Fresh breeses. The Wind as usual. Rafted of the Water. Emp^d^ filling the Hold. got the Wood on board.

Sunday 13th. The Wind and Weather much the same. Emp^d^ Watring the Vessel. Got on board some Spruce beer & [ ] it.

Monday 14th. D Weather. The People on Shore as usual. The gunner drying the Powder on Shore. The Wind from the NW.

Tuesday 15th. In the afternoon gloomy weather inclinable to rain. At 5 it came on and rain'd incipantly during the Night. The Wind in the SE Quarter.

Wednesday 16th. The Wind the same as yesterday with Constant Rain. At 4 the Boats ret^d^. Emp^d^ occasionally on board.

Thursday May 17th 1792. In the Afternoon it clear'd up. Emp^d^ getting the things on board from the Shore. The Observatory and Tents were got on board. This Harbour Captain Vancouver named Port Discovery which lays in Latitude 48° 02' N Longitude 237° 22' 19" East of Greenwich and Variation 21° 50' East.

Friday 18th. Fresh breeses with rain. Everything being on board at 1 veer'd away on the Stream Cable and took up the Best Bower-hoisted in the Cutter and Loos'd the Topsails. At 6 Weigh'd and turn'd to Wind^d^. At 7 brought up again on the North Side of the Harbour. During the night Calm with rain. At 4 Weigh'd with a Light breese and Stood out of the Harbour—

Saturday 19th. Light airs. Capt Vancouver came on board. When he went away parted Company with the *Discovery* and Stood over to the North^d^ to look into an Opening while the *Discovery* went up the Arm the Boats had been. ½ past 8 brought up in 12 fathom. In the morning M^r^. Johnstone in the Cutter with M^r^. Sheriff in the Launch went to Survey the Inlet while the Vessel proceed further up. At Noon brought up of a Sandy Point where an excellent run of Water was. Haul'd the Seine but caught no fish-in the Evening M^r^. Johnstone ret^d^. In the Morning he went again. At 8 Weigh'd and Stood further up the arm. At Noon being Calm brought up. The Cutter ret^{d}. Fine Serene Pleasant Weather.

Sunday 20th. It Continued Calm. The People emp^{d} occasionally. The Boats Surveying. During the night much the same Weather.

Monday 21st. Fine Weather. At 1 the Launch ret^{d}. ½ past 2 the Tide Setting Strong to the Southward & East^{d} Weigh'd with a light breese from the Westward. At 4 found the Tide against us. Sent the Cutter a Surveying. Came too in 27 fathom water. [Then] Sent away to look into an opening where some Natives came to her having some young fawns which they Sold for buttons &c. In the Evening both Boats ret^{d}. At 7 AM both boats went away. Weigh'd and Stood further up the Arm. The Boats ret^{d} at 11 having got near the head of an opening. Saw several Canoes but none came to us. Clean'd below.

Tuesday 22nd. Fine clear Weather Light Airs. The Boats towing the Vessel through a narrow passage the Tide running amazingly fast. When through found a different Tide. The Tow rope broke and the Tide being on the Starb^{d} Bow the Vessel before the boats Could lay hold was alongside of a Steep rock 20 fathoms water. In a few minutes she went off. The Tide so strong. Brought up in a Small Bay at Noon.

Wednesday May 23rd 1792. Fine fresh breezes. Fird a Swivel for the Small Boat but could not observe where she was. At 2 brought up in a fine Sandy Bay in 12 fathoms water. Sent the Launch to haul the Seine. An exceedingly fine run of Water. Fill'd the Water Casks. The Bank along the Shore was an entire Bed of Onions which was got for the People. Caught some fine Trout. During the night it rained. At 6 AM Weighed and Brought to Windward with the Tide. In opening the Entrance of a passage had a fresh breese. The Latitude at Noon was 48° 16' N having come out 5 Miles to the South^{d} & Eastward. Sandy Island N 25 W 5 Miles.

Thursday 24th. Fine pleasant weather. At 1 entered the Inlet that the *Discovery* had gone up. Some Canoes came off with some fish. At 5 the Tide being done brought up in 8 fathoms Water ½ a Mile from the North Shore — and about 6 Leagues from the Entrance. At 5 AM Weighed and Stood over to the South Shore. At 9 brought up again in 9 fathom. Sent the Launch on Shore to Cut Wood. Seamen emp^{d} Setting up the Topmast & Top Gallant Rigging. Some of the Natives came to the Party on Shore.

Friday 25th. Fine clear weather. ½ past 1 Weighed turning to Windward keeping the Starboard Shore on board finding the Tide stronger. At 6 brought up in 10 fathoms Water. Sent the People on Shore to amuse themselves. At 4 AM Weigh'd with the flood Tide. Found we did not gain much. At 8 Came too again. Several Canoes came alongside.

Saturday 26th. Light airs. ½ past 2 Weigh'd the Boats towing the Vessel. A breese from the Southward and Westward. At 5 Saw the *Discovery* laying on the Star[b] Shore. At 6 brought up in 40 fathom water abreast of the *Discovery* about 3 miles from the Shore. A Village abreast of us where there seem'd a numerous Inhabitants. AM. In the Morning M[r] Johnstone in the Cutter accompanied Captain Vancouver a surveying. Being to far from the Shore Weighd and towed further in Shore. At 11 brought up in 25 fathom water. Sent the Water Casks on Shore.

Sunday 27th. Fine clear weather. The People on Shore Washing their Clothes. AM. At 4 Sent the Launch to an Island[2] abreast of us to haul the Seine. Caught some fine Trout and flat fish. The Wind from the South[d] & Eastward attended with drisling rain. Mustrd the People.

Monday 28th. In the Afternoon it clear'd up. In the Evening it came to rain again. In the Morning M[r]. Whidby return'd. Got on board a turn of Water. Sent the Carpenters on Shore to Cut Wood. At 7 Weighd. At 9 M[r]. Whidby in the *Discovery* Launch came on board then proceed up another opening to the Northward. The Latitude at Noon was 48° 04' North a light breeze—

Tuesday 29th. Mod with Pleasant weather. At 4 finding the Tide against us and no Wind Came too in 17 fathom water. Hauled the Seine. At 6 the Tide answering, Weigh'd with a fine breeze from the North[d] and Westward. At 8 came too again in 75 fathom 1½ mile off Shore. During the night it rained. At 5 in the Morning the *Discoverys* Launch and our own left the Vessel with a Week Provision.[3] Finding the situation not Suitable for the Vessel at 7 Weigh'd made Sail up the Arm to find a more Eligible Situation for refitting & brewing Beer.

Wednesday May 30th 1792. Moderate with fine Weather. Sent the Small Boat in Search of Water but found none. At 7 in the Evening brought up in 35 fathoms Muddy bottom 1 Cable Length from the Shore. The Wind Variable from SW to NW.

Thursday 31st. Light airs. People emp[d] in the Hold. At 3 arrived His Majesty Ship *Discovery*. M[r]. Johnstone return'd on board. People emp[d] with the Boatswain.

Friday June 1st. At 1 Weighed with little or no wind. The Tide drifting the Vessel down the Inlet. At 3 a breese sprung up from the Westward. Made Sail. At 9 brought up in 13 fathom water on the Larb[d] Shore. At noon the mouth of the Entrance from S 40° E to S 26° E. White Cliff Island from S 29° E to S 34° E. The low land at the Bottom of the Harbour N 11° W to N 22° W.

---

[2]Blake Island.

[3]According to Vancouver's and Bell's (the Unsigned Journal) Narratives, Mr. Whidbey and Lt. Hanson explored the two northward openings (Port Susan and Saratoga Passage). For whatever reason, Hanson did not acknowledge the survey in his journal.

Saturday 2nd. Moderate breezes. Weigh'd. At 4 got aground upon a Soft Mud bank. Fird 2 Guns and made the Signal of Distress. The *Discoverys* Boats came to our Assistance. Run out the Stream Cable and hove taught. Till high Water took the opportunity of repairing the Bow where a piece of Copper was rubb'd off. When aground the Point of Entrance from S 32° E to S 27° E. The low Sand at the bottom of the Bay from N 19° W to N 31° W. Down Top Gallant Yards. Struck the Masts. Punished David Dorman Seamen with 36 Lashes for Neglect of Duty. At 12 hove off. At 2 Warp'd her into 9 fathom water. At 9 Weigh'd per Signal. At Noon brought up in 40 fathom. Wash'd & Clean'd Ship.

Sunday 3rd. Mod Weather. People emp^{d} occasionally. In the Evening the Launch return'd. In the night fresh breezes from the North^{d} & Westw^{d}. In the forenoon Sent the Cutter to haul the Seine. Got fish Enough for the People for two Days. Hoisted in the Launch.

Monday 4th. The Wind and Weather much the same. Being the Kings birth Day the People had grog & Beer. Capt Vancouver with of his Officers went on Shore and took Possession in His Majestys Name.

Tuesday 5th. Light winds with Showers of rain. The Wind variable. In the Morning hauld the Seine. A fresh breese from the Northward and a Strong Ebb Tide. At 7 answ^{d} the Signal to Weigh, Weigh'd and made Sail with the *Discovery*. At Noon a Light breese.

Wednesday 6th. Mod breezes and Clear Weather. Working down the Arm. In the Evening the Tide Setting Strong and little wind brought up in 37 fathom 1½ Mile from the Shore. During the Night Calm. In the Morning a light breese from the North^{d}. At 7 Weighed and turned down the Arm. The Carpenters repairing the Launch.

Thursday 7th. The Wind much the same. Finding the flood Tide Setting up Strong ½ past 1 brought up in 7 fathoms 1½ Mile from the Shore. Sent the Cutter on board the *Discovery*. Protection Island from S 57° W to S 48° W. Dungesess Spit S 40° W. At 6 Weigh'd with the Ebb. ½ past 10 brought up again in 32 fathom. Dungeness Spit S 54° W. Protection Island from S 26° W to S 22° W. the Tide of Ebb Setting at the Rate of 3½ Miles per hour. People emp^{d} occasionally.

Friday June 8th 1792. Calm with Clear Weather. The Ebb Tide still running Strong. At 5 a breeze sprung up from the Northward and Westward. The *Discovery* sent two Boats a Surveying. ½ past 5 Weighed. Made Sail to the North Side of the Strait. The Wind failing us Sent the Cutter to tow the Vessel. The *Discovery* being well in with the Land could not see her. At 10 fird a Swivel which she answer^{d}. Finding ourselves loosing ground brought up in 48 fathom. At 3 Weighed and stood for the *Discovery*. At 6 passed her. Sent the Cutter on board. At 7 brought up in 29 fathom water Sandy Island N 51° W to N 48° W. The Winds variable. Sometimes a fresh breese then Calms. Sailmakers making Boat Sails.

Saturday 9th. Light airs but variable. People empd working up Junk. ½ past 1 we Weigh'd in Company with the *Discovery*. The Tide Strong in our favor. Turn'd up with a light breese. Finding the Tide setting the Vessel Strong into a Small bight hoisted out the Launch to tow the Vessel round the the [sic] Tide so rapid, brought with the Stream Anchor. Soon after it parted. Let go the Best Bower. The Tide running 5 Miles per hour. Veer'd away to a whole. At Slack Water Sent the Boats to sweeps for the Anchor. [ ] the *Discoverys* Rounded the Point.

Sunday 10th. Fine pleasant weather. It being Slack Water the Boats empd sweeping but without success. In the Morning it was Cloudy. To the Southwd little Tide. Hove up the Anchor and proceeded to Join the *Discovery*. At 9 brought up in 7 fathom ¾ of a Mile from the Shore. Sent the Cutter to haul the Seine and the Launch for Water.

Monday 11th. Light Winds. In the morning got on board the Water Casks. Answd the Signal to weigh. Weighed and made Sail up the Inlet to find a more Suitable Situation for the Vessels to lay. At 10 Enter'd an extensive opening. The People empd working up Junk. Variable Winds.

Tuesday 12th. Mod and Clear Weather, Sailmakers making a new Jibb. At 6 in the Evening brought up in a Bay on the Starboard Shore in 5 fathom Water 2 Mile of Shore. Received a Stream Anchor and Cable from the *Discovery*. During the night Calm. At 4 Capt V in the Pinnace and Launch went a Surveying. The Observatory was Erected. Finding ourselves to far off Weigh'd and towed further in. Moored with a kedge. Got all the empty Casks & forge on Shore. The Extremes of the Bay from N 55° W to S 20° W. The Wind from the Southward.

Wednesday 13th. Fine agreeable pleasant weather. Empd watering the Vessel. Down Top Gallant Yards. AM. Hauld the Seine. Sent the Boilers for brewing Spruce Beer on Shore. The different [ ] on Shore. The rest overhauling the rigging on board. A fresh breese from SE.

Thursday June 14th 1792. The weather much the same. ½ past 2 Mr. Whidby with the *Discoverys* Cutter and our went to Explore an Inlet to the SE. At Sunset they saw two Vessels coming down the Arm. The Boats retd and gave the information. In the Morning they had passed us. Mr. Whidby went again. The *Chatham* got under Way to Speak Them. At 10 Saw them. Found they were Spanish Vessels one a Brig the other a Schooner Surveying the Straits.

Friday 15th. Moderate breezes and Cloudy. Tack'd occasionally working up into the Bay in the light airs. At 7 South Extreme of Birch Bay NEbE Distance 3 or 4 Leagues. Some rain during the. At 6 Fresh breezes & Squally. The Wind at East nearly in the Bay.

Saturday 16th. Fresh breese and Squally attended with Shower of Rain. At 1 brought up in 5 fathom water abreast the Observatory. Down Top Gallant Yards. The Carpenter with his Crew on Shore Cutting Spars. Steaded the Vessel with a Kedge. At Noon the Wind from East to NE.

Sunday 17th. The Wind fresh from the Southward and Eastward. The [ ] on Shore. ½ past 5 the Cutter retd from Surveying. Mustered the People.

Monday 18th. Do. Wr. At Daylight Mr. Johnstone in the Cutter accompanied by one of the *Discovery* Boats to finish an Inlet he had left undone in his former route.

Tuesday 19th. Fine Clear Weather. Empd occasionally on board. The People on Shore as—Received on Board Water and Wood.

Wednesday 20th. Fine pleasant weather. The Wind from the Southd and Eastward. The People on Shore. Mr. Johnstone retd having compleated. AM. Haul'd the Seine. Empd getting provisions out of the After Hold.

Thursday 21st. Light airs and Cloudy Weather. Hauld the Cutter up on Shore. Empd Cutting Wood. AM. Scrubb'd Hammocks. One Large Canoe with 25 Men pass'd by the Bay. The Seamen empd about the Rigging.

Friday 22d. Fine Serene Weather. In the Afternoon Set up the Rigging fore and Aft. AM. In the morning hauld the Seine. Got the Sails upon Deck to air. Seamen employed airing & Pointing them.

Saturday 23d. Fine Pleasant Weather. The *Discoverys* Launch retd having parted Company with the Pinnace. Empd getting everything on board. At Noon Cloudy Weather.

Sunday 24th. Do. Wr. Capt Vancouver retd in the Pinnace. The observatory and Tents were got on board. Got everything from the Shore. AM. At 4 Weighed the Kedge and hove up the Best Bower. Hoisted in the Cutter and made Sail. This Bay was named Birch Bay by Capt V. in Latitude 42° 53' 30" N Longitude 237° 32' East and Variation 19° 15' East. Being a commodious place for Vessels to refit having an exceeding fine river to Water at.

Monday June 25th, 1792. Fine Clear Weather. ½ past 12 Saw the two Spanish Vessels. At 4 Joined them. The Wind variable. At 8 luft the Topsails. During the night Tack'd occasionally. In the morning a light breese from the SE. Out Reefs and made Sail. At Noon the Extreme of the Land from SEbE to SbE. Distance 1½ Mile from each Shore. The *Discovery* and two Spanish Vessels in Company.

11

Unsigned Journal

Edmond Meany, the noted University of Washington professor, initially published *Vancouver's Discovery of Puget Sound* in 1907. Several years later, Alexander H. Turnbull of Wellington, New Zealand, contacted him. Turnbull purchased an unsigned journal from the library of R.T. Pritchett of London. The journal was clearly written by a member of the *Chatham*, but the author was unclear. Historians believed it to be written by either Edward Bell, a clerk, or the surgeon, William Walker.

The following was extracted from the *Washington Historical Quarterly*, Volume V, Numbers 2 and 3 (April and July 1914). It was also published in Meany's 1957 edition of his text.

[No. 2 p. 133] On the 28th [April 1792] at Noon our Lat: was 47.32 N and in the Evening the 29th falling calm, we came to an anchor with the *Discovery* near Destruction Island, the place where a Boat's Crew of the *Imperial Eagle* commanded by Mr. Berkley were barbarously murdered by the Natives as mention'd in Mears's Voyage. None of the natives came off to us but we observ'd two canoes entering a small Bay abreast of us. At about 3 we weigh'd per Signal and at 5 set Studding Sails with a moderate Soly: Breeze, but rainy weather. At daylight a strange Sail was seen in the N. W. quarter standing towards us, she hoisted American Colours. About 7 we spoke her, she proved to be the Ship *Columbia* of Boston commanded by a Mr Grey, on the Fur trade. She had wintered on the Coast in Port Clynquot in Berkley's Sound.[1] This Mr. Grey being the man who Mr Mears in his Chart has published having entered the Streights of De Fuca, and after proceeding a considerable distance up,

[1]Port Clayoquot is actually in Clayoquot Sound.

return'd to sea again by another passage to the Northward of that by which he entered —

Captn: Vancouver was desirous of obtaining from him some information respecting the Streights, he therefore hoisted a boat out, and sent an officer on board the *Columbia*. Mr Grey very civilly offered him any information he could possible give him, but at the same time told him that Mr Mears had been very much mislead in his information and had published what never had happened; for though he (Mr Grey) did enter the Streights of De Fuca, and proceeded a considerable distance, where he still saw an unbounded horizon, he return'd, but return'd by the same way he entered. He had been two & twenty months from Boston, and had obtained a valuable cargo of Furs. He had built a small sloop of about 45 tons at Clyoquot which was now trading to the Northward.

He gave no very favourable account of the Northern Indians whose daring and insolent spirit had carried them to very unwarrantable lengths. Several attempts had been made by them to seize his, and other Vessels on the Coast. Several people of different Ships had been treacherously murdered, and Mr Grey's Chief Mate with two of the seamen were in this manner murder'd while fishing round a point of Land, a small distance [p. 134] from the Ship. This happen'd somewhere about the Lat: of 54¼°. After the Boat with the Officer return'd we made sail to the Nd. And the *Columbia* stretched in for the Shore. About noon we were nearly abreast of the much talked of Streights of Juan De Fuca, the *Discovery* made our Signal to lead in. The weather was thick and Hazy and prevented our having an observation. Cape Classet at Noon bore N 20 E 2 miles. This Cape is settled by Captn: Vancouver in the Lat: of 48.23 N and the Longe: 235.38 Et.

At one o'clock we haul'd round Green Island, and as we pass'd had a view of the Spiral Rock, which is remarkable. On Green Island is a very large Village, and from it and the Villages on the Main, a number of canoes came off. The Natives brought a number of Otter Skins to sell, but wou'd part with none for anything but Copper & Blue Cloth Cloathing with Metal Buttons they were very eager after and we saw several with Blue Coats & round Hats. Mr Mears is very much out in the distance he makes the entrance of these Streights, he says they are 15 leagues wide, whereas the Entrance is no more than 12 leagues in breadth. In the Evening having but little wind and it coming on thick we brought up on the S. shore in 12 fathoms water and then observed the *Columbia* following us. She had just entered the Streights. After we came too a few fish were caught with the hook & line.

May. The following morning the 1st of May with a fine breeze at West and clear pleasant weather we got under weigh and proceeded up the Streights, and left the *Columbia* off Green Island laying too, bartering with the Natives for Skins. Several canoes follow'd us with skins, fish &c., to sell but the rage was copper; next to this article Cloth & wearing apparel with Brass Buttons, Copper wrist bands, Musquets & Swords were chiefly in demand.[2]

Among other articles offered for sale was their children, several were offered for a Musquet or a Sheet of Copper. The women being the first we had seen since leaving the Sandwich Islands, had not a few attacks of Gallantry made on them by the Sailors though they were by no means inviting. But however great the difference between them and the Sandwich Islands in point of Beauty much greater was it in point of behaviour, for here the smallest degree of indelicacy towards one of these Ladies, [p. 135] shock'd their modesty to such a degree, and had such an effect on them, that I have seen many of them burst into tears, they would endeavour to hide themselves in the bottom of their canoes and discover the most extreme degree of uneasiness and distress.

Some of the canoes were very large and contain'd a whole family of men & women and a considerable part of their Household furniture, large Bladders full of their delicious Whale Oil was in every canoe and the little Infants in their Cradles were plied with large quantities of it by their Mothers. As we got the Breeze fresher, the canoes soon dropp'd off.

About 6 o'clock in the evening having run about 20 leagues from the Entrance in a Bite on the S. side in 8 fathoms, from this the Streights appear'd to widen, but we saw some very distant land in which there were many apparent large openings. So far as we had yet proceeded up these Streights, we had seen no opening, nor the appearance of any Harbour, on the Southern, or Continental Shore; now two or three openings presented themselves, and as the great object of the voyage was if possible to discover a communication by water between this Coast and the Lakes situated on the other side of America, the Continental Shore must of course be kept always aboard and all openings minutely explored.

Captain Vancouver was now anxious to get the Vessels into a Harbor, and while the Vessels were refitting it was intended that the boats should be sent to explore the openings now in sight. Accordingly the next morning he went himself in the Pinnace, accompanied by our Cutter (both well arm'd) to look for a Harbour. This they found at a short distance from us, and the next morning we weigh'd and made sail for it. The Harbour was a very complete one and shelter'd from all winds but the

[2]None of the other journals made any reference to the Indians in possession of firearms. While this is not conclusive, it is certainly obvious the Indians understood their purpose.

water was deep and we anchor'd in 25 fathoms water not a quarter of a mile from the Shore. This place at first was named Port Discovery, conceiving ourselves the first that had been in it, but we afterwards found ourselves mistaken, it having been visited by two Spanish Vessels, and call'd Port Quadra, by which name it was continued and we settled its Lat: to be 48.2.30 N and the Long: 237.22.19 E.

Opposite to where the Vessels lay a low Point of Land run out, where there was an excellent run of Freshwater. Here the Tents and Observatory were set up, and there being plenty of Spruce Pine here a party from each Ship was sent on shore to brew Spruce Beer for the Ships' Companies. As this Beverage was well known to be a great Antiscorbutic, the people were allow'd to drink freely of it in lieu of their [p. 136] Grog. As the *Chatham* was very open in her upper works the Carpenters of both Vessels were employ'd in Caulking her.

Not having met the Store ship at the Sandwich Islands as was expected and fearing that we might probably not see her till the next Season at those Islands, and possible not then, should any unfortunate accident have happen'd to her in which case we should have been somewhat distress'd for Provisions particularly Bread & Flour, it was only proper to guard against such disappointments and delays. The Ships Company was therefore on the 5th put to two-thirds allowance of Bread only. This on the coast of American cou'd be not hardship as Fish is always to be got. We haul'd the Seine here generally every day, and in general with success, and we frequently got Salmon Trout in it.

On the 17th Captn: Vancouver, with Lieut: Paget, and Mr. Johnstone our Master set out in 3 Boats well Mann'd and arm'd, and victuall'd for a week, to explore the openings between this and our last anchorage which I spoke of. In the meantime the Vessels were refitting for sea. The Powder was sent on shore to dry, and being in want of Plank the Carpenters were employ'd, after the Caulking was finished, in sawing up a fine large tree, of which there were plenty, and very convenient. As there were no Inhabitants here we carried on all our operations with facility; now and then a couple or 3 canoes wou'd come in with a little Fish to sell, but this was not often, and they were very quite and inoffensive. They were evidently a tribe that visited the Sea Coast but seldom, as they were generally clad in skins of Land animals, and during our stay here, they brough[t] but one Sea Otter skin to sell. Once or twice they brought some fresh kill'd Venison which was very acceptable to us, for though we could everywhere observe the track of Deer, and shooting excursions were frequently made, we were never so fortunate to shoot any here.

When the time arrived for the expected return of the Boats, we began impatiently to look out for them, but it was not till the 16th that they return'd to the Ships after nine days absence. They had examined several arms or openings, which after running some distance inland closed, and they had left some extensive openings unexplored to the Eastward of this Port, where it was now intended to proceed to with the Ships. Having got everything ready for Sea, on the 18th we sail'd out of Port Quadra. The weather was fair and pleasant, indeed we had enjoy'd much fine weather in Port. After getting outside, by desire of Captn: Vancouver, we parted company with the *Discovery*, in order to examine an opening in the N. W. quarter, whilst she proceeded up an arm to which the Continent had been brought, to the Eastd. of Port Quadra. We cross'd [p. 137] the Streights with a fine Breeze, and entered the opening about 6 o'clock in the evening and came to an anchor for the night. In the morning boats were dispatched to examine the branches which run within this opening, which employ'd us till the 23rd. It is very extensive being full of Islands. The land is delightful, being in many places clear and the soil so rich that the grass in several parts grew to man height. We were surprised in such a fine country to find scarce and inhabitants, not a smoke or a village was seen, and only two small canoes with 3 people in each were met by the Boats in all their cruizing; from these, three young Fawns just kill'd were purchased. We saw several Deer on the sides of the rising grounds, but could never kill any. The navigation in this place is so full of Rocks and small Islands was intricate and dangerous. On the 21st we touch'd a Rock on one side, whilst at the other we had twenty-two fathoms water.

On the 23rd we again enter'd the Streights but a different opening to that we came in at. We cross'd over and about Noon got into the arm which the *Discovery* went when we parted from her. Here we met with a small tribe of Indians who came off to sell a little fish, Bows & Arrows, and some few skins of Land Animals. We observ'd among them some articles we knew they must have got our [out] of the *Discovery*, and they soon made sufficient that she was up the arm. The people spoke a different language from the Indians we saw at the entrance of Dufuca's Streights though little else bout them appeared different for they were equally as dirty. It seemed evident that their intercourse with Ships had been limited (if indeed they ever had any) from their surprize and astonishment at many things, and their not having about them any European articles whatever except it might be a knife, but they had a very good idea of bartering and wou'd not part with anything without the value of it. Copper was yet the rage.

[No. 3 p. 215] We were detained by the Tides, which were rapid, from joining the *Discovery* before the 26th when we found her at anchor off a Point of a small opening called by Captn: Vancouver Restoration

Point. Here there was a small village, containing, I shou'd suppose, about 60 or 70 Inhabitants. It was situated on a fine rising ground, and the Country round it was extremely pleasant to appearance and clear. The Natives had brought a good supply of Venison to the *Discovery*. Two of her boats with Lt: Paget & Mr Whidby were now absent on a surveying expedition up the continuation of this & the Arms round us, and the morning after our arrival Captn: Vancouver with Mr Johnstone set out with two Boats on another expedition. Though I have but just before mentioned that I conceived the Natives hereabouts had but little intercourse with Europeans, we had here a proof that they were not entirely unaccustomed to Trading Vessels for two very good Sea Otter Skins were brought off for sale, and the price was copper. However they took so reasonable a price, and their having no more than these two skins among them makes me think that the knowledge they have of Trading Ships is acquir'd by their own commerce with Tribes between them and the Sea.

On the 27th at night Mr Whidby & Lt. Paget return'd from their cruize having closed up the Arms. In one place they met with a considerable [p. 216] tribe of Indians from whom he had nearly met with some trouble, but by early good management nothing material happened. After being very well treated by the Boats party the Natives seized the opportunity of their stopping at a Beach to Dinner, to attack them. They were observed to string their Bows & sling their Quivers and were making for the Wood behind the party at Dinner from whence it was no doubt their intention to fire on them but as this was observ'd Mr Menzies & Mr Manby catching up their Muskets ran up and drove them back to their Canoes. As there were some opening to look into the Northd, we weigh'd anchor and quitted this place the next day the 28th and as Mr Johnstone was still absent in our Cutter with Captn: Vancouver we took Mr Whidby and the *Discovery's* Launch with us to carry on the survey and when we came abreast of the opening she was dispatched along with our Launch in which went Ltd: Hanson with a week's provisions. In the meantime we anchored off a place called Rose Point from the numerous trees of that name that were on the low ground; besides this there were plenty of currant, Gooseberry, & Raspberry bushes, and large beds of Strawberries but very little if any of these Fruits were yet ripe.

June. On the 30th we were join'd by the *Discovery* and we proceeded with her on the further examination of this tedious Inland Navigation. Nothing remarkable occurred till the 2nd of June when sailing up a place called Port Gardner in Possession Sound, by the negligance of the man in the chains about one o'clock in the afternoon we run aground upon a Muddy Bank. We immediately gave the *Discovery* the alarm and at the same time made the Signal for assistance. She was astern of us and directly anchor'd and dispatched her Boats to our relief. On sounding astern of the Ship it was found that we had run a considerable distance over a Shoal and before we could carry an anchor our [out] into water sufficiently deep we veer'd away four Hawsers on end. At Highwater we hove off without any damage whatever and brought up in 9 fam. water. As we found this place like all the others shut up, we weigh'd the next morning and sail'd out of the Port and the following day anchor'd in a Bay to wait the return of Lt Hanson & Mr Whidby and to celebrate His Majesty's Birthday. The Boats return'd on the 4th and on that day possession was taken on shore by Captn: Vancouver in His Majesty's name of all the Land in the Streights, and the part in which we now were call'd Gulph of Georgia. On this occasion the *Discovery* fired 21 guns on the Flag of possession being hoisted and as the King's Birth Day the Ship's Companies were served double allowance of Grog to drink his health.

There was in the Bay a fine Sandy Beach where the Seine was [p. 217] haul'd with pretty good success. We saw no Village nor Inhabitants near this place but on the point of the beach there stood a remarkable high pole, strongly supported by props at the Bottom, and at the top of it was fixed a human skull. What the reason of so curious a thing could be no one could devine. Many such had been seen in different parts of the Inland Navigation and in Mr Hanson's late cruize. No less than three of these Poles with skulls on them were seen at one place contiguous to which was a very large burying Ground. Some bodies were wrapp'd up in Mats & Skins and laid in canoes, whilst some that appear'd but recently dead were thrown into a deep hole in the earth and not covered.

On the 5th we left this Bay and proceeded on our exploration, crossing over to the opening out of which we came the 23rd of May, having to that place carried the Continent. We found Tides here extremely rapid and on the 9th in endeavouring to get round a point to a Bay in which the *Discovery* had anchor'd, we were swept to Leeward of it with great impetuosity. We therefore let go the Stream anchor in 28 fathoms water but in bringing up, such was the force of the Tide that we parted the Cable. We immediately let go the Bower with which we brought up. On trying the Tide we found it running at the rate of 5½ miles an hour. At slack water we swept for the anchor but could not get it, after several fruitless attempts to get it we were at last obliged to leave it and join the *Discovery* in Strawberry Bay. This Bay obtain'd its name from a tolerable quantity of Strawberries we found there. As the *Discovery* had only been waiting for us here we left it the following day and steered for a very extensive opening trending about N. and came to an anchor in a very pleasant Bay which was called Birch Bay. From this place two Boat expeditions were undertaken one by Captain Vancouver and the other by Mr

Whidby. In the meantime the Observatory was set up for the purpose of regulating the watches and Spruce Beer brew'd for the Ships Companies. Our operations on shore were carried on in a very convenient place there being a fine Grass plot of nearly a mile in length with a fine fresh water River at the back of it. Captn: Vancouver set out with his two Boats and 10 days provisions on the 12th to the Westward and Mr Whidby with two Boats and a weeks provisions towards an opening to the Eastward of us. The same Evening we were surprized to see Mr Whidby's Boats return but much more so when we learnt from them that they had seen two Vessels, a Brig and a Schooner coming down the Arm which lay round the point of the Bay. It was immediately conjectured from the improbability of trading vessels being in this inhospitable part of the Coast and the distance from the entrance [p. 218] of the Streights that they were foreign Vessels employed on the same service as ourselves and which conjecture we afterwards found to be right. A lookout for them was kept during the night and nothing been seen of them. In the morning a boat was dispatched to the Entrance of the arm but she returned without seeing them. It was thought they had pass'd during the night. Mr Broughton therefore got under weigh in the *Chatham* and the boats were redispatched on their examination. Whilst the *Chatham* was getting under way the Vessels were observed by the help of the Glasses a considerable way to the Westward of us so that they must have pass'd in the night.

We soon came up with them and they hoisted Spanish Colours. A Boat with an officer was sent on board the Brig where he was very politely received by the Commander. They proved to be His Catholic Majesty's Brig *Soutile* commanded by Don Dionisio Galiano and the Schooner *Mexicana*, Don Cayetano Valdez, Commander; both Captains of Frigates in the Royal Navy of Spain and employed in surveying these Streights to complete the parts left unfinished by Seigr. Malespini with whom these two gentlemen had been Lieutenants. They left Nootka late in May where there were at that time lying 3 Frigates and a Spanish Brig of War, Don Quadra, Commodore.

Don Galiano offered us every information & civility in his power and sent on board some milk & cabbages that he had brought from Nootka. The Vessels were very small, the Brig not being more than 45 tons Burthen. They had each a Lieutenant, a Pilot, and twenty men and carried two Brass Guns each. After receiving the necessary information we parted from them and made for our old anchorage, whilst they continued their route to the Westd. From this time to the 23rd we were employed in taking the necessary observations for determining the rates of the watches, and in other ways and Mr Whidby's party having returned after an absence of six days, closing the places up which he went to explore. We cut here some remarkably fine Plank, of the Pine tree, and there was a good deal of Alder & Birch here. We had tolerable good luck with the Seine, the Bay affording plenty of Flat fish, some Salmon Trout and a small kind of Bream and we now and then shot some Ducks. Though there was no village near us and we were but very seldom visited by canoes, Mr Whidby in his last Cruize, at no great distance from the Ships, met with a numerous Tribe of Indians, not less than 300, that were just shifting their Village. They had very little connexion with them as the Indians shew'd no desire for their landing near them. On the 23rd Captn: [p. 219] Vancouver returned after an absence of twelve days; he had met with the two Spanish Vessels and been on board them and now was by agreement going to join them as our destination was much the same as theirs and as we shou'd be obliged to visit at the place to which Captn: Vancouver had carried the Continent during a further expedition of the Boats we shou'd have an opportunity of being sociable.

On the 24th we quitted the Bay which is in the Lat: of 48.53.30 N and the Long: 237.32 Et. and stood to the Westward. About Noon we came up with the Spanish Vessels with whom we kept company till the 26th when we came to the situation from whence our next surveying cruize was to commence, and late at night the whole Squadron anchored, in a place which from its unenviting shore and the few refreshments beyond water which it produced was call'd by us Desolation Reach, its Lat: is 50.11 N and Longe: 235.27 Et.

12

Thomas Heddington

Thomas Heddington was born June 1, 1774, in Chatham. He entered the navy at age twelve and served on several ships before joining the *Chatham* as a midshipman. He was promoted to lieutenant in November 1795 and served on several more ships until "retiring" to land service in 1802 when he was put in charge of the Hawkesley Signal Station. He was promoted to commander in 1806 and to captain on the retired list in 1851. He died in Exter April 2, 1852.

Saturday 28th. At 1 Sounded in 30 fms Fine black Sand. At 7 Sounded in 25 fms Fine black Sand. Extremes of the Land from North to S 40° E^{t}. Offing 4 or 5 miles. In Royals. At ½ past 1 the wind shifted suddenly & took us aback, fill'd & stood to the North^{d}. At 2 Tack'd per signal. At ½ past 5 sounded in 30 fms black stones. At 7 made sail & bore away along shore. At 8 the Land from SSE to NNW. Sounded in 25 fms clay & black stones. Offing 4 or 5 [NW]. At Noon the Land from S 40° [ ] to N 28° W. Sounded in 13 fms Fine Black Sand.

Sunday 29th. In Studding sails. At 12 Tacked. At 3 anchor'd per signal in 16 fms fine black sandy bottom on the South^{d} of Destruction Island. Found a Current Setting NNE ½ a mile per Hour. At ½ past 2 ans^{d} the sign^{l} to weigh. At 4 weigh'd & made Sail with the *Discovery*. The *Discovery* fir'd a gun. Ans^{d} it with another. At 5 Set Studding Sails. At 6 the N^{o} Ea of the Land bore N 20° W. Saw a [Strange] Sail in the NW Quarter. At ½ past [7] spoke the American Ship *Columbia*, Gray from Boston. She has wintered on the Coast in Port [ ]. At 11 the *Discovery* made the signal to lead into Port or Places bearing that appearance. At Noon [in 1st reefs]. Cape Classet the South^{d} [Extremes] of the Entrance of Juan De Fuca Streights bearing N 20° E. From the thickness of the weather we could not procure an observation

"As we have been in with the Coast ever since we made it on the 18th I though it very unnecessary to work the Days works to this Period."

T Heddington

At 1 haul'd round Tatooch Isld in the Entrance of the Streight passing between it & a small rock which lays to the North^{d} of it. At ¼ past 7 answ^{d} the Signal to anchor & at ½ past anchor'd in 12 fms with the Best Bower hard stony bottom. Extremes of the [Land] seen from E ½ S to W^{t}. Off shore ¼ of a Mile. Canoes occassionally [ ] with small [shells]. At ½ 6 weigh'd per Signal & made Sail to the East^{d} of the Streights. At 8 Extremes of the Land from E by N to West. At Noon Ext^{m} of the N^{o} Shore from [ ] to W b N. The South^{n} Shore from East to W b S.

Tuesday 1st May. At 7 ans^{d} the Signal to prepare to anchor. At ¾ past anchor to the North^{d} of a low sandy spit [ ]; the Streight from this situation had same appearance of being clos'd. Hoisted out the Cutter. Wash'd & smok'd below. Cooper setting up Casks. Sail makers repairing the Main Sail. Several Canoes visited us, not ornamented like Classet.

Wed May 2^{d}. P.M. Moderate Breezes and Clear Weather. Employ'd about the rigging. The night nearly calm. A.M. Moderate [Breezes] & Clear Weather. ½ past 5 answ^{d} [the signal] to weigh. Weigh'd [ ] with the *Discovery* & made sail to the [Eastward keeping] to the South^{d} of a Small Green Isl^{d} in a Harbour which the Boat had discover'd the preceding afternoon. [At 11] brought up in 25 fms water. Hoisted out the Launch & moor'd with the Best Bower to the north^{d} & Stream to the South^{d}.

Thurs 3^{d}. P.M. Employ'd [overhauling] and airing the Sail Room. Unbent the Sail. Down T G^{l} Yards & masts upon Deck & Struck Lower Yards of Top Masts. In the night calm. A.M. Mod & Clear. Scrubb'd Hammocks. Employ'd overhauling the Rigging. Sent the Cooper on Shore with the Empty Casks. Carpenters Caulking the Top Sides. Sway'd up Lower Yards, Top Masts & T G^{l} Masts.

Friday 4th. P.M. Mod & Clear. Employ'd about the Rigging. A.M. D^{o} weather. Employ'd in the Hold. Got 2 Caulkers from the *Discovery.*

Sat 5th. P.M. Ditto weather. Sent the Sail Maker on shore to repair the Fore Top Sail and a party to cut wood & Brew. A.M. D^{o} W^{r}. D^{o} Employ'd. Sent the armourer's Forge on shore. Put the Ships Company to ⅔^{d} allowance of Bread.

Sun 6th. P.M. Ditto weather. Employ'd as before. [ ]. Punished Thos Townsend Quarter Master & Jno Clark Marine with 12 lashes each for Insolence to their superior officer.

Mon 7th. P. D^{o} weather. Employ'd wooding & Brewing. A.M. Ditto Weather. Sent the Cutter to attend Cap^{tn} Vancouver exploring the Streights.

Tues 8th. Calm & Thick foggy weather. Fir'd two Swivels in answer to two heard from the Boats. A.M. Ditto weather. Employ'd as yesterday. Sent the Powder on shore to air.

Wed 9th. P.M. Light Breezes with Rain. Parties as before. P.M. Moderate and Clear. Ditto Employ'd.

Thursday 10th. P.M. Mod Breezes & Clear Weather. Ditto Employ'd. A.M. Ditto weather. Rec^{d} wood.

Friday 11th. Ditto weather. Employ'd as yesterday.

Saturday 12th. Mod & Clear. Rec^{d} wood & water per Launch. A.M. D^{o} weather. Parties as before. Rec^{d} wood & water. Having finish'd Caulking returned the 2 Men belonging to the *Discovery*.

Sunday 13th. P.M. Light wind & Cloudy. Rec^{d} water & a Cask of Spruce Beer per Launch. A.M. D^{o} Weather. [Scraped the] Sides. Rec^{d} water per Launch. Muster'd the Ships Company. Parties as before.

Mon May 14th. P.M. Light wind and Cloudy. Clean'd the [ ] & Bread Room. A.M. D^{o} weather. Sent some Barrels of Powder on shore to air. Rec^{d} 2 turns of water per Launch. Cooper, Sail Maker, Brewers &c Employ'd as before.

Tues 15th. P.M. D^{o} Weather. Parties on shore as before. Carpenters Carpenters [sic] preparing a tree to be saw'd into Plank. A.M. Thick Rainy weather. Employ'd occasionally on board.

Wed 16th. P.M. Thick Rainy weather. The Cutter return'd. Rec^{d} a turn of wood. A.M. Mod & Cloudy. Employ'd occasionally with the Boatswain.

Thursday 17th. P.M. Light airs and Cloudy. Rec^{d} on board 12 Casks of Spruce Beer. Secur'd it upon Deck. A.M. Light airs with Showers of Rain. Bent Sails, up Top Gall^{t} Yards & got every thing from the Shore.

Friday 18th. P.M. Light Variable airs with Showers of Rain. Weigh'd the Best Bower anchor & hove into half the Stream Cable. Got the Forge of the armourer from the Shore & hoisted in the Cutter. At ½ past 6 weigh'd and work'd nearer the mouth of Harbour. At 8 brought up on the Northern Shore in 26 fms with the Stream anchor. A.M. D^{o} weather. At ½ past 3 weigh'd and made Sail out of the Harbour. Light Variable airs & Clear weather.

Saturday May 19th. At 1 Parted Company with the *Discovery* to Explore an opening which appear'd to the N^{o} of West^{d}. At ½ past 5 hove & sent the Cutter to Sound the Entrance of an opening which had been discover'd. At 6 Enter'd the Harbour, Sounded in 19 fms. At ½ 7 anchor'd with the Stream in 9 fms. Scrubb'd Hammocks. At 10 sent the Launch and Cutter to Explore an arm which branch'd off to the North^{d}. At 10 weigh'd and made sail up an Eastern branch. At 11 brought up with the

Stream in 24 fms about 1½ up the Arm. Distant from the shore a fine Sandy beach 2 Cables Length.

Sunday May 20th. P.M. Mod and Clear. In the Evening the Launch and Cutter return'd having left a spacious inlet to be Explor'd. A.M. Light winds and Clear weather. Sent the Cutter to Explore the Entrance. At 7 weigh'd and made Sail up the arm. At ½ past 10 brought up in 25 fms [½] a Cables Length off Shore. Sent the Launch further up the arm. At Noon the Cutter return'd.

Mon 21st. P.M. Calm weather. At 1 the Launch return'd. At ½ past 2 weigh'd but it being calm & the Tide making against us. At 4 brought up in 26 fms. Sent the Launch & Cutter away to explore two Branches in this [Eastern] opening. At 9 the Boats return'd. They met with a few Indians who [behav'd] Friendly and sold them some young Fawns. One of them was alive. A.M. Light Wind & Cloudy. At [ ] weigh'd and made sail farther up the arm. Clean'd below.

Tues 22d. P.M. Light Winds & Cloudy. At ½ past [10 dropp't] through the Narrows. When through [touch'd on a rock] on the Larboard [ ]. At 2 brought up in 19 fms in a spacious Bay. Sent the Cutter to explore it. A.M. Calm & [ ]. At 9 weigh'd and with the Tide dropp'd [towards an] opening into the Streights.

Wed 23d. P.M. Clear weather. At 1 a Moderate Breeze sprung up. At 3 brought up between a small island and the Main in 12 fms. Sent the Launch [on Shore]. Receiv'd a turn of water. From the [Vast] quantity of straw Berries found here this Place obtained the name of Straw Berry Bay. Squally weather. A.M. Mod and Clear. At ½ past 5 weigh'd and made Sail into the Streights. Tack'd occasionally [passing] to the Eastward of Sandy Island which at Noon bore N 25° Wt 5 Miles and the opening of which the *Discovery* stood was open.

Thurs 24th. P.M. Moderate and Clear. At 1 Enter'd the Inlet with a strong Flood Tide. At ½ past 5 brought up on the North Shore in 8 fms ¾ of a mile offing & 5 or 6 Leagues from the Mouth of the Inlet. Squally weather. A.M. Mod and Cloudy. At 3 weigh'd with the last quarter of Flood and stood over towards the South Shore and at 7 brought up [9] fms ½ a mile from the Shore. Sent the Launch on Shore and recd a turn of wood. Set up the Top Mast & Top Gallt Rigging. At Noon weigh'd & with the Flood work'd up the Inlet.

Friday May 25th. P.M. Moderate Breezes and Cloudy weather. At 5 brought up in 19 fms Sandy bottom. A.M. Do weather. At 3 weigh'd & with the Flood work'd up the Inlet. At finding no tide with us and gaining no Ground at 7 brot up on the Eastn shore in 12 fms water Sandy bottom ½ a mile from the Shore.

Sat 26th. P.M. Cloudy weather. A Light Breeze sprung up from the

North[d]. Weigh'd and made Sail up the Inlet. At 4 saw the *Discovery* at an anchor in a Harbour on the west[n] Shore. Stood for it & at 4 brought up near her in 38 fms 3 Miles off shore. A.M. Mod Breezes. At 4 the Cutter was sent to accompany Cap[tn] Vancouver in exploring the Inlet. At 9 weigh'd & made Sail farther in Shore. At 11 brought up in 25 fms Sandy bottom ¾ of a mile off shore.

Sun 27th. P.M. Mod and Clear. Sent the Empty water casks on shore. Carpenters Painting the sides. Wash'd and smok'd. A.M. Calm and Cloudy. Haul'd the Seine. Mod Breezes and thick Rains.

Mon 28th. P.M. Moderate and Cloudy. At 8 weigh'd and made sail out of the Bay accompanied by the *Discovery* Launch. A.M. D[o] weather. At Noon Entered an arm trending to the North[d] & West[d].

Tues 29th. P.M. Moderate Breezes and Clear weather. At 8 brought up with the Stream anchor in 75 fms Sandy bottom 1½ Cables length off shore. A.M. D[o] weather. Sent the Launch to accompany the *Discovery's* Launch in Exploring the arm. At 7 weigh'd & made sail up the arm in search of a convenient place to anchor in.

Wed 30th. P.M. Mod Breezes and Clear weather. Sent the Small Boat on Shore upon an Island to look for water but found none. At 7 brought up in 35 fms muddy bottom 1 Cables length off shore. Down T G[l] yards. Sent the Carpenter on shore to saw Plank & Brewers to Brew Spruce Beer. Punish'd Henry Barfleur Seaman with 12 lashes for Insolence to his Superior Officer.

Thursday 31st. P.M. Light wind and [Clear Weather]. Haul'd up the Best Bower Cable to get [ ] from under it. Arriv'd here H. M. Ship *Discovery* and the Cutter came on board. A.M. Cloudy with Showers of Rain. [Employed occasionally about the ship.]

Frid June 1st. P.M. Cloudy with Showers. At 1 weigh'd but there being but little wind the Tide drifted us down the Inlet. At 3 a Breeze sprung up from the South[d] & [Eastward & made] sail up the Inlet again. At 9 brought up in 13 fms [on] the Larboard Shore. A.M. Ditto weather. At 4 weigh'd and in Company with the *Discovery* made Sail up the Inlet. At 11 Enter'd a Harbour. At Noon the Mouth of the Harbour from S 40° E[t] to S 26° E. White Cliff Island from S 29° E[t] to S 34° E. The low Land at the Head of the Harbour from N 11° W[t] to N 22° W[t].

Sat 2[d]. P.M. Mod Breezes and Cloudy weather. At 1 got aground upon a soft muddy bottom. Fird 2 guns & [made] signal of distress. The *Discovery* sent her [boats to our] assistance. Run out the Stream anchor with 4 Hawsers on end & hove taught till high water. Took this opportunity of repairing part of the [copper] on the Star[b] Bow which had rubb'd off by the Bill of the anchor. When aground the Points of Entrance bore from S 32° E[t] to S [27]° E[t]. The [W[t]] end of White Cliff Island S 28° E[t] &

the Low land of the Head of the Bay from N 19° W[t] to N 31° W[t]. Down Top gallant Yards & Top gall[t] Masts. Punish'd David Dornan Seaman with 36 lashes for neglect of Duty. At 12 hove off the Tide having flood. At 2 Warp[d] into 9 fms soft bottom where we brought up with the Stream anchor. A.M. D° weather. At 9 weigh'd per Signal and made sail out of the Harbour. At noon brought up in 40 fms. White Cliff Island from S 27° [ ] to S [ ].

Sun 3[d]. P.M. Mod breezes and Clear weather. Employ'd occasionally. The Launch return'd. A.M. D° weather. Rec[d] a turn of water per Launch & hoist'd her in to paint.

Mon 4th. P.M. Mod & Cloudy. Employ'd occasionally. A.M. Light winds & Cloudy. Scrubb'd Hammocks. Rec[d] 2 turns of water per Cutter. Carpenters painting the Launch.

Tues 5th. P.M. Light wind with Showers of Rain. Employ'd occasionally. A.M. Light wind & Cloudy. Haul'd the Seine. At 7 weigh'd & made Sail out of the Gulf in Company with the *Discovery*. Mod Breezes & Clear.

Wed. 6th. P.M. Moderate breezes and Clear. At 10 brought up in 33 fms 1½ mi off shore. In the night Light Wind. A.M. Mod and Clear. At 7 weigh'd & with the Tide in our favour work'd down the Gulf. Carpenters as before.

Thursday 7th. P.M. Mod & Clear. At ½ past 1 brought up in [7] fms 1½ off shore. Protection Isl[d] bear [S 48° W[t]] to [S 51° W[t]]. Dungeness Spit [ ]. At 6 [ ]. Light winds. At ½ past 10 A.M. brought up in 13 fms 2 or 3 miles off Shore. Dungeness Spit bearing S 54°W[t], Protection Isl[d] from S 26° W[t] to S 22° W[t]. Clear Weather.

Friday June 8th. P.M. Calm & Clear. At 5 a Breeze sprung up. Ans[d] the Signal to weigh. Weigh'd & made Sail towards the North Part of the Straits. At 10 Fir'd a swivel to know the *Discovery's* situation. She ans[d] it bearing NNW. At 11 brought up in 33 fms. A.M. Light wind. At ½ past 3 weigh'd & made Sail towards the *Discovery*. At 7 brought up in 29 fms Sandy Island from N 51° W to N 40° W[t]. Laying in the Entrance of a opening with N[d] of westw[d]. Employ'd working up Junk.

Sat 9th. P.M. Light Variable airs & Clear weather. Sail Makers making a new jib. A.M. Light wind. At ½ past 1 weigh'd in the Company with the *Discovery* & with the Tide in favor turned into the opening. At ½ past 2 the Tide swept us at the Back of [ ] Sandy Island & finding it set against us, brought up with the Stream in 20 fms. At 3 parted the Stream Cable, let go the Small Bower & veer'd to a whole Cable. Found the tide running 5¼ Knots per Hour. At Slack Tide Swept for the anchor but could not hook it.

Sun 10th. P.M. Light wind and Clear. Wash'd & smok'd below. At

Slack water swept again for the Stream anchor but without success. A.M. Mod & Cloudy. Swept a third time for the Stream anchor but without success. At 7 weigh'd and made Sail for Strawberry Bay where we found the *Discovery.* At 10 brought up in 7 fms ½ a mile off Shore at our former anchorage. We were visited by Mrs Puget & Whidby in the *Discovery's* Boats. We began painting the vessel [but as] Cap^{n} Vancouver refus'd to assist us with a little oil which we wanted, we were oblig'd to leave the sides one yellow and the other we painted black as we had black paint [mix'd]. Sent the empty water casks on shore.

Mon 11th. P.M. Light wind. A.M. Light wind & Clear. Rec^{d} the water casks from the Shore. Ans^{d} the Signal to weight. At 6 weigh'd & made Sail up the Inlet. At 10 Enter'd a very extensive opening. Many Indians visited [among] whom were two pretty young women.

Tues June 12th. P.M. Mod Breezes and Clear weather. Sail makers [ ] a new jib. At 6 brought up in a Bay on the [Star^{b}] Shore of the Arm [in 5 fms 1½ or 2 Miles] off Shore. Rec^{d} a Stream anchor and cable from the *Discovery.* [ ] Small Bower to the NW & a Kedge to the [ ]. The Forge & the empty Beer & water Casks [on shore]. When moor'd the Extreme of the Bay from [ ] to S 20° W^{t}. Rec^{d} a turn of water per Launch. Birch Bay is by far the most pleasant Place we have been at on the Coast of [America]. Round it is [spacious] beach of level land extending for Miles. [Saw a Canoe] in a tree with a Dead Body in it. Mod & Clear.

Wed 13th. P.M. Employ'd occasionally. Rec^{d} a turn of water per Launch which compleated the [Butts] in the Fore hold. Down Top gall^{t} yards. A.M. Haul'd the Seine. Armour employ'd at the Forge. A Party brewing.

Thurs 14th. P.M. Light wind & Clear. At 5 Mod & Cloudy. Sent our Cutter accompanied by one of the *Discovery's* to explore the Inlet. At 10 the Cutters returned having seen two vessels with Spanish Colours. The one appeared to be a Brig, the other a [ ]. These vessels were standing towards us. A.M. D^{o} weather. At Day light the Cutters were again sent on their expedition. At 4 unmoor'd. At 5 weigh'd and made Sail to the [North^{d}] to speak the Vessels seen by the Boats the preceeding Evening. Previous to our weighing a Lieutenant [(Baker)], a midshipman [(Nicholas)] & a party of men were sent on board by Captn Vancouver.[1] Clear'd Ship for action. At 10 Found them to be a Spanish Brig & Schooner. Hail'd the Brig, hove too along side of her and sent a Boat on board. At 11 by return of the Boat we rec^{d} the following intelligence

---

[1] I believe the reference here meant that Broughton "filled out" the crew of *Chatham* with a few from the *Discovery.* From Heddington's comment, it is possible that he was unaware that Vancouver was out exploring in the small boats.

"That the Brig & Schooner, *Sutile* & *Mexicana* were employ'd by the Spanish Government in carrying on a Survey of these Streights [recently begun by a] Spanish Frigate; that the Commanders we met were Don Dionisio Alcala Galiano & Don Valdez both Captains of Frigates in the Spanish Navy but the former who commanded the Brig is chief of the Expedition. The vessels are each of 45 Tons Burthen & were fitted out from the Port of Acapulco from where they Proceeded to Nootka Sound which was the last Port they were in till they enter'd the Streights. They inform'd us that the Governor's Name is Don [ ] Quadra who is waiting impatiently our arrival when he means to cede that [place] to us. The *Active* Brig is laying there to take him to [ ].

Friday 15th. P.M. Mod Breezes and Cloudy weather. Tack'd occasionally working up towards the Bay. At 7 the South Extreme of Birch Bay NE b [ ] distant 3 or 4 Leagues. Light wind. Tack'd occasionally during the night. A.M. Fresh Breezes and squally with Rain. At 4 In 1st Reef of the Top Sails. At Day Light South Extreme of Birch Bay NE 3 or 4 Leagues. Employ'd occasionally. At Noon enter'd Birch Bay.

Sat 16th. P.M. Fresh Breezes and Squally weather. At 1 brought up in 5 fms in the Bay with the Small Bower. Down Top Gallt Yards. A.M. Mod Breezes and Cloudy. Sent the Carpenters on shore to cut a tree down for Plank. A Party on shore wooding. Run a Kedge and Towline out to the SE and moor'd with it. Sail makers repairing the jib. Armourer &c as before. When moor'd bearings Extremes of the Bay N [62°] Wt & S 24° Wt. A Snowy Mountain N 86° Et.

Sun 17th. P.M. Fresh Breezes and Cloudy weather. Recd a turn of wood and a Cask of Spruce Beer. A.M. Mod and Cloudy. Employ'd occasionally. Muster'd the Ships Company.

Mon 18th. P.M. Mod Breezes and Clear weather. Employ'd occasionally. A.M. Haul'd the Seine. Sent the Cutter and Launch to explore the Western Side of the Inlet. Employ'd wooding. Carpenters Sawing Plank. Sail makers making a new Jib.

Tues 19th. P.M. D° Weather. Employ'd wooding. Sail makers &c. &c. as before. A.M. D° weather. D°. Employ'd wash'd & smok'd between Decks and the Boatswain's store room. Recd a turn of wood.

Wed 20th. P.M. Ditto weather. Ditto Employ'd. The Cutter and Launch return'd. A. M. D° weather. Employ'd getting provision out of the Main hold. Air'd the Gunners Store room.

Thurs 21st. P.M. Light wind & Cloudy weather. Haul'd the Cutter up on shore to clean her bottom. Employ'd wooding. Recd a turn of wood per Launch. A.M. Ditto weather. Scrubbd hammocks. Recd a turn of water per Launch. Armourer and Carpenter &c. Employ'd on shore. Seamen necessarily on board.

Friday 22^{d}. P.M. Ditto weather. Employ'd over hauling & [airing] the [Sail Room]. Party [wooding]. A.M. D^{o} weather. Empd [ ] on shore the same.

Saturday June 23^{d}. P.M. Moderate Breezes & Cloudy weather. Rec^{d} a turn of wood per Launch. A.M. Set the Main Rigging up and the Fore & [ ] Top Mast Rigging.

June 24th. P.M. Mod Breezes & Cloudy weather. Launch the Cutter and brought the Beer and water off. A.M. Light wind and Clear weather. At 4 weigh'd the Kedge. At ½ past 5 ans^{d} the Signal to weigh'd. Weigh'd the Bower and made Sail in Company with the *Discovery* out of the Bay. Sent the Boats to bring off the Plank. At ½ past 6 hove too and at 8 the Boats return'd. Hoisted them in and made Sail to the Westward. Wash'd & smok'd below. At Noon Birch Bay on with the Snowy Mountain [ ]. Spanish P^{t} S 55° E. Lat^{d} Obs^{d} 48° 59' N.

Mon 25th. P.M. Mod Breezes and Cloudy weather. At 3 join'd company with the Spanish vessels *Sutile* & *Mexicana*. At 8 in 1st reef of the Top Sails. Made & shorten'd Sail occasionally during the night. A.M. D^{o} weather. At 6 out reefs. At Noon the East^{n} of the arm from SE b E to S b E. Dist [ ] miles. Lat Obs^{d} 49° 36' N.

Bibliography

Baker, Joseph, 3rd Lieutenant. *A Log of His Majesty's Ship* Discovery *from 22nd December 1790 to 27 November 1792*. Microfilm copy #A49. Seattle: University of Washington.

Ballard, V. V. *A Log of the Proceedings of His Majestys Ship* Discovery *George Vancouver Commander Beginning March 1st 1791 and Ending October 16, 1796*. Microfilm copy #A123. Seattle: University of Washington.

Bell, Edward. "A New Vancouver Journal on the Discovery of Puget Sound." Ed. Edmond S. Meany. *Washington Historical Quarterly*, Vol. V, nos. 2, 3 and 4; Vol. VI, no. 1 (April, July, October 1914; January 1915).

Blumenthal, Richard W., ed. *The Early Exploration of Inland Washington Waters: Journals and Logs from Six Expeditions, 1786–1792*. Jefferson, NC: McFarland, 2004.

Broughton, William R. "Broughton's Log of a Reconnaissance of the San Juan Islands in 1792," Ed. J. Neilson Barry, *Washington Historical Quarterly*,Vol. XXI (January, 1930) pp. 55–60

_____. *Journal* (untitled). Microfilm copy #A137. Seattle: University of Washington.

Brown, John A. *The Log of the Proceedings of His Majesties Ship* Discovery. London: Public Record Office Ref: Adm 51/4533.

Clark, Joseph G. *Lights and Shadows of Sailor Life, as Exemplified in Fifteen Years' Experience, Including the More Thrilling Events of the U.S. Exploring Expedition, and Reminiscences of an Eventful Life on the "Mountain Wave."* Boston: Benjamin B. Mussey & Co., 1848.

Cook, James. *A Voyage to the Pacific Ocean Undertaken, By the Command of His Majesty, for Making Discoveries in the Northern Hemisphere. To Determine the Position and Extent of the West Side of North America; its Distance from Asia; and the Practicability of a Northern Passage to Europe. Performed Under the Direction of Captains Cook, Clerke, and Gore, in his Majesty's Ships the* Resolution *and* Discovery. *In the Years 1776, 1777, 1778, 1779, and 1780*. London: Published by Order of the Lords Commissioners of the Admiralty, printed by W. and A. Strahan, 1784.

Fisher, Robin, and Hugh Johnstone, eds. *From Maps to Metaphors: The Pacific World of George Vancouver*. Vancouver: UBC Press, 1993.

Gough, Barry M. *The Northwest Coast: British Navigation, Trade and Discoveries to 1812*. Vancouver: UBC Press, 1992.

Hanson, James. *Journal* (untitled). London: Public Record Office Ref: Adm 51/4146.

Heddington, Thomas. *Journal* (untitled). London: Public Record Office Ref: Adm 55/15.

Hilson, Stephen E. *Exploring Puget Sound & British Columbia*, Holland, MI: Van Winkle Publishing Co., 1975.

Hitchman, Robert. *Place Names of Washington*. Pasco: Washington State Historical Society, 1985.

Howay, Frederic W. *Voyages of the* Columbia *to the Northwest Coast 1787–1790 & 1790–1793*. Portland: Oregon Historical Society Press, 1990.

Humphries, Harry. *A Journal of a Voyage to the Northwest Coast of America and Round the World Performed in His Majesty's Sloop* Discovery *& Brig* Chatham *in the Years 1791, 1792, 1793, 1794, and 1795*. Microfilm copy #A124. Seattle: University of Washington.

Johnstone, James. *Journal* (untitled). London: Public Record Office Ref: Adm 53/339.

Kendrick, John. *The Men with Wooden Feet: The Spanish Exploration of the Pacific Northwest*. Toronto: NC Press, 1986.

_____. *The Voyage of* Sutil *and* Mexicana *1792*. Spokane: Arthur H. Clark, 1991.

Lamb, W. Kaye, ed. *George Vancouver: A Voyage of Discovery to the North Pacific Ocean and Round the World 1791–1795*. London: The Hakluyt Society, 1984.

Manby, Thomas. *Journal* (untitled). London: Public Record Office Ref: Adm 53/403.

_____. *Journal* (untitled). New Haven: Yale Collection of Western Americana, Beineke Rare Book and Manuscript Library.

McDonald, Lucile S. *Making History: The People Who Shaped the San Juan Islands*. Friday Harbor WA: Harbor Press, 1990.

McDowell, Jim. *José Narváez. The Forgotten Explorer including His Narrative of a Voyage on the Northwest Coast in 1788*. Spokane WA: Arthur H. Clark, 1998.

McKenzie, Charles George. *Continuation of the Proceedings of His Majesty's Ship* Discovery, *George Vancouver Esq. Commander* Microfilm copy #A125. Seattle: University of Washington.

Meany, Edmond S. *Vancouver's Discovery of Puget Sound*. Portland: Binfords & Mort, 1957.

Meares, John, Esq. *Voyages Made in the Years 1788 and 1789 from China to the N. W. Coast of America: with an Introductory Narrative of a Voyage Performed in 1786, from Bengal, in the Ship* Nootka *to which are annexed, Observations on the Probable Existance of a North West Passage*. Vol. 1. London: Logographic Press, 1791.

Menzies, Archibald. *Menzies' Journal of Vancouver's Voyage*. Edited, with Botanical and Ethnological Notes, by C.F. Newcombe, M.D., and a Biographical Note by J. Forsyth. Victoria BC: William H. Cullin, 1923.

Morgan, Murray C. *Peter Puget on Puget Sound*. http://www.tpl.lib.wa.us/V2/NWROOM/Morgan/Puget.htm. Seattle: University of Washington Press, 1979. Pp 4–14.

Mudge, Zachary. *Remarks on Board H.M. Sloop* Discovery. Microfilm copy #A336. Seattle: University of Washington.

Nokes, Richard J. *Almost a Hero: The Voyages of John Meares, R.N., to China, Hawaii and the Northwest Coast*. Spokane WA: Washington State University Press, 1998.

Pethick, Derek. *The Nootka Connection. Europe and the Northwest Coast 1790–1795*. Vancouver: Douglas & McIntyre, 1980.

Phillips, *Washington State Place Names*. Seattle: University of Washington Press, 1976.

Puget, Peter. "The Vancouver Expedition: Peter Puget's Journal of the Exploration of Puget Sound, May 7–June 11, 1792." Ed. Bern Anderson. *The Pacific Northwest Quarterly*, Vol. XXX, nos. 1 thru 4, 1939.

Roberts, Edward. *A Log of His Majestys Sloop* Discovery *Round the World in the Years 1791, 1792, 1793, 1794 and 1795 Under the Command of George Vancouver Esq*[r]. Microfilm copy #A125. Seattle: University of Washington.

Robson, John. http://pages.quicksilver.net.nz/jcr/index.html
Scott, James Woodward. *Journal* (untitled). London: Public Record Office Ref: Adm 55/14.
Sherriff, John. *Journal* (untitled). London: Public Record Office Ref: Adm 53/334.
Stewart, John. *Log HMS* Discovery *1791–1794.* Microfilm copy #A135. Seattle: University of Washington.
Swaine, Spelman. *A Log of the Proceedings of His Majesty's Ship* Discovery *George Vancouver Esq*[r] *Commander Commencing December 18 1790 and Ending the 30th of August 1792 Kept by Spelman Swaine.* Microfilm copy #A126. Seattle: University of Washington.
Sykes, John. *A Log of the Proceedings of His Majesty's Sloop* Discovery *from Dec 18*[th] *1790 to February 28*[th] *1795 kept by John Sykes.* Microfilm copy #A127. Seattle: University of Washington.
Taylor, E.G.R. and M.W. Richey. *The Geometrical Seaman, a book of early nautical instruments.* Hollis & Carter for the Institute of Navigation, Cambridge: Cambridge University Press, 1962.
Vancouver, George. *A Voyage of Discovery to the North Pacific Ocean, and Round the World in Which the Coast of North-West America Has Been Carefully Examined and Accurately Surveyed.* London: Printed for G.G. and J. Robinson, Paternoster-Row and J. Edwards, Pall-Mall, 1798.
Wagner, Henry R. *Spanish Explorations in the Strait of Juan de Fuca.* Santa Ana, CA: Fine Arts Press, 1933.
Walbran, John T. *British Columbia Coast Names: 1592–1906. Their Origin and History.* Seattle: University of Washington Press, 1972.
Whitebrook, Robert Ballard. *Coastal Exploration of Washington.* Palo Alto, CA: Pacific Books, 1959.
Wing, Robert C. *Joseph Baker: Lieutenant on the Vancouver Expedition for Whom Mt. Baker was Named.* Seattle: Grey Beard Publishing, 1992.
_____. with Gordon Newell. *Peter Puget: Lieutenant on the Vancouver Expedition, Fighting British Naval Officer, The Man for Whom Puget Sound Was Named.* Seattle: Grey Beard Publishing, 1979.
With Pride in Heritage: History of Jefferson County. Port Townsend WA: Jefferson County Historical Society, 1966.

Index